THE PHANTOM STRANGER

VOLUME 1 A STRANGER AMONG US

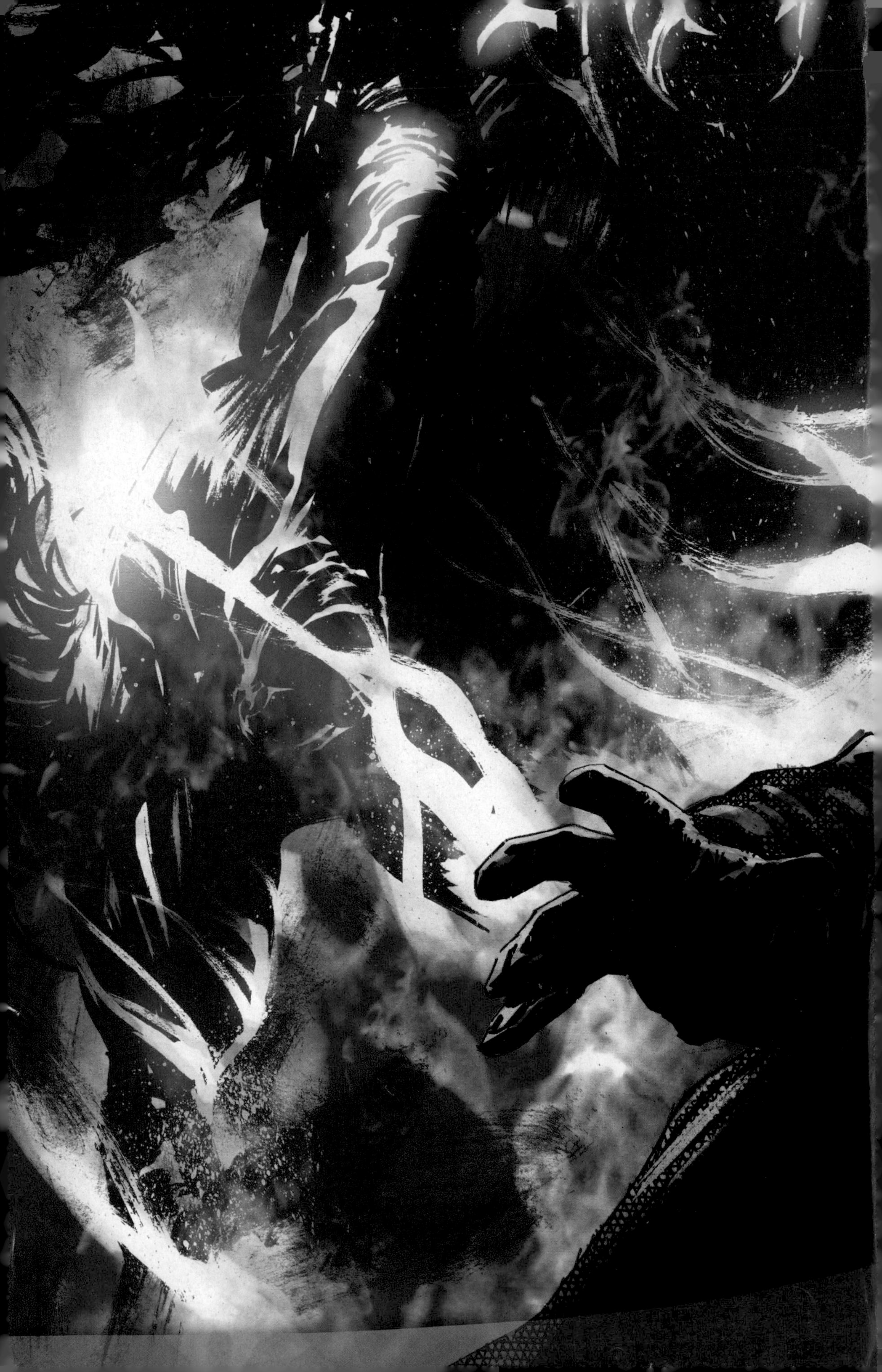

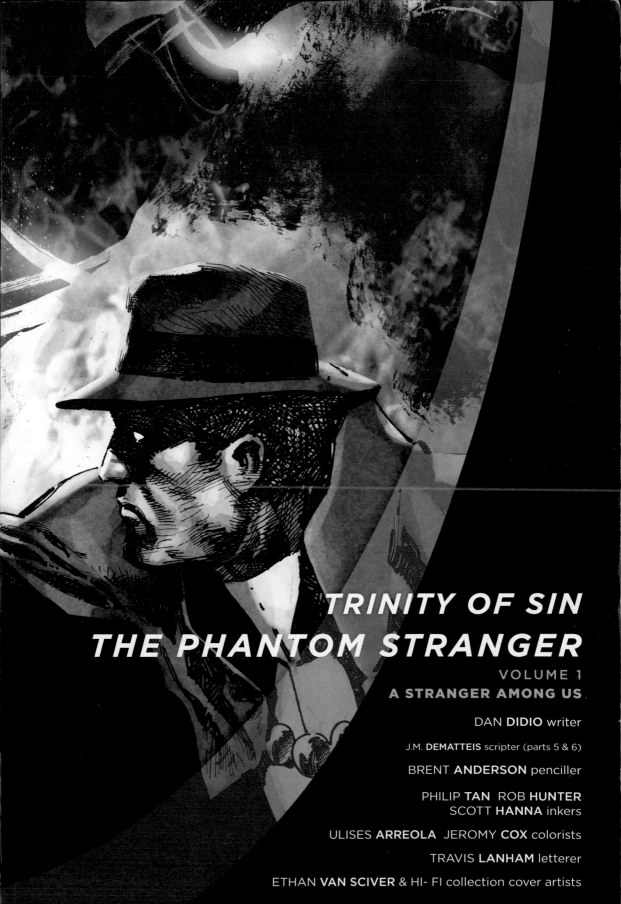

TRINITY OF SIN
THE PHANTOM STRANGER

VOLUME 1
A STRANGER AMONG US

DAN **DIDIO** writer

J.M. **DEMATTEIS** scripter (parts 5 & 6)

BRENT **ANDERSON** penciller

PHILIP **TAN** ROB **HUNTER**
SCOTT **HANNA** inkers

ULISES **ARREOLA** JEROMY **COX** colorists

TRAVIS **LANHAM** letterer

ETHAN **VAN SCIVER** & HI- FI collection cover artists

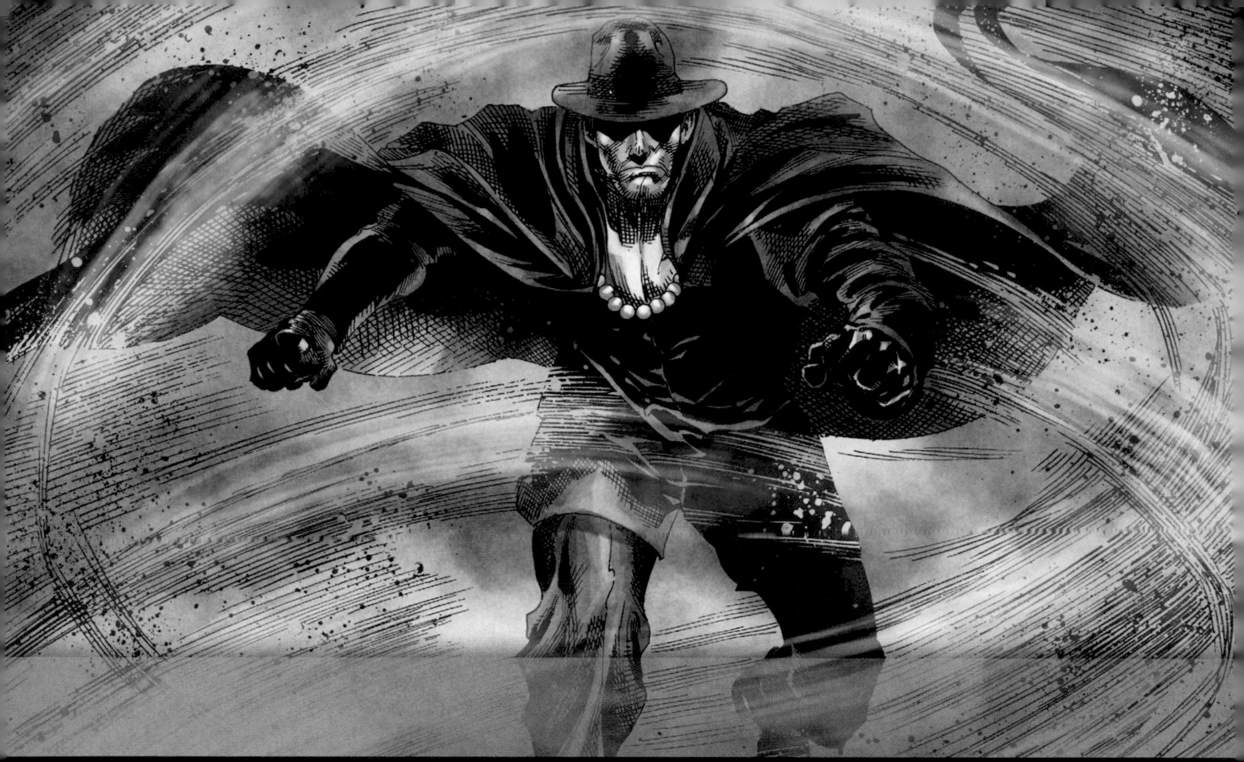

WIL MOSS Editor - Original Series ROBIN WILDMAN Editor
ROBBIN BROSTERMAN Design Director - Books ROBBIE BIEDERMAN Publication Design

BOB HARRAS Senior VP - Editor-in-Chief, DC Comics

DIANE NELSON President DAN DIDIO and JIM LEE Co-Publishers GEOFF JOHNS Chief Creative Officer
JOHN ROOD Executive VP - Sales, Marketing & Business Development AMY GENKINS Senior VP - Business & Legal Affairs
NAIRI GARDINER Senior VP - Finance JEFF BOISON VP - Publishing Planning
MARK CHIARELLO VP - Art Direction & Design JOHN CUNNINGHAM VP - Marketing
TERRI CUNNINGHAM VP - Editorial Administration ALISON GILL Senior VP - Manufacturing & Operations
HANK KANALZ Senior VP - Vertigo & Integrated Publishing JAY KOGAN VP - Business & Legal Affairs, Publishing
JACK MAHAN VP - Business Affairs, Talent NICK NAPOLITANO VP - Manufacturing Administration SUE POHJA VP - Book Sales
COURTNEY SIMMONS Senior VP - Publicity BOB WAYNE Senior VP - Sales

TRINITY OF SIN - THE PHANTOM STRANGER VOLUME 1: A STRANGER AMONG US

DC Comics, 1700 Broadway, New York, NY 10019
A Warner Bros. Entertainment Company.
Printed by RR Donnelley, Salem, VA, USA. 4/26/13. First Printing.
ISBN: 978-1-4012-4088-2

Library of Congress Cataloging-in-Publication Data

DiDio, Dan, 1959- author.
Trinity of Sin : The Phantom Stranger. Volume 1, A stranger among us / Dan DiDio, Brent Anderson, Scott Hanna.
pages cm
"Originally published in single magazine form in Phantom Stranger 0-5."
ISBN 978-1-4012-4088-2
1. Graphic novels. I. Anderson, Brent Eric, illustrator. II. Hanna, Scott, illustrator. III. Title. IV. Title: Stranger among us.
PN6728.P526D53 2013
741.5'973—dc23
2013000118

SUSTAINABLE FORESTRY INITIATIVE
Certified Chain of Custody
At Least 20% Certified Forest Content
www.sfiprogram.org
SFI-01042
APPLIES TO TEXT STOCK ONLY

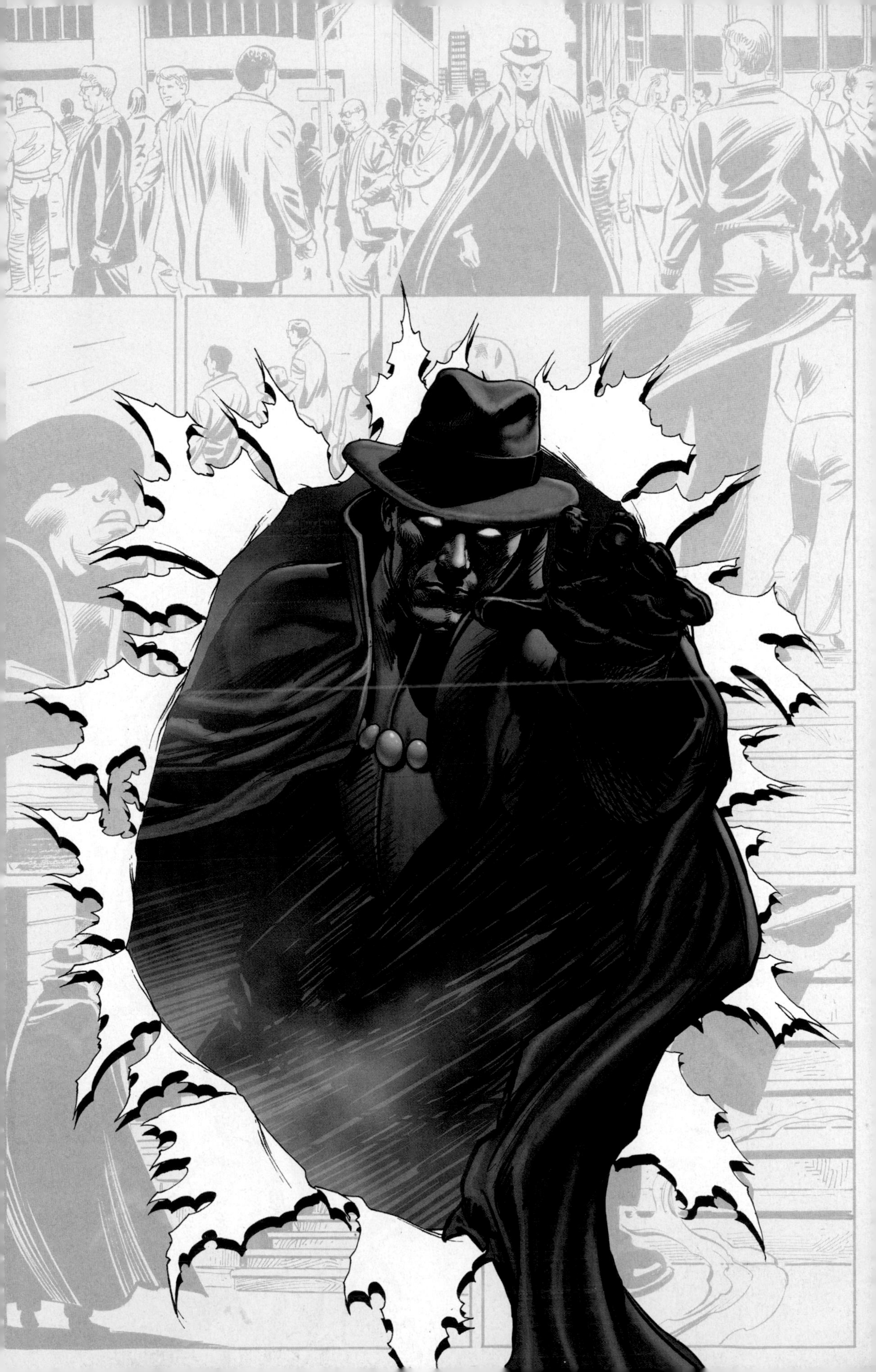

Cover by Brent Anderson & Jeromy Cox

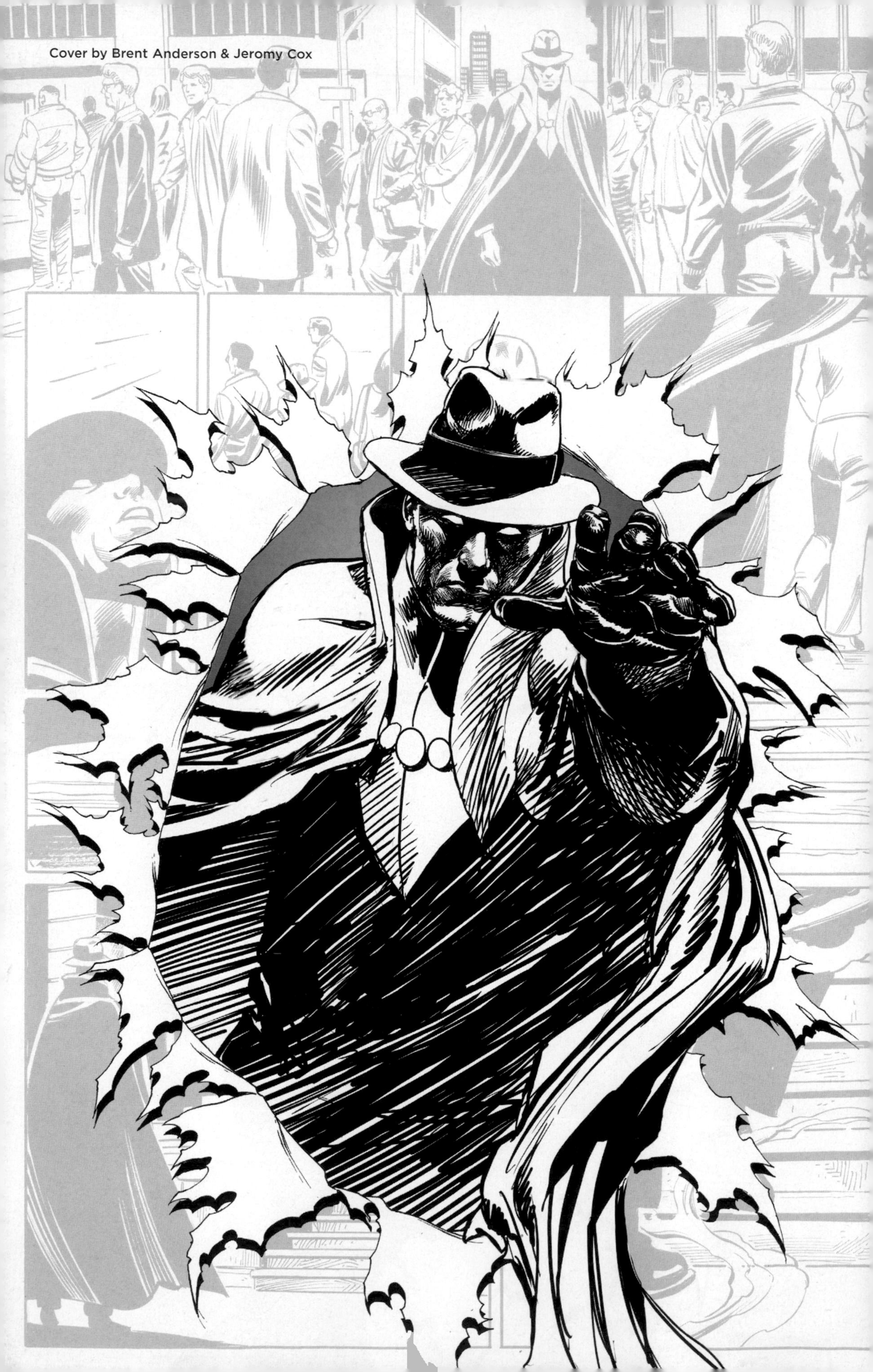

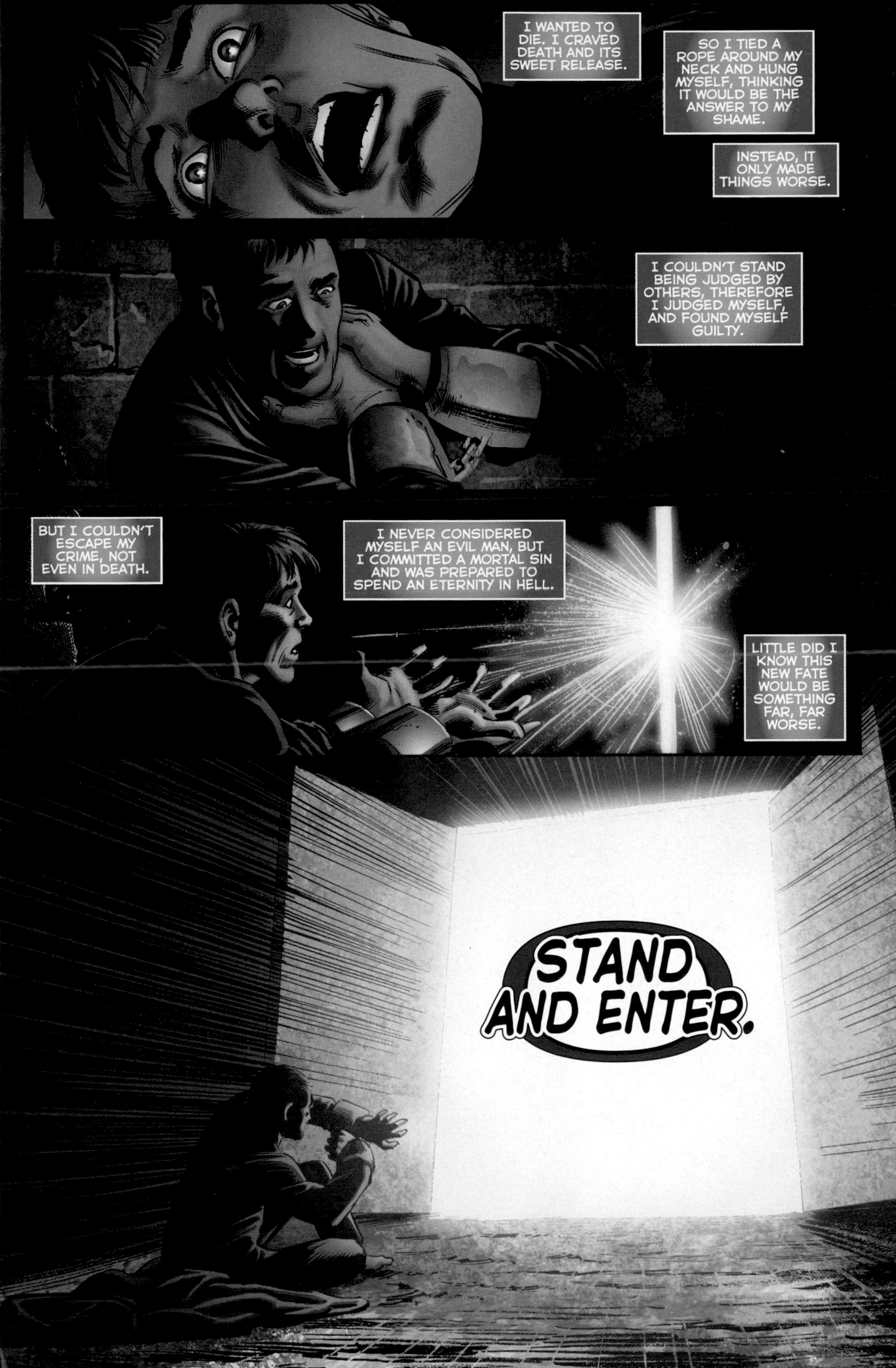
I WANTED TO DIE. I CRAVED DEATH AND ITS SWEET RELEASE.
SO I TIED A ROPE AROUND MY NECK AND HUNG MYSELF, THINKING IT WOULD BE THE ANSWER TO MY SHAME.
INSTEAD, IT ONLY MADE THINGS WORSE.
I COULDN'T STAND BEING JUDGED BY OTHERS, THEREFORE I JUDGED MYSELF, AND FOUND MYSELF GUILTY.
BUT I COULDN'T ESCAPE MY CRIME, NOT EVEN IN DEATH.
I NEVER CONSIDERED MYSELF AN EVIL MAN, BUT I COMMITTED A MORTAL SIN AND WAS PREPARED TO SPEND AN ETERNITY IN HELL.
LITTLE DID I KNOW THIS NEW FATE WOULD BE SOMETHING FAR, FAR WORSE.
STAND AND ENTER.

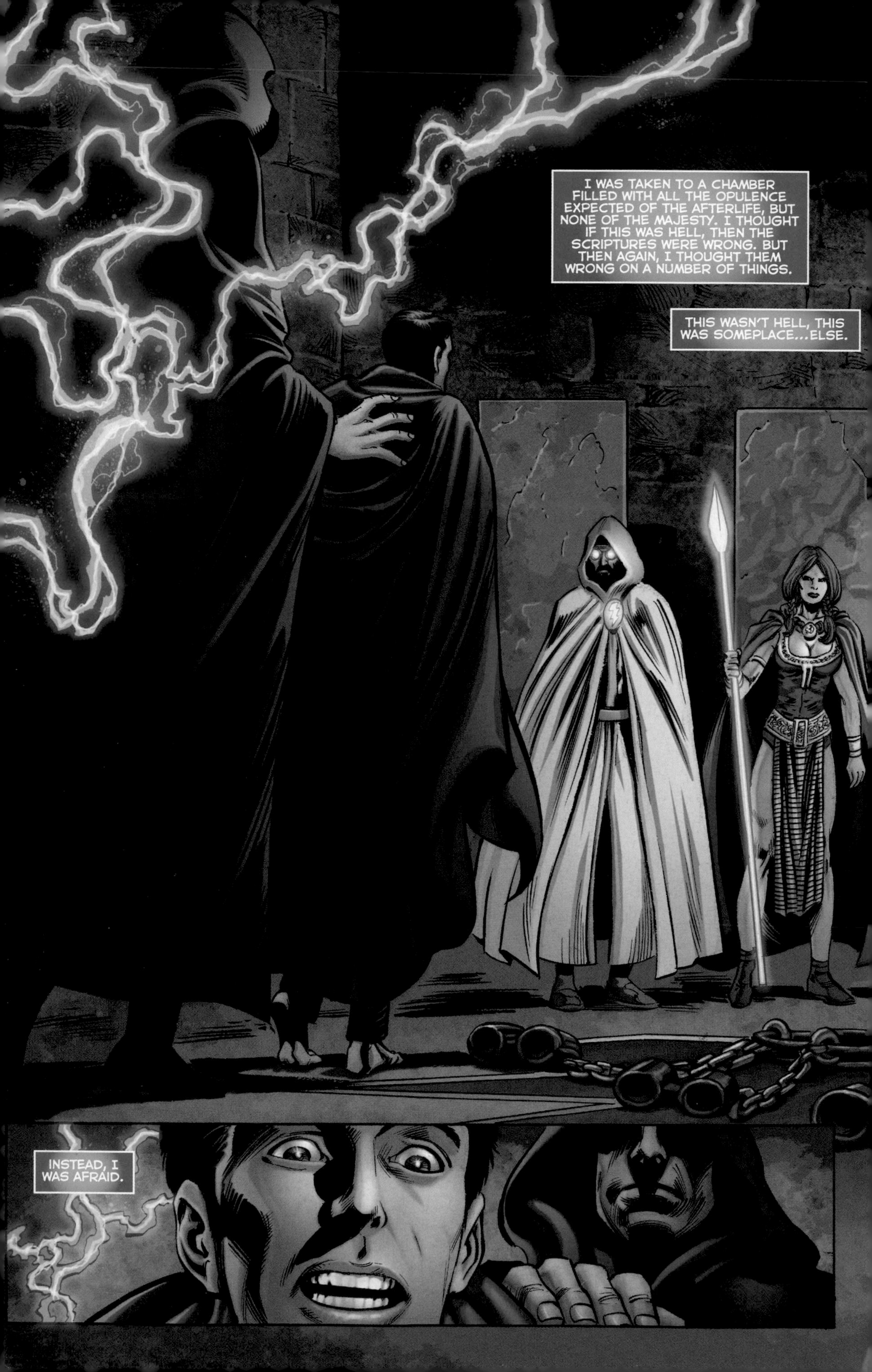
I WAS TAKEN TO A CHAMBER FILLED WITH ALL THE OPULENCE EXPECTED OF THE AFTERLIFE, BUT NONE OF THE MAJESTY. I THOUGHT IF THIS WAS HELL, THEN THE SCRIPTURES WERE WRONG. BUT THEN AGAIN, I THOUGHT THEM WRONG ON A NUMBER OF THINGS.
THIS WASN'T HELL, THIS WAS SOMEPLACE...ELSE.
INSTEAD, I WAS AFRAID.

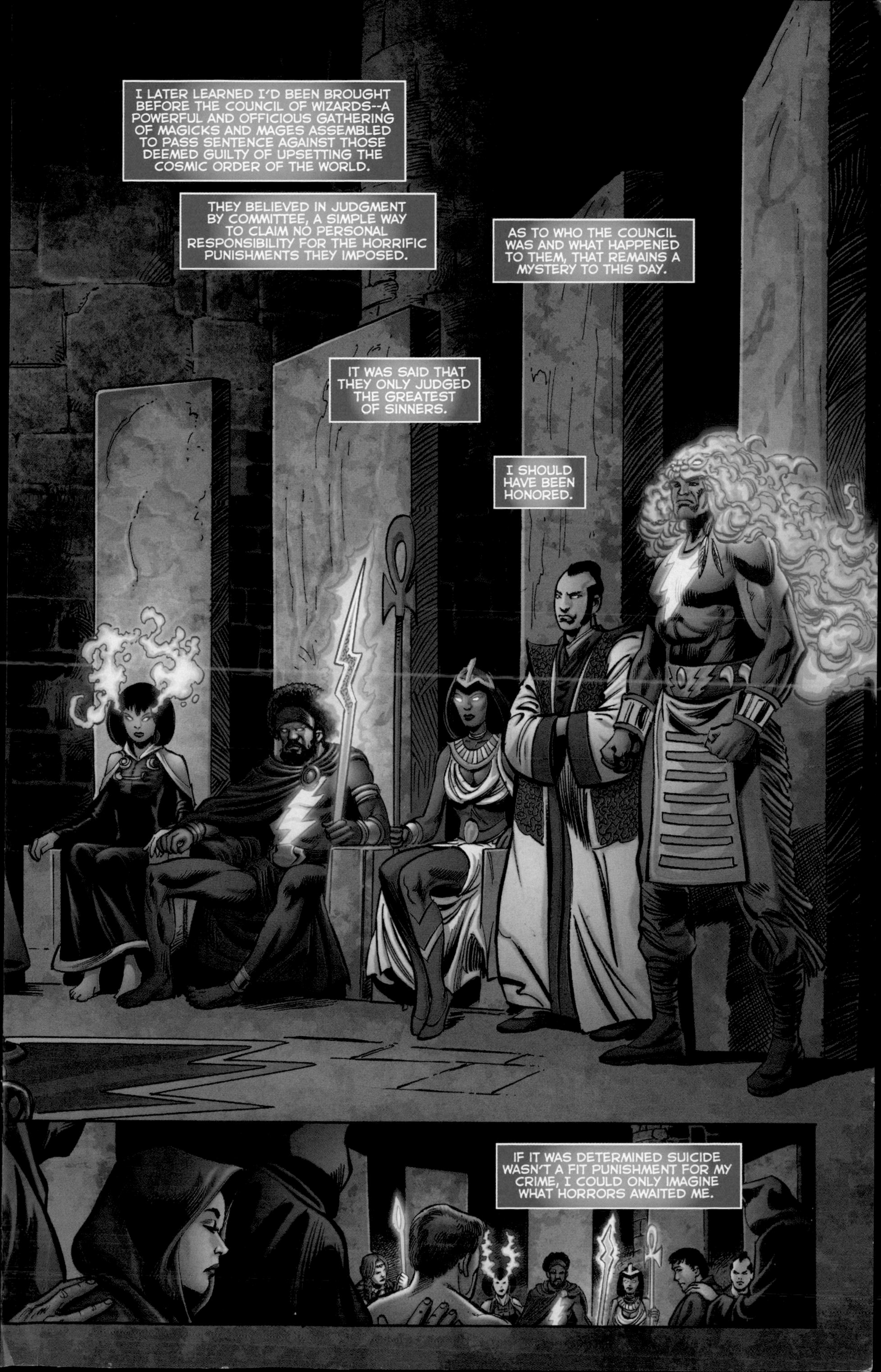
I LATER LEARNED I'D BEEN BROUGHT BEFORE THE COUNCIL OF WIZARDS--A POWERFUL AND OFFICIOUS GATHERING OF MAGICKS AND MAGES ASSEMBLED TO PASS SENTENCE AGAINST THOSE DEEMED GUILTY OF UPSETTING THE COSMIC ORDER OF THE WORLD.
THEY BELIEVED IN JUDGMENT BY COMMITTEE, A SIMPLE WAY TO CLAIM NO PERSONAL RESPONSIBILITY FOR THE HORRIFIC PUNISHMENTS THEY IMPOSED.
AS TO WHO THE COUNCIL WAS AND WHAT HAPPENED TO THEM, THAT REMAINS A MYSTERY TO THIS DAY.
IT WAS SAID THAT THEY ONLY JUDGED THE GREATEST OF SINNERS.
I SHOULD HAVE BEEN HONORED.
IF IT WAS DETERMINED SUICIDE WASN'T A FIT PUNISHMENT FOR MY CRIME, I COULD ONLY IMAGINE WHAT HORRORS AWAITED ME.

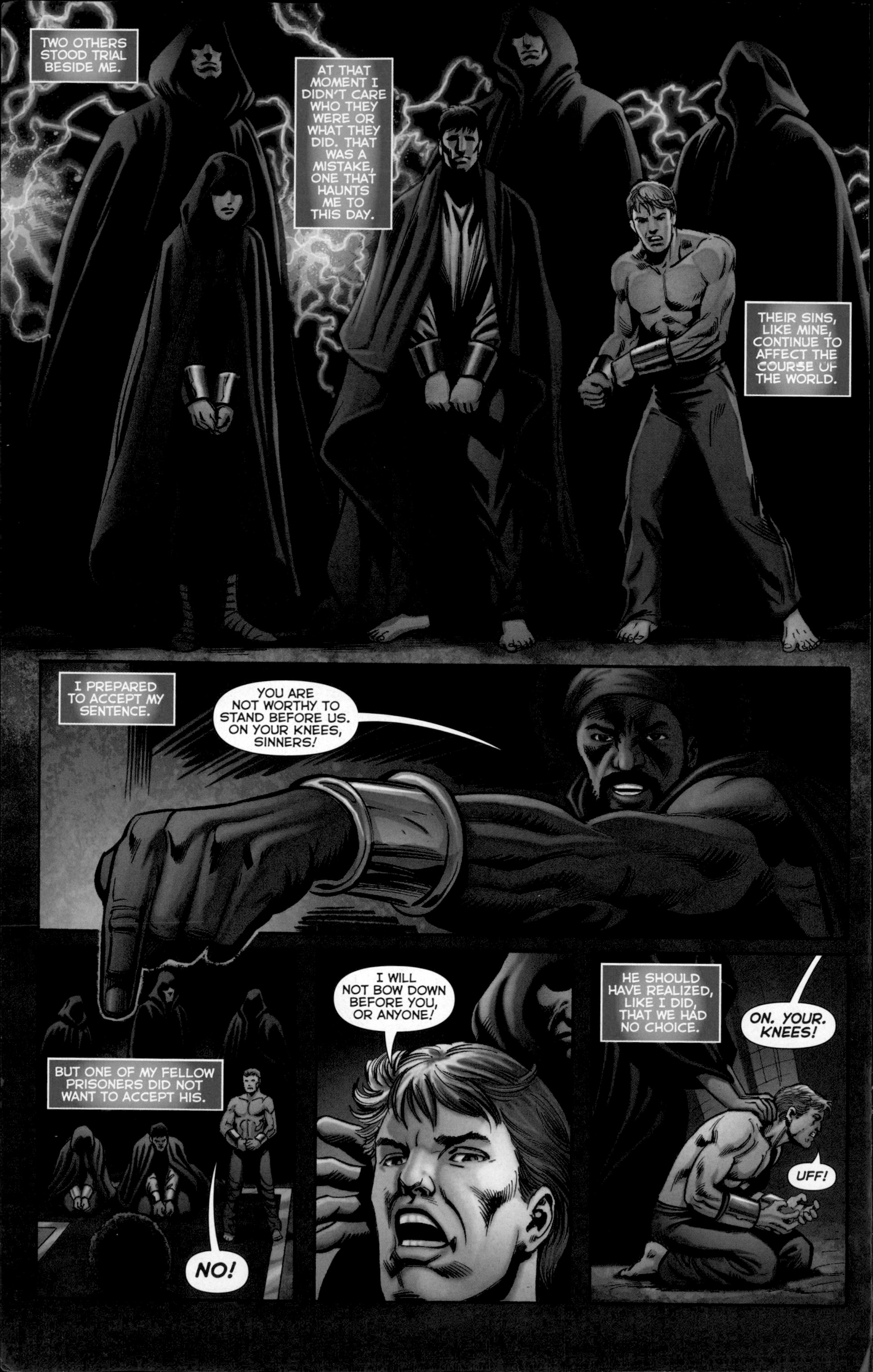
TWO OTHERS STOOD TRIAL BESIDE ME.
AT THAT MOMENT I DIDN'T CARE WHO THEY WERE OR WHAT THEY DID. THAT WAS A MISTAKE, ONE THAT HAUNTS ME TO THIS DAY.
THEIR SINS, LIKE MINE, CONTINUE TO AFFECT THE COURSE OF THE WORLD.
I PREPARED TO ACCEPT MY SENTENCE.
YOU ARE NOT WORTHY TO STAND BEFORE US. ON YOUR KNEES, SINNERS!
BUT ONE OF MY FELLOW PRISONERS DID NOT WANT TO ACCEPT HIS.
NO!
I WILL NOT BOW DOWN BEFORE YOU, OR ANYONE!
HE SHOULD HAVE REALIZED, LIKE I DID, THAT WE HAD NO CHOICE.
ON. YOUR. KNEES!
UFF!

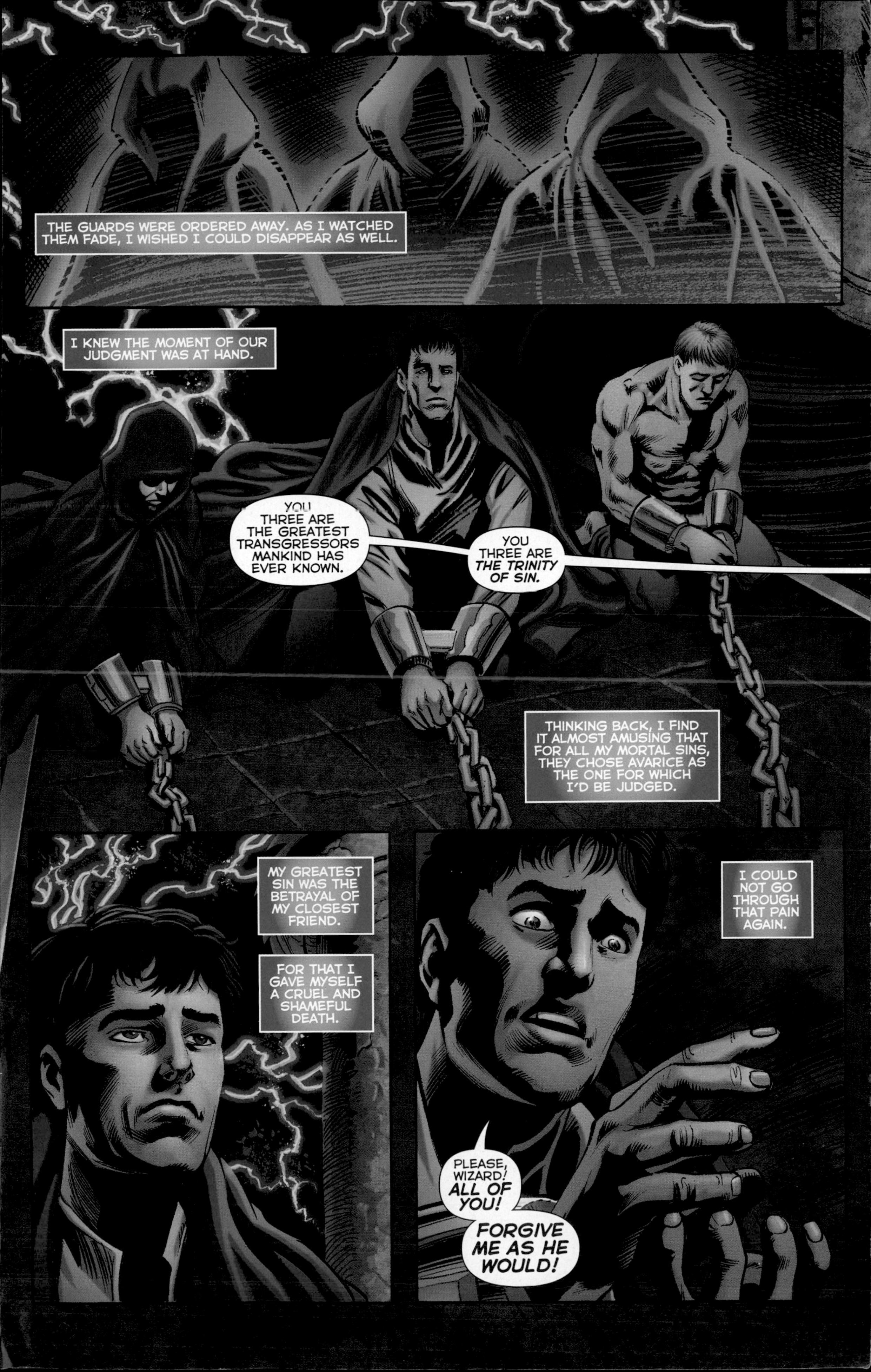
THE GUARDS WERE ORDERED AWAY. AS I WATCHED THEM FADE, I WISHED I COULD DISAPPEAR AS WELL.
I KNEW THE MOMENT OF OUR JUDGMENT WAS AT HAND.
YOU THREE ARE THE GREATEST TRANSGRESSORS MANKIND HAS EVER KNOWN.
YOU THREE ARE *THE TRINITY OF SIN.*
THINKING BACK, I FIND IT ALMOST AMUSING THAT FOR ALL MY MORTAL SINS, THEY CHOSE AVARICE AS THE ONE FOR WHICH I'D BE JUDGED.
MY GREATEST SIN WAS THE BETRAYAL OF MY CLOSEST FRIEND.
FOR THAT I GAVE MYSELF A CRUEL AND SHAMEFUL DEATH.
I COULD NOT GO THROUGH THAT PAIN AGAIN.
PLEASE, WIZARD! ***ALL OF YOU!***
FORGIVE ME AS HE WOULD!

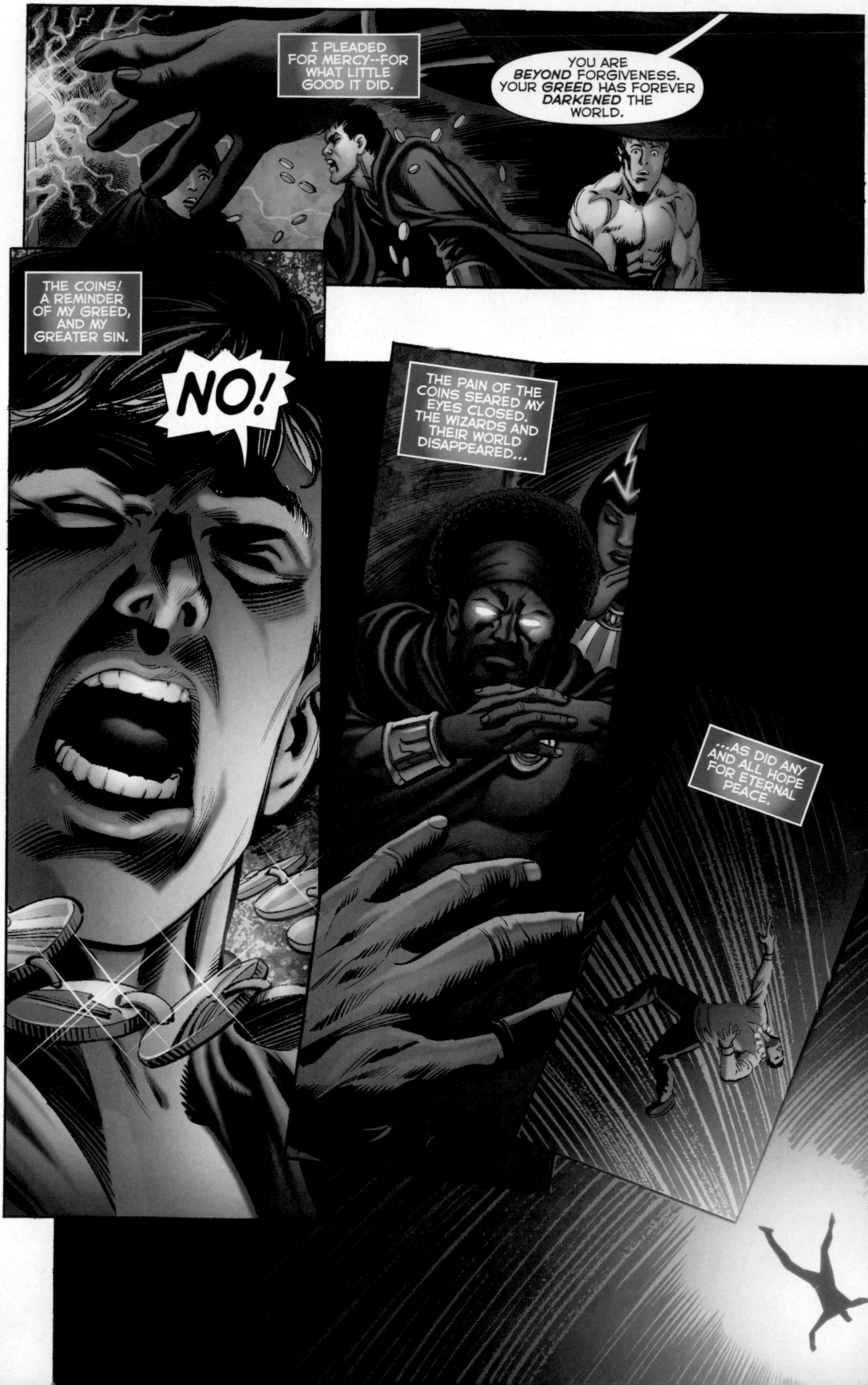
I PLEADED FOR MERCY--FOR WHAT LITTLE GOOD IT DID.
YOU ARE BEYOND FORGIVENESS. YOUR GREED HAS FOREVER DARKENED THE WORLD.
THE COINS! A REMINDER OF MY GREED, AND MY GREATER SIN.
NO!
THE PAIN OF THE COINS SEARED MY EYES CLOSED. THE WIZARDS AND THEIR WORLD DISAPPEARED...
...AS DID ANY AND ALL HOPE FOR ETERNAL PEACE.

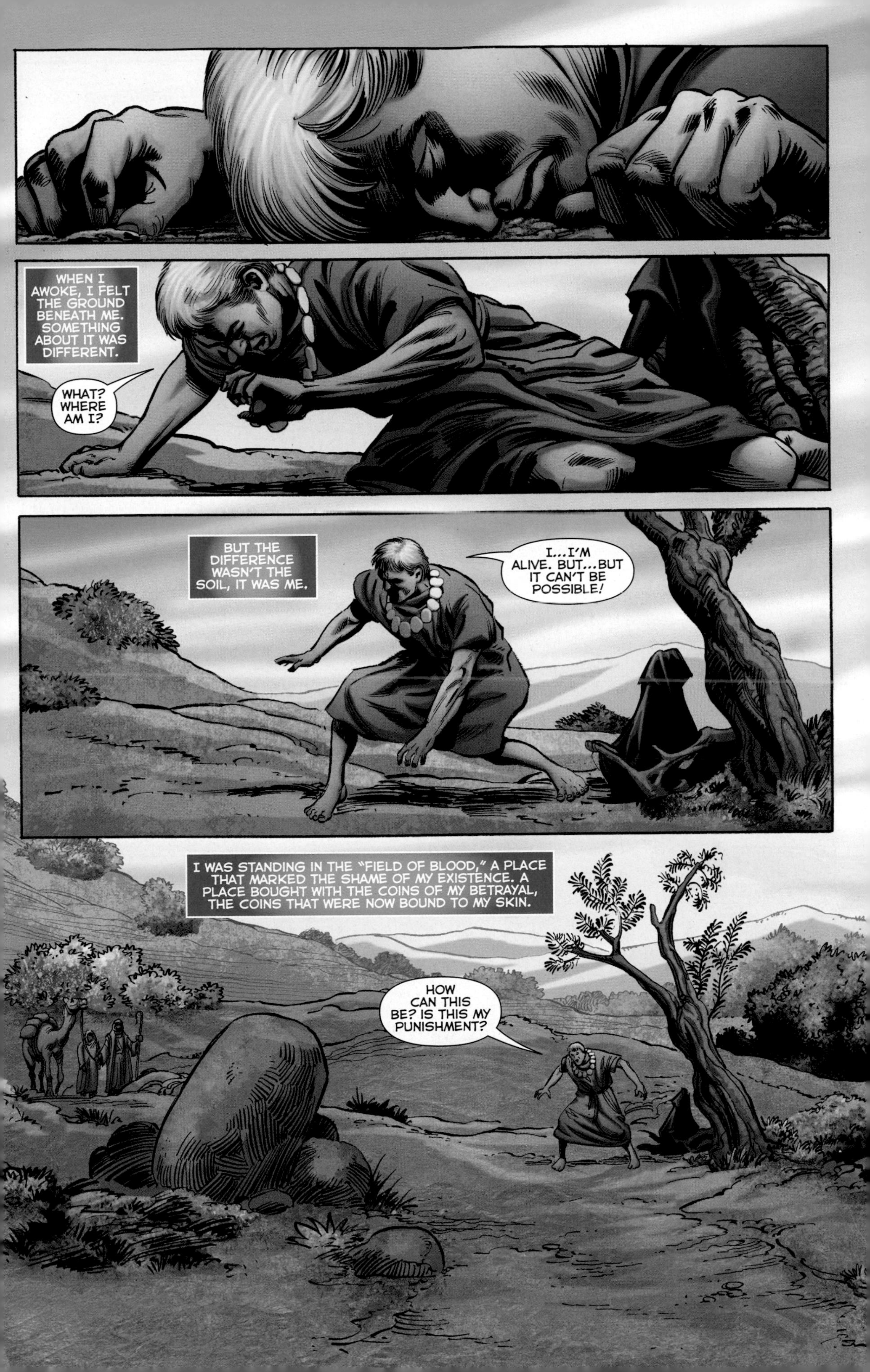
WHEN I AWOKE, I FELT THE GROUND BENEATH ME. SOMETHING ABOUT IT WAS DIFFERENT.
WHAT? WHERE AM I?
BUT THE DIFFERENCE WASN'T THE SOIL, IT WAS ME.
I...I'M ALIVE. BUT...BUT IT CAN'T BE POSSIBLE!
I WAS STANDING IN THE "FIELD OF BLOOD," A PLACE THAT MARKED THE SHAME OF MY EXISTENCE. A PLACE BOUGHT WITH THE COINS OF MY BETRAYAL, THE COINS THAT WERE NOW BOUND TO MY SKIN.
HOW CAN THIS BE? IS THIS MY PUNISHMENT?

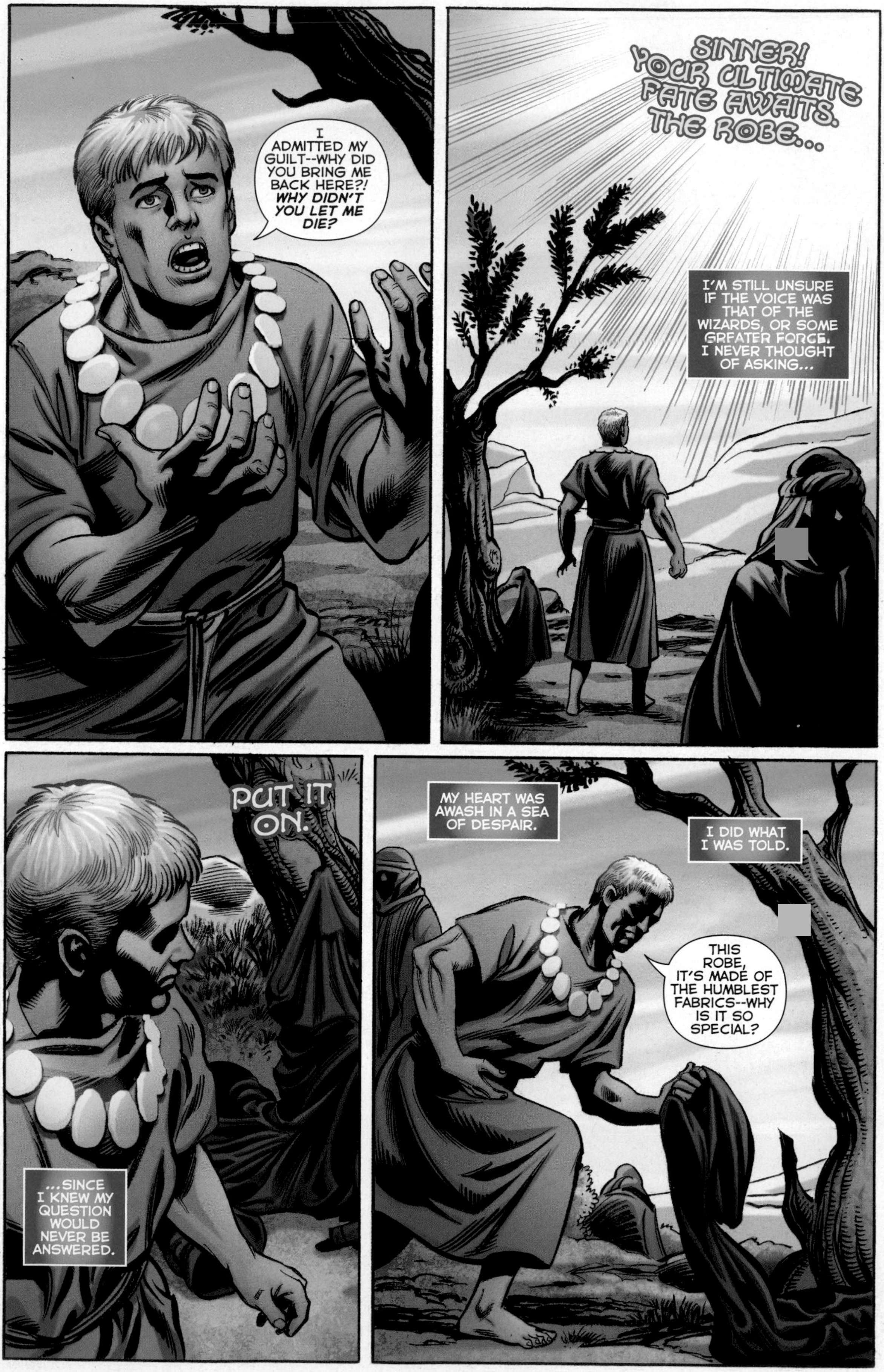
I ADMITTED MY GUILT--WHY DID YOU BRING ME BACK HERE?! *WHY DIDN'T YOU LET ME DIE?*
SINNER! YOUR ULTIMATE FATE AWAITS. THE ROBE...
I'M STILL UNSURE IF THE VOICE WAS THAT OF THE WIZARDS, OR SOME GREATER FORCE. I NEVER THOUGHT OF ASKING...
PUT IT ON.
...SINCE I KNEW MY QUESTION WOULD NEVER BE ANSWERED.
MY HEART WAS AWASH IN A SEA OF DESPAIR.
I DID WHAT I WAS TOLD.
THIS ROBE, IT'S MADE OF THE HUMBLEST FABRICS--WHY IS IT SO SPECIAL?

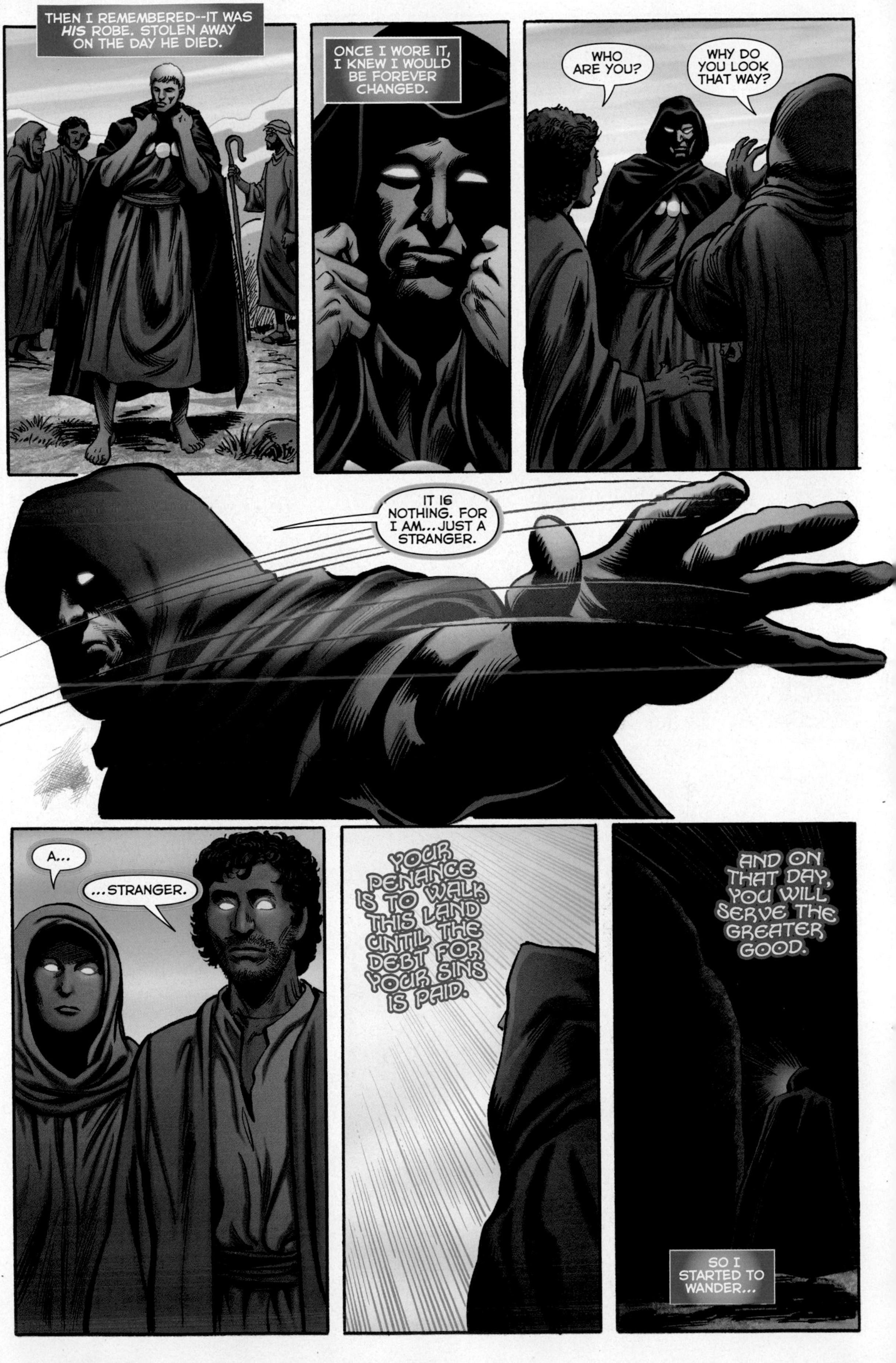
THEN I REMEMBERED--IT WAS HIS ROBE. STOLEN AWAY ON THE DAY HE DIED.
ONCE I WORE IT, I KNEW I WOULD BE FOREVER CHANGED.
WHO ARE YOU?
WHY DO YOU LOOK THAT WAY?
IT IS NOTHING. FOR I AM...JUST A STRANGER.
A...
...STRANGER.
YOUR PENANCE IS TO WALK THIS LAND UNTIL THE DEBT FOR YOUR SINS IS PAID.
AND ON THAT DAY, YOU WILL SERVE THE GREATER GOOD.
SO I STARTED TO WANDER...

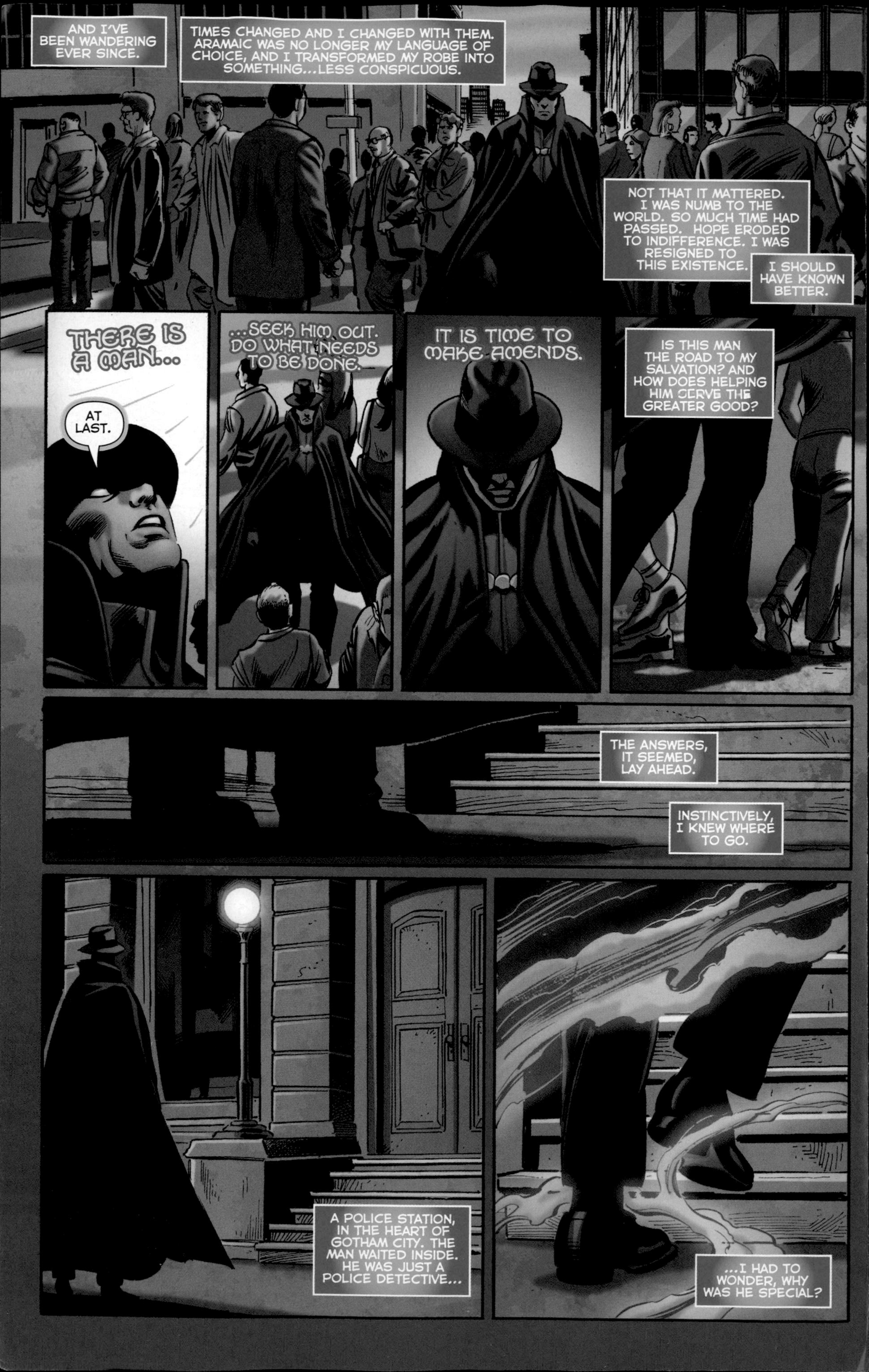
AND I'VE BEEN WANDERING EVER SINCE.
TIMES CHANGED AND I CHANGED WITH THEM. ARAMAIC WAS NO LONGER MY LANGUAGE OF CHOICE, AND I TRANSFORMED MY ROBE INTO SOMETHING...LESS CONSPICUOUS.
NOT THAT IT MATTERED. I WAS NUMB TO THE WORLD. SO MUCH TIME HAD PASSED. HOPE ERODED TO INDIFFERENCE. I WAS RESIGNED TO THIS EXISTENCE.
I SHOULD HAVE KNOWN BETTER.
THERE IS A MAN...
AT LAST.
...SEEK HIM OUT. DO WHAT NEEDS TO BE DONE.
IT IS TIME TO MAKE AMENDS.
IS THIS MAN THE ROAD TO MY SALVATION? AND HOW DOES HELPING HIM SERVE THE GREATER GOOD?
THE ANSWERS, IT SEEMED, LAY AHEAD.
INSTINCTIVELY, I KNEW WHERE TO GO.
A POLICE STATION, IN THE HEART OF GOTHAM CITY. THE MAN WAITED INSIDE. HE WAS JUST A POLICE DETECTIVE...
...I HAD TO WONDER, WHY WAS HE SPECIAL?

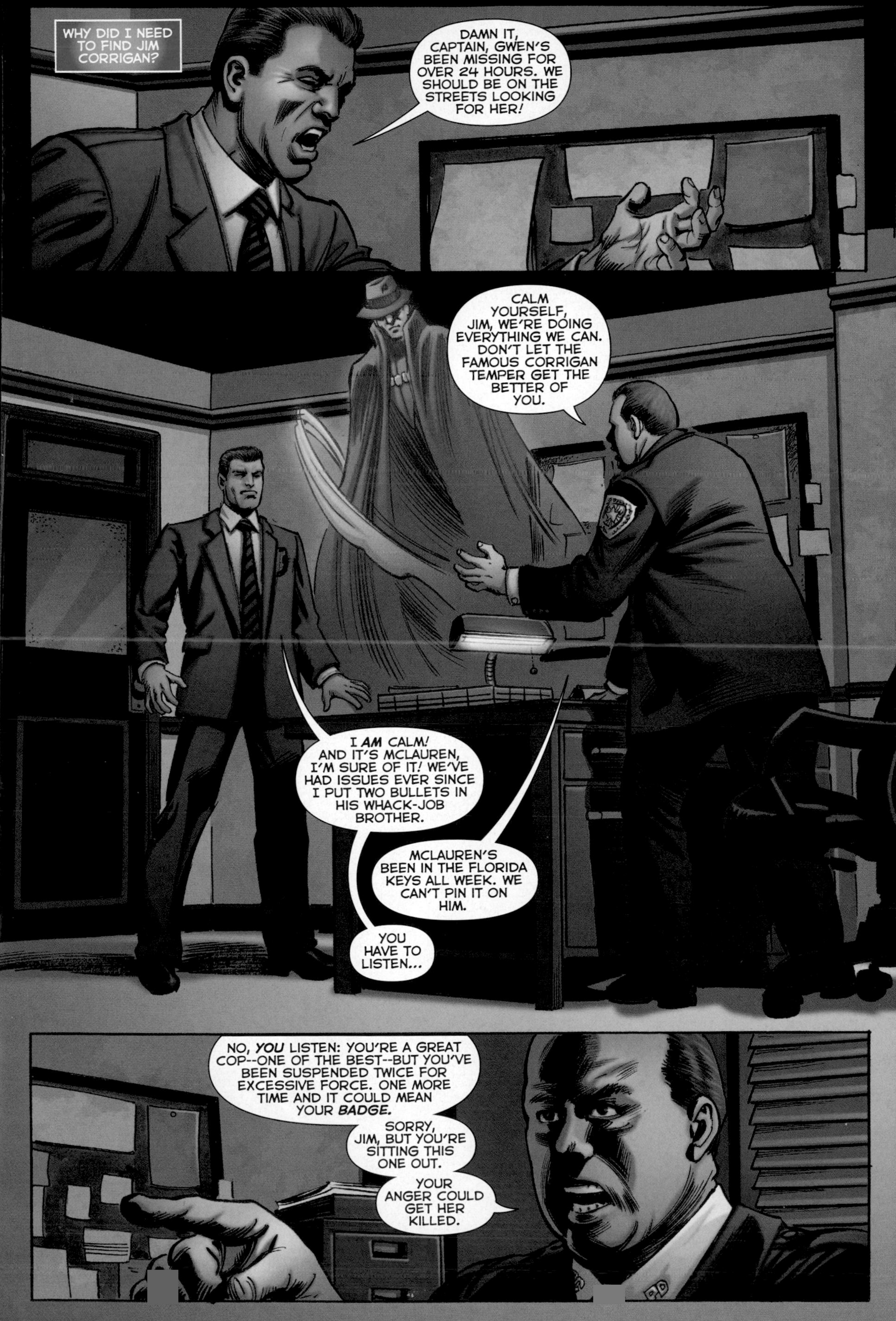
WHY DID I NEED TO FIND JIM CORRIGAN?
DAMN IT, CAPTAIN, GWEN'S BEEN MISSING FOR OVER 24 HOURS. WE SHOULD BE ON THE STREETS LOOKING FOR HER!
CALM YOURSELF, JIM, WE'RE DOING EVERYTHING WE CAN. DON'T LET THE FAMOUS CORRIGAN TEMPER GET THE BETTER OF YOU.
I AM CALM! AND IT'S MCLAUREN, I'M SURE OF IT! WE'VE HAD ISSUES EVER SINCE I PUT TWO BULLETS IN HIS WHACK-JOB BROTHER.
MCLAUREN'S BEEN IN THE FLORIDA KEYS ALL WEEK. WE CAN'T PIN IT ON HIM.
YOU HAVE TO LISTEN...
NO, YOU LISTEN: YOU'RE A GREAT COP--ONE OF THE BEST--BUT YOU'VE BEEN SUSPENDED TWICE FOR EXCESSIVE FORCE. ONE MORE TIME AND IT COULD MEAN YOUR BADGE.
SORRY, JIM, BUT YOU'RE SITTING THIS ONE OUT.
YOUR ANGER COULD GET HER KILLED.

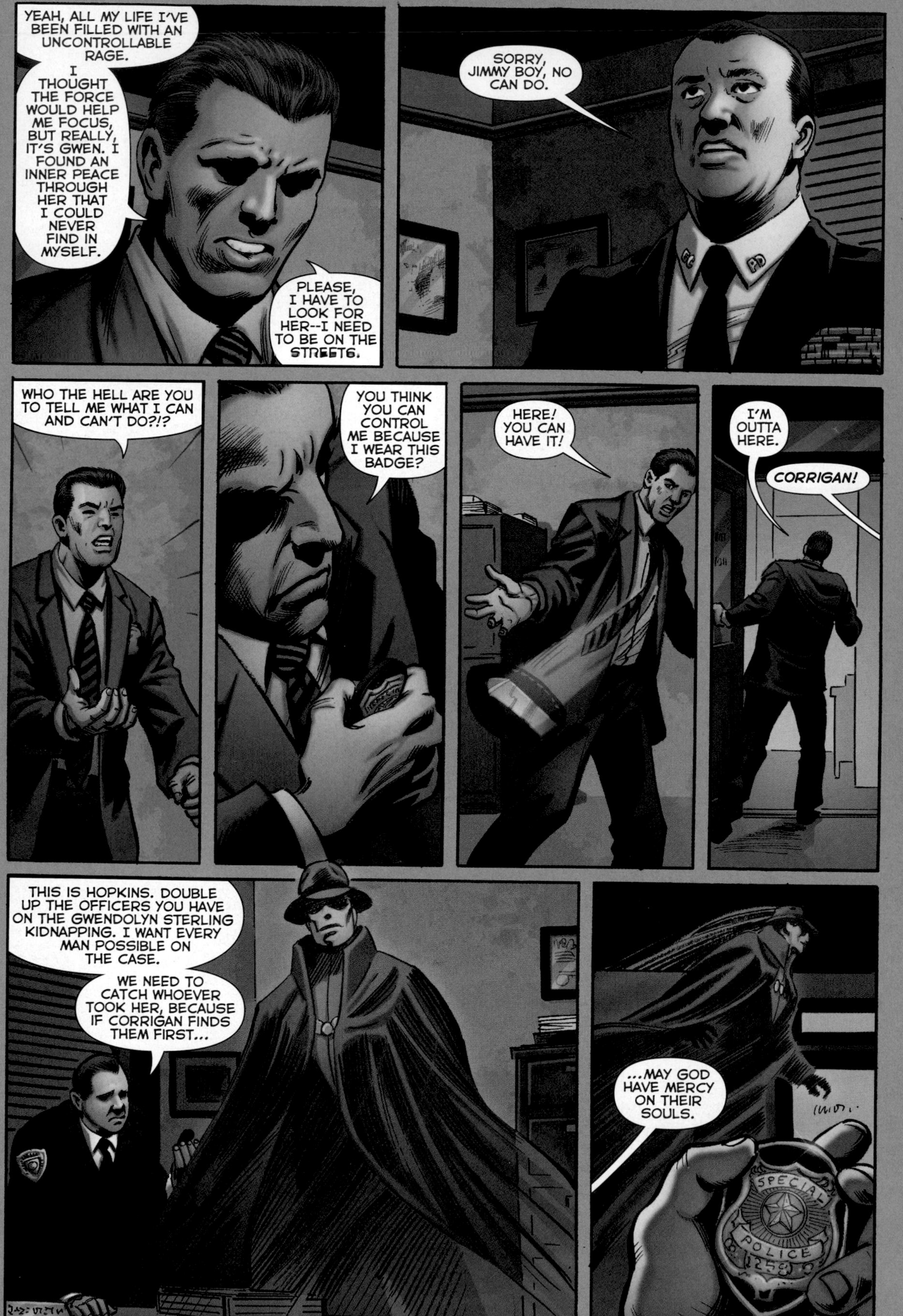
YEAH, ALL MY LIFE I'VE BEEN FILLED WITH AN UNCONTROLLABLE RAGE.
I THOUGHT THE FORCE WOULD HELP ME FOCUS, BUT REALLY, IT'S GWEN. I FOUND AN INNER PEACE THROUGH HER THAT I COULD NEVER FIND IN MYSELF.
PLEASE, I HAVE TO LOOK FOR HER--I NEED TO BE ON THE STREETS.
SORRY, JIMMY BOY, NO CAN DO.
WHO THE HELL ARE YOU TO TELL ME WHAT I CAN AND CAN'T DO?!?
YOU THINK YOU CAN CONTROL ME BECAUSE I WEAR THIS BADGE?
HERE! YOU CAN HAVE IT!
I'M OUTTA HERE.
CORRIGAN!
THIS IS HOPKINS. DOUBLE UP THE OFFICERS YOU HAVE ON THE GWENDOLYN STERLING KIDNAPPING. I WANT EVERY MAN POSSIBLE ON THE CASE.
WE NEED TO CATCH WHOEVER TOOK HER, BECAUSE IF CORRIGAN FINDS THEM FIRST...
...MAY GOD HAVE MERCY ON THEIR SOULS.
SPECIAL
POLICE
1258

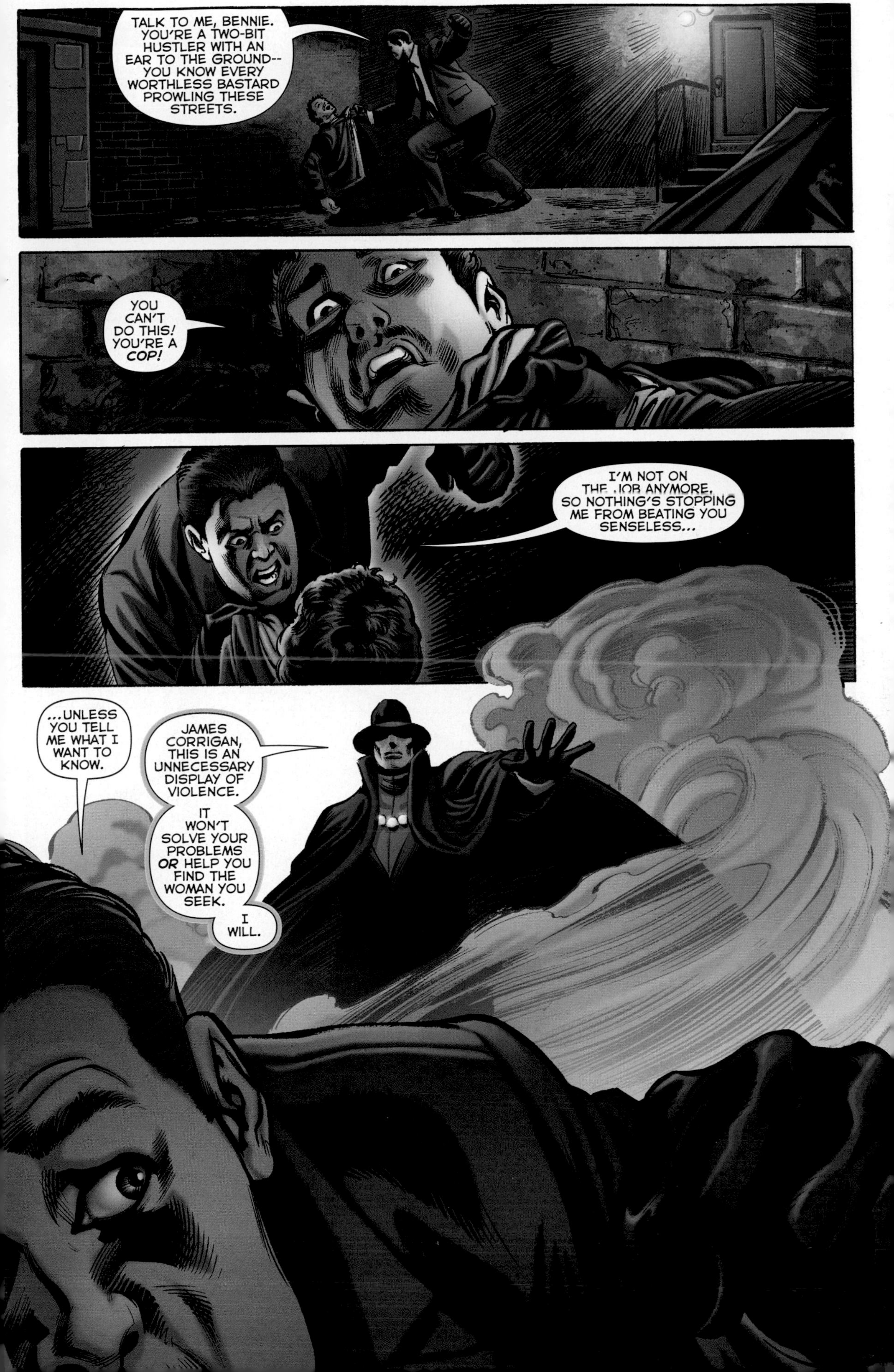
TALK TO ME, BENNIE. YOU'RE A TWO-BIT HUSTLER WITH AN EAR TO THE GROUND-- YOU KNOW EVERY WORTHLESS BASTARD PROWLING THESE STREETS.
YOU CAN'T DO THIS! YOU'RE A COP!
I'M NOT ON THE JOB ANYMORE, SO NOTHING'S STOPPING ME FROM BEATING YOU SENSELESS...
...UNLESS YOU TELL ME WHAT I WANT TO KNOW.
JAMES CORRIGAN, THIS IS AN UNNECESSARY DISPLAY OF VIOLENCE.
IT WON'T SOLVE YOUR PROBLEMS OR HELP YOU FIND THE WOMAN YOU SEEK.
I WILL.

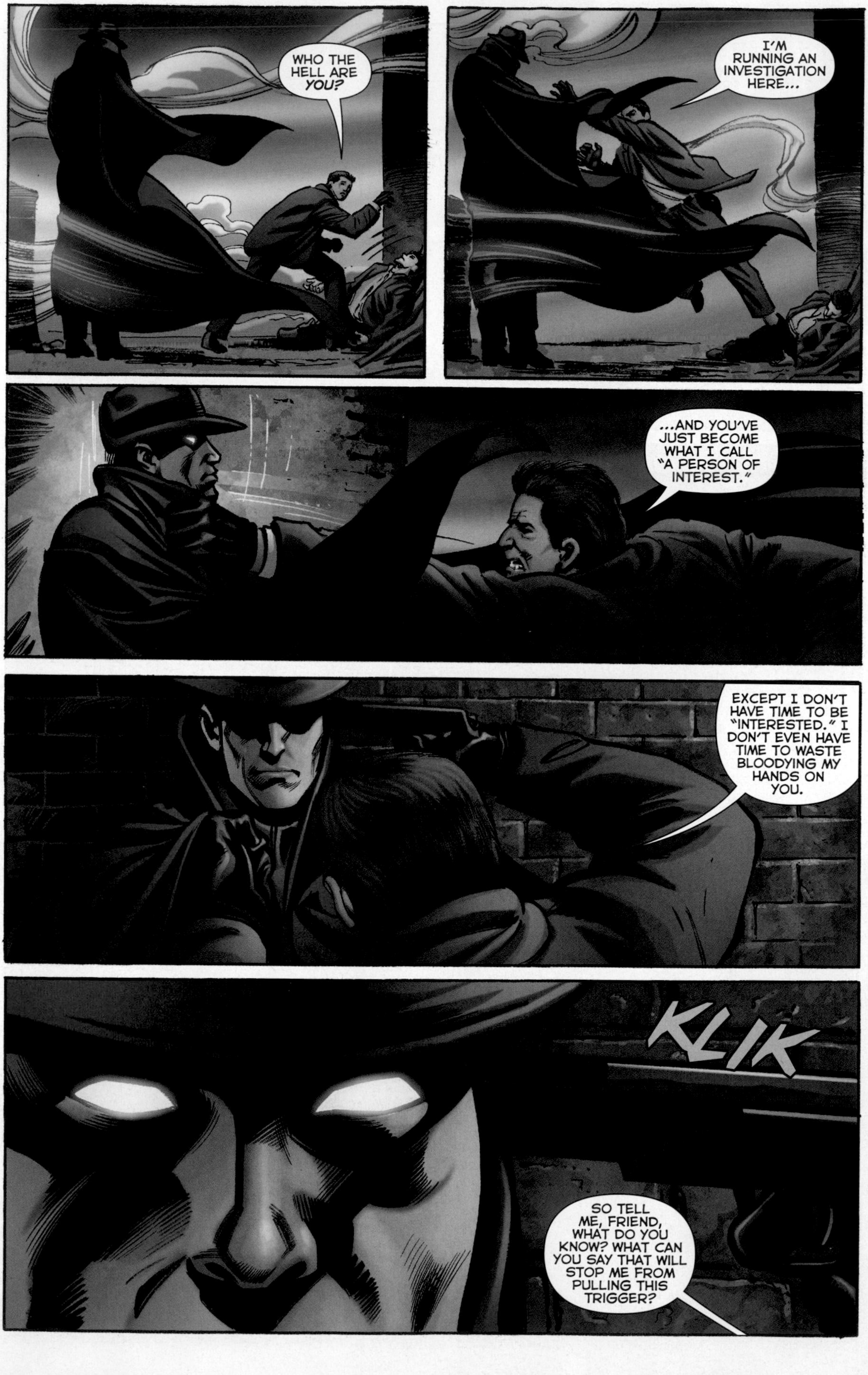
WHO THE HELL ARE *YOU?*
I'M RUNNING AN INVESTIGATION HERE...
...AND YOU'VE JUST BECOME WHAT I CALL "A PERSON OF INTEREST."
EXCEPT I DON'T HAVE TIME TO BE "INTERESTED." I DON'T EVEN HAVE TIME TO WASTE BLOODYING MY HANDS ON YOU.
KLIK
SO TELL ME, FRIEND, WHAT DO YOU KNOW? WHAT CAN YOU SAY THAT WILL STOP ME FROM PULLING THIS TRIGGER?

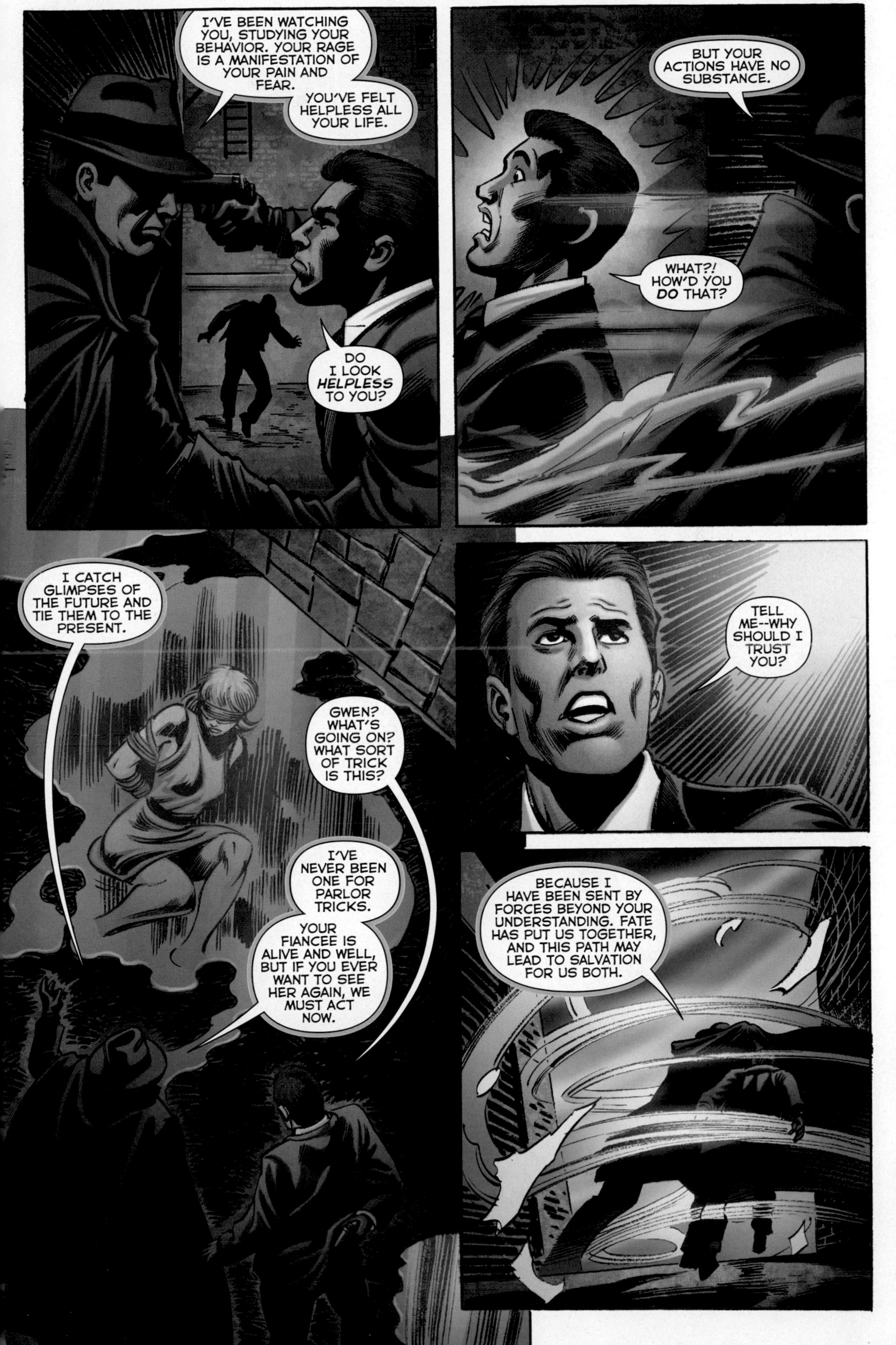
I'VE BEEN WATCHING YOU, STUDYING YOUR BEHAVIOR. YOUR RAGE IS A MANIFESTATION OF YOUR PAIN AND FEAR.
YOU'VE FELT HELPLESS ALL YOUR LIFE.
DO I LOOK *HELPLESS* TO YOU?
BUT YOUR ACTIONS HAVE NO SUBSTANCE.
WHAT?! HOW'D YOU *DO* THAT?
I CATCH GLIMPSES OF THE FUTURE AND TIE THEM TO THE PRESENT.
GWEN? WHAT'S GOING ON? WHAT SORT OF TRICK IS THIS?
I'VE NEVER BEEN ONE FOR PARLOR TRICKS.
YOUR FIANCEE IS ALIVE AND WELL, BUT IF YOU EVER WANT TO SEE HER AGAIN, WE MUST ACT NOW.
TELL ME--WHY SHOULD I TRUST YOU?
BECAUSE I HAVE BEEN SENT BY FORCES BEYOND YOUR UNDERSTANDING. FATE HAS PUT US TOGETHER, AND THIS PATH MAY LEAD TO SALVATION FOR US BOTH.

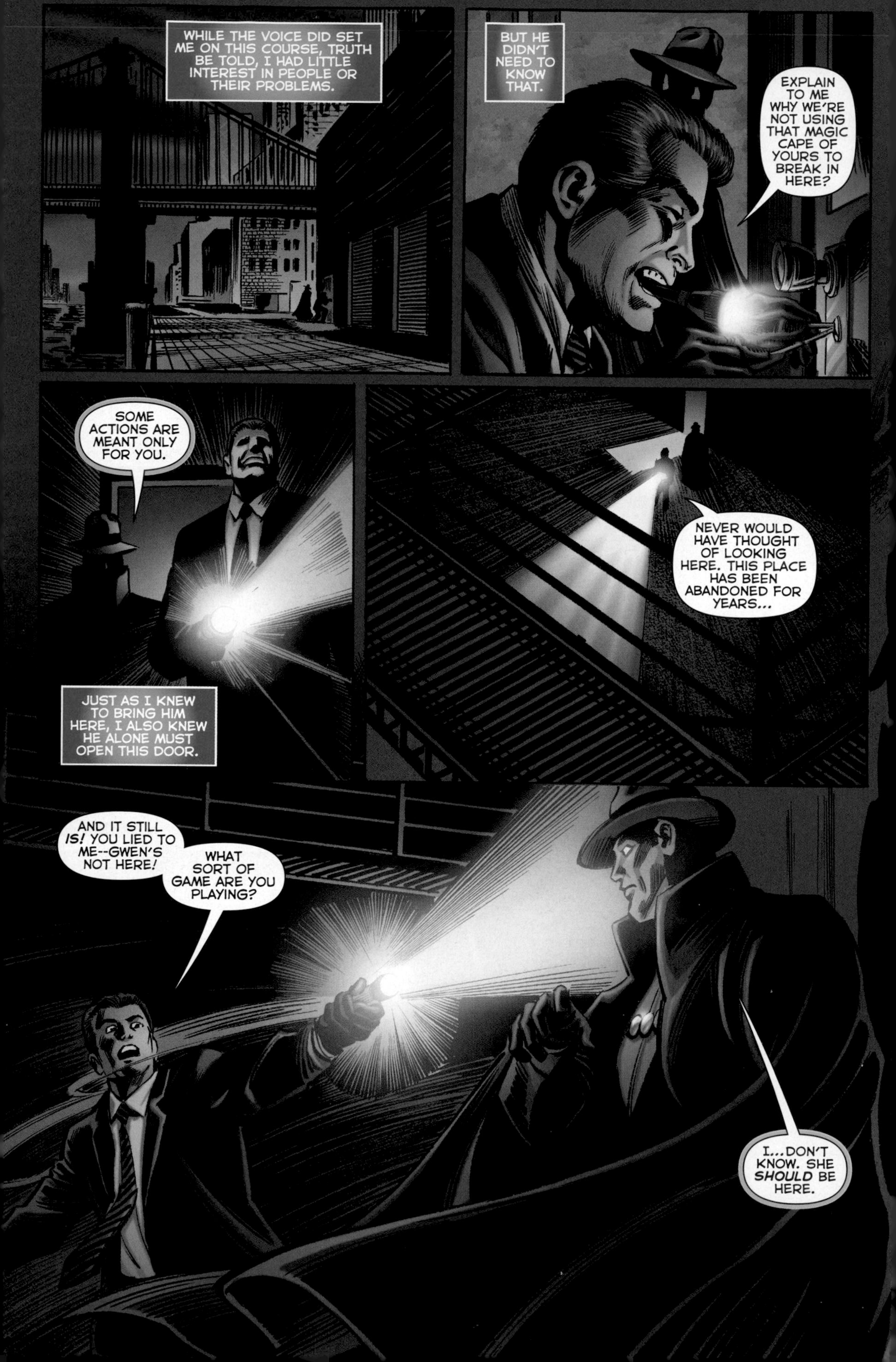
WHILE THE VOICE DID SET ME ON THIS COURSE, TRUTH BE TOLD, I HAD LITTLE INTEREST IN PEOPLE OR THEIR PROBLEMS.
BUT HE DIDN'T NEED TO KNOW THAT.
EXPLAIN TO ME WHY WE'RE NOT USING THAT MAGIC CAPE OF YOURS TO BREAK IN HERE?
SOME ACTIONS ARE MEANT ONLY FOR YOU.
JUST AS I KNEW TO BRING HIM HERE, I ALSO KNEW HE ALONE MUST OPEN THIS DOOR.
NEVER WOULD HAVE THOUGHT OF LOOKING HERE. THIS PLACE HAS BEEN ABANDONED FOR YEARS...
AND IT STILL IS! YOU LIED TO ME--GWEN'S NOT HERE!
WHAT SORT OF GAME ARE YOU PLAYING?
I...DON'T KNOW. SHE SHOULD BE HERE.

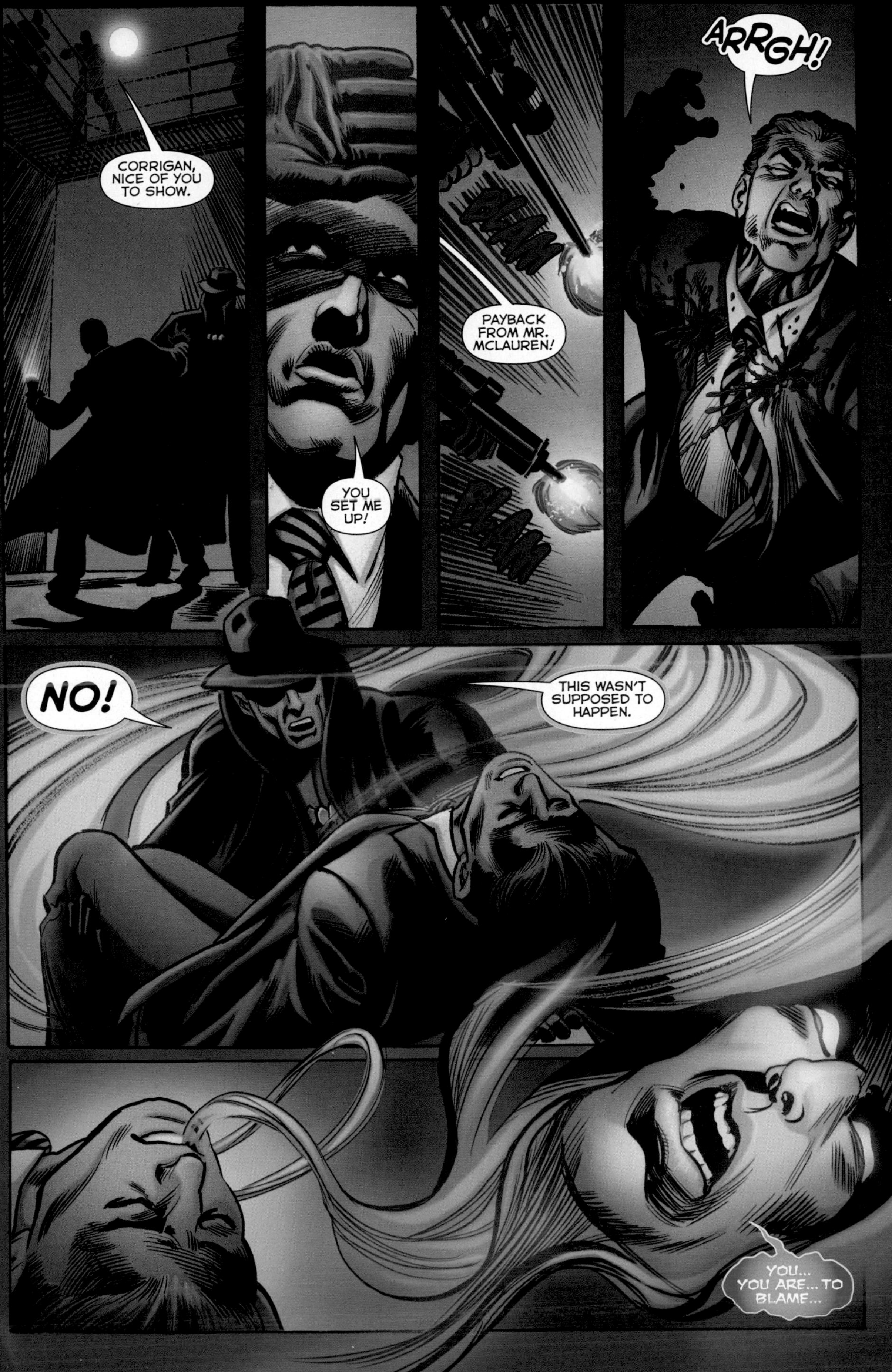
CORRIGAN, NICE OF YOU TO SHOW.
YOU SET ME UP!
BLAM
PAYBACK FROM MR. MCLAUREN!
BLAM
ARRGH!
NO!
THIS WASN'T SUPPOSED TO HAPPEN.
YOU... YOU ARE... TO BLAME...

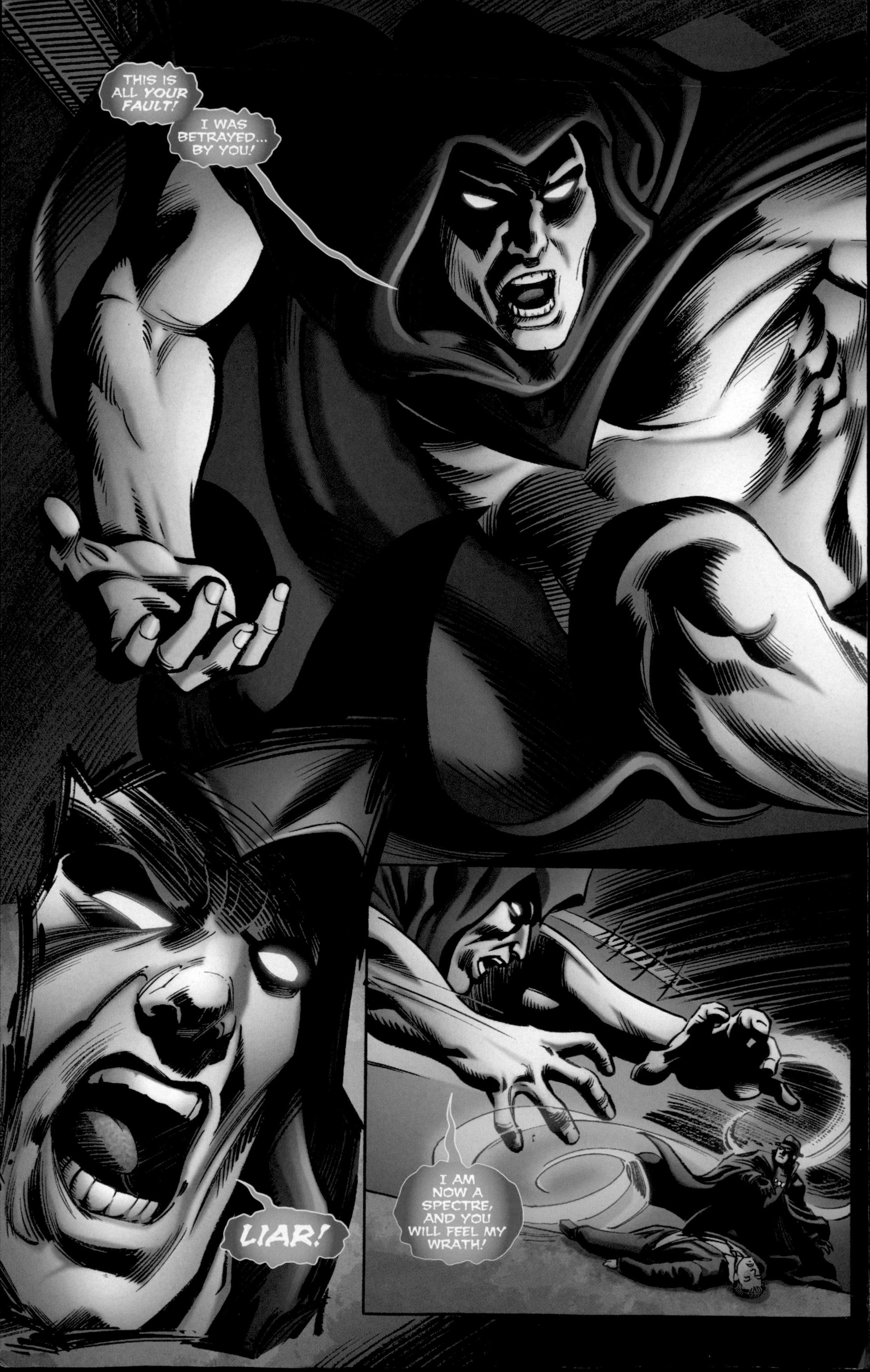
THIS IS ALL YOUR FAULT!
I WAS BETRAYED... BY YOU!
LIAR!
I AM NOW A SPECTRE, AND YOU WILL FEEL MY WRATH!

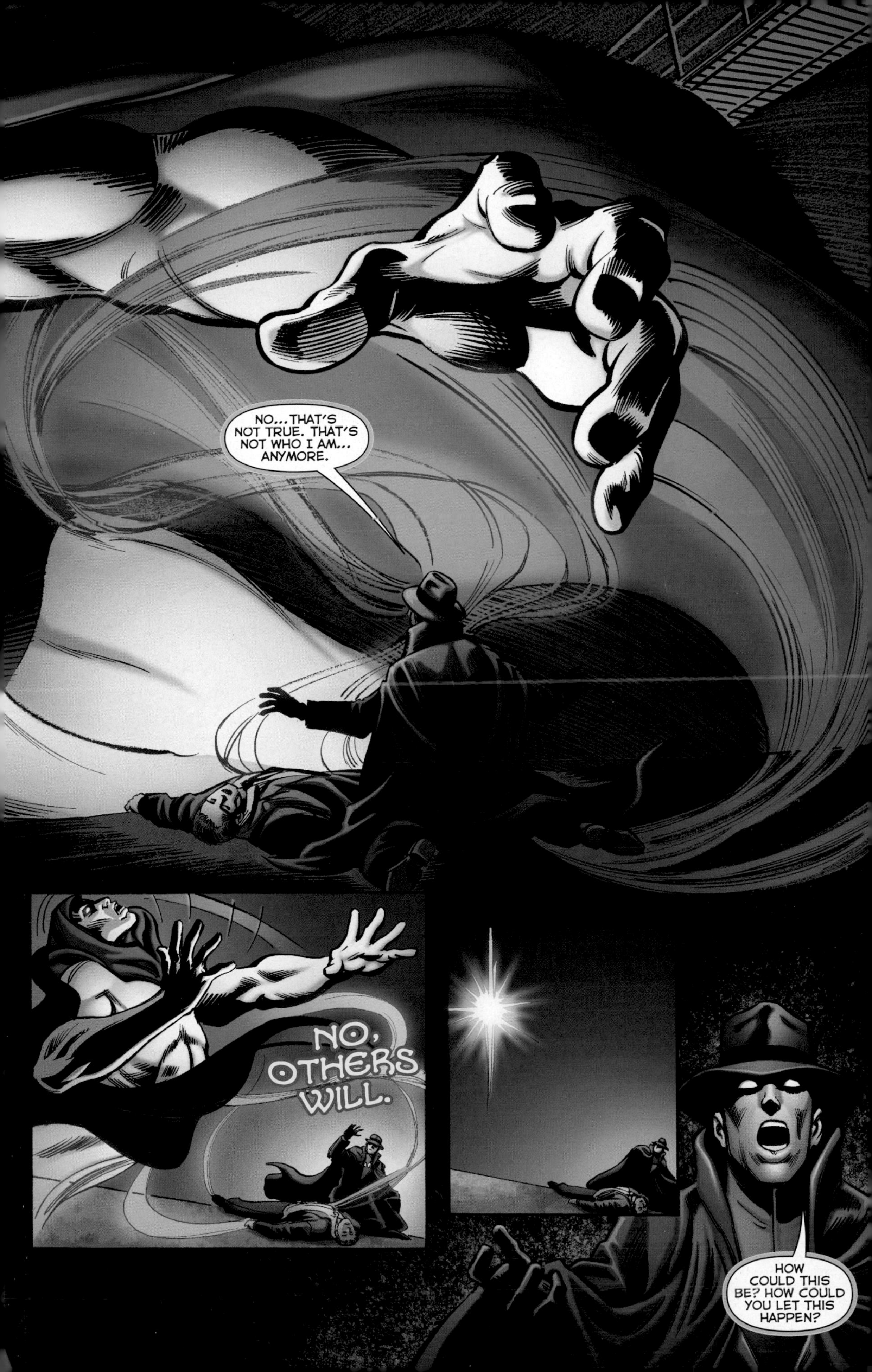
NO... THAT'S NOT TRUE. THAT'S NOT WHO I AM... ANYMORE.
NO, OTHERS WILL.
HOW COULD THIS BE? HOW COULD YOU LET THIS HAPPEN?

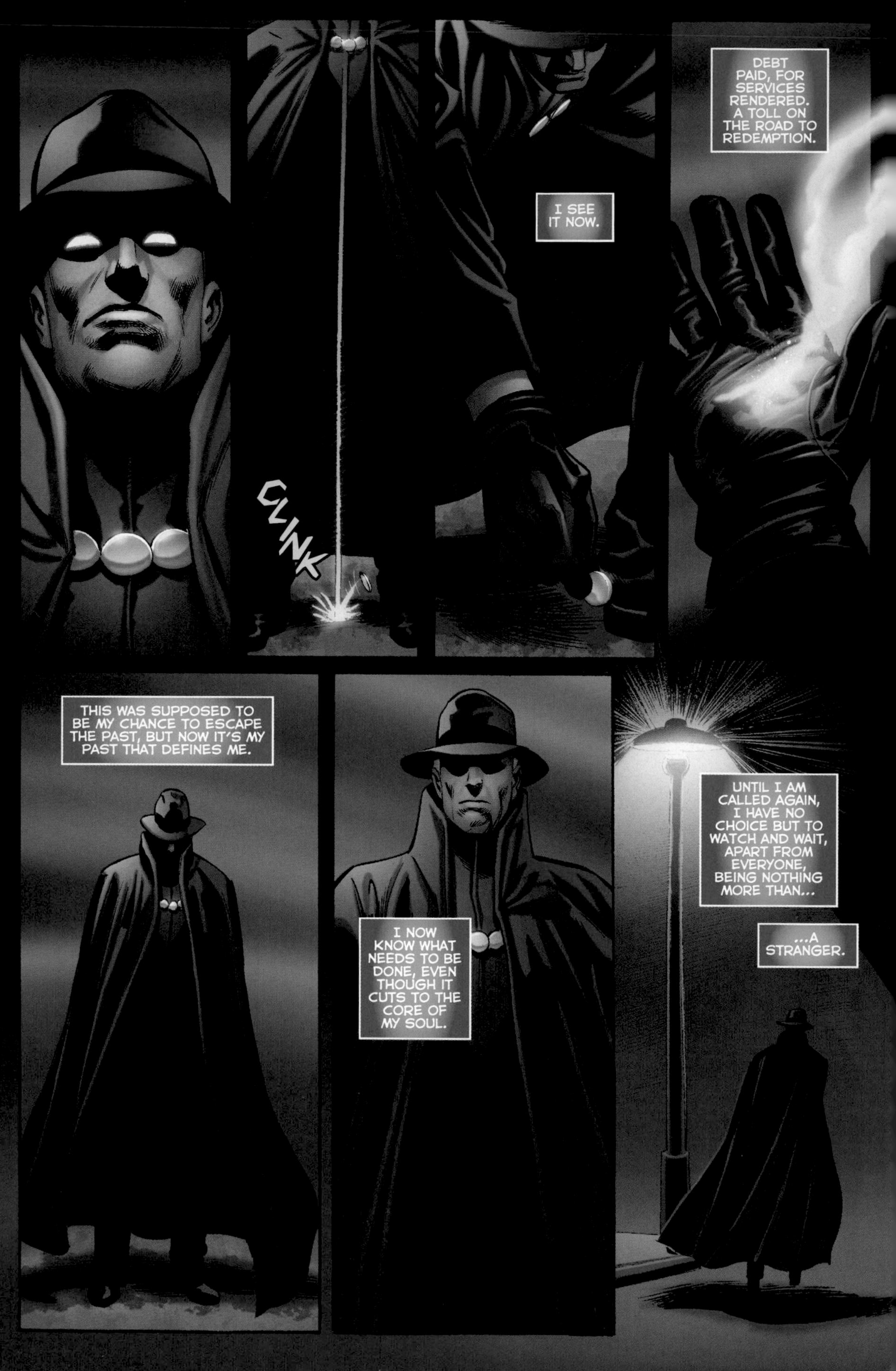
CLINK
I SEE IT NOW.
DEBT PAID, FOR SERVICES RENDERED. A TOLL ON THE ROAD TO REDEMPTION.
THIS WAS SUPPOSED TO BE MY CHANCE TO ESCAPE THE PAST, BUT NOW IT'S MY PAST THAT DEFINES ME.
I NOW KNOW WHAT NEEDS TO BE DONE, EVEN THOUGH IT CUTS TO THE CORE OF MY SOUL.
UNTIL I AM CALLED AGAIN, I HAVE NO CHOICE BUT TO WATCH AND WAIT, APART FROM EVERYONE, BEING NOTHING MORE THAN...
...A STRANGER.

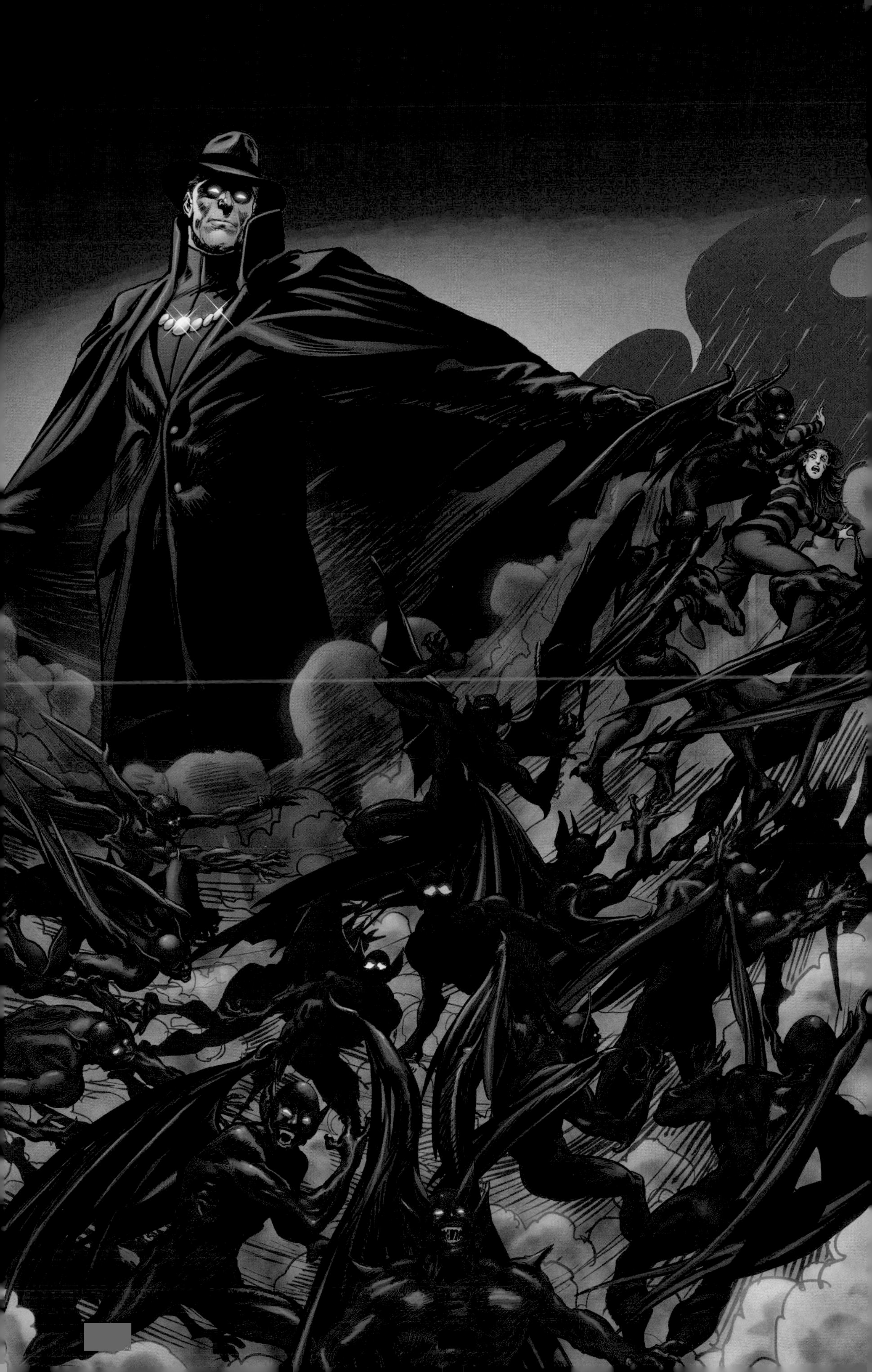

PENCILLER BRENT ANDERSON INKER PAGES COVER
TITLE PHANTOM STRANGER ISSUE # #1 MONTH
INTERIORS

Cover by Brent Anderson & Jeromy Cox

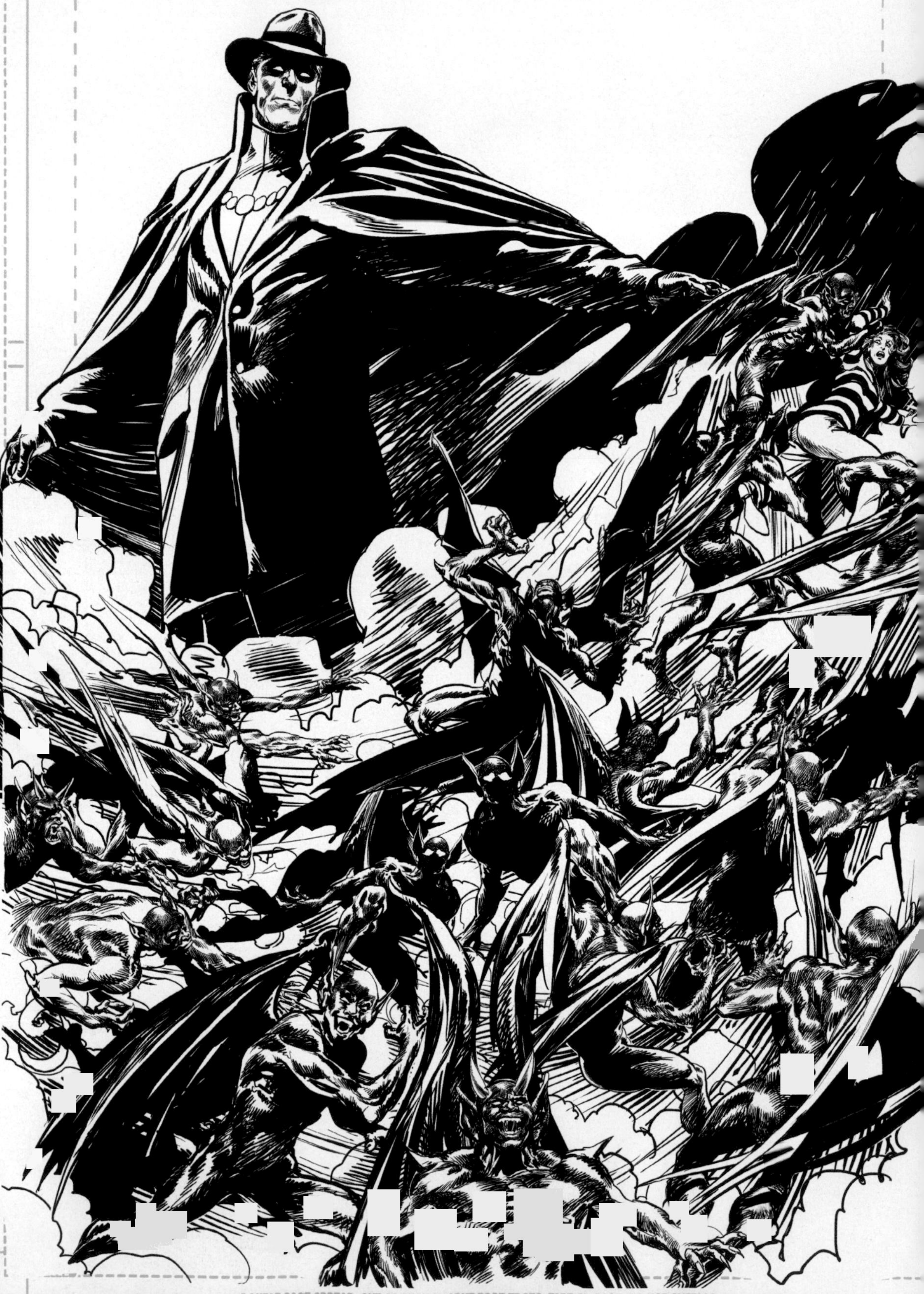

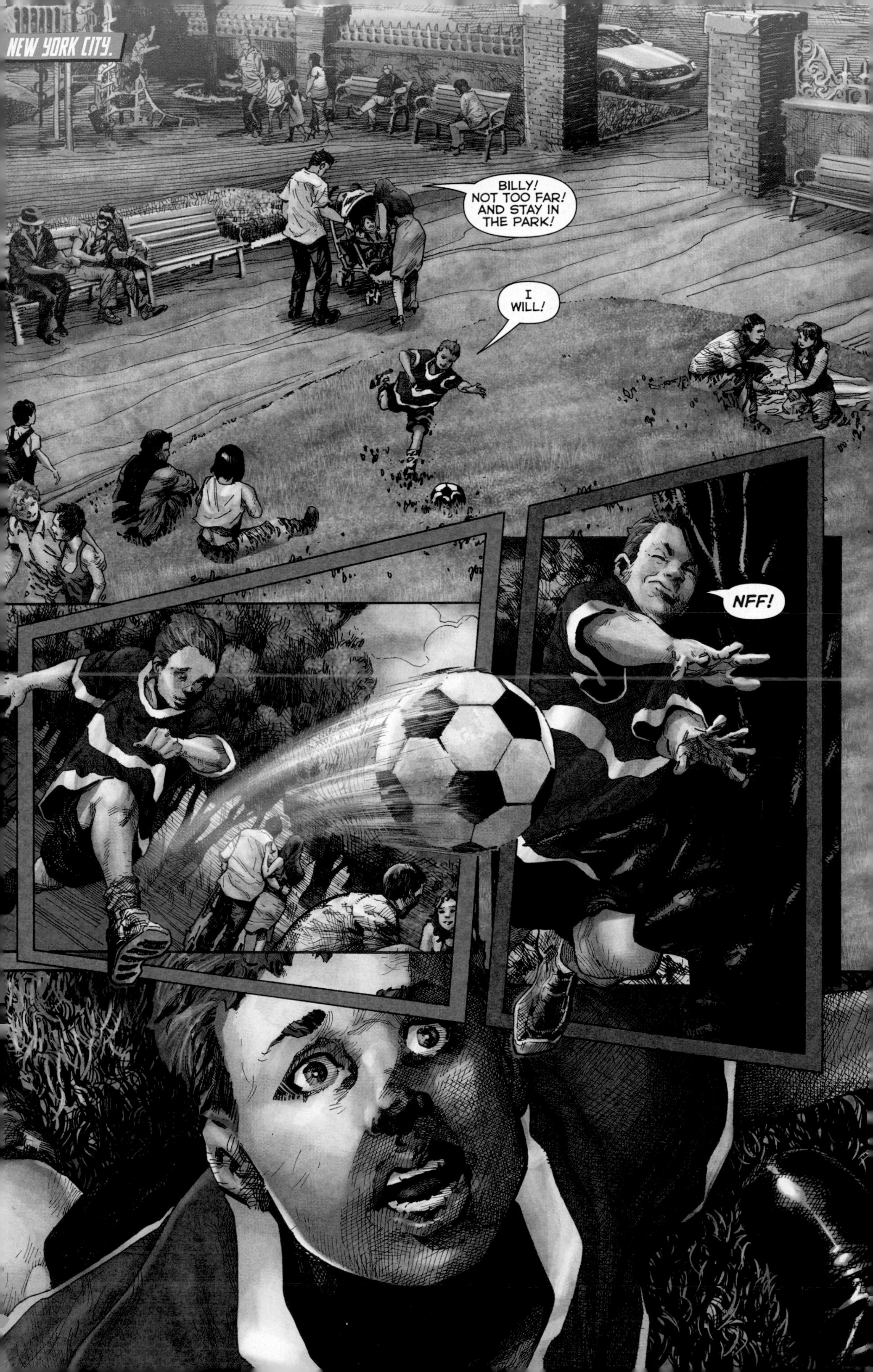
NEW YORK CITY.
BILLY! NOT TOO FAR! AND STAY IN THE PARK!
I WILL!
NFF!

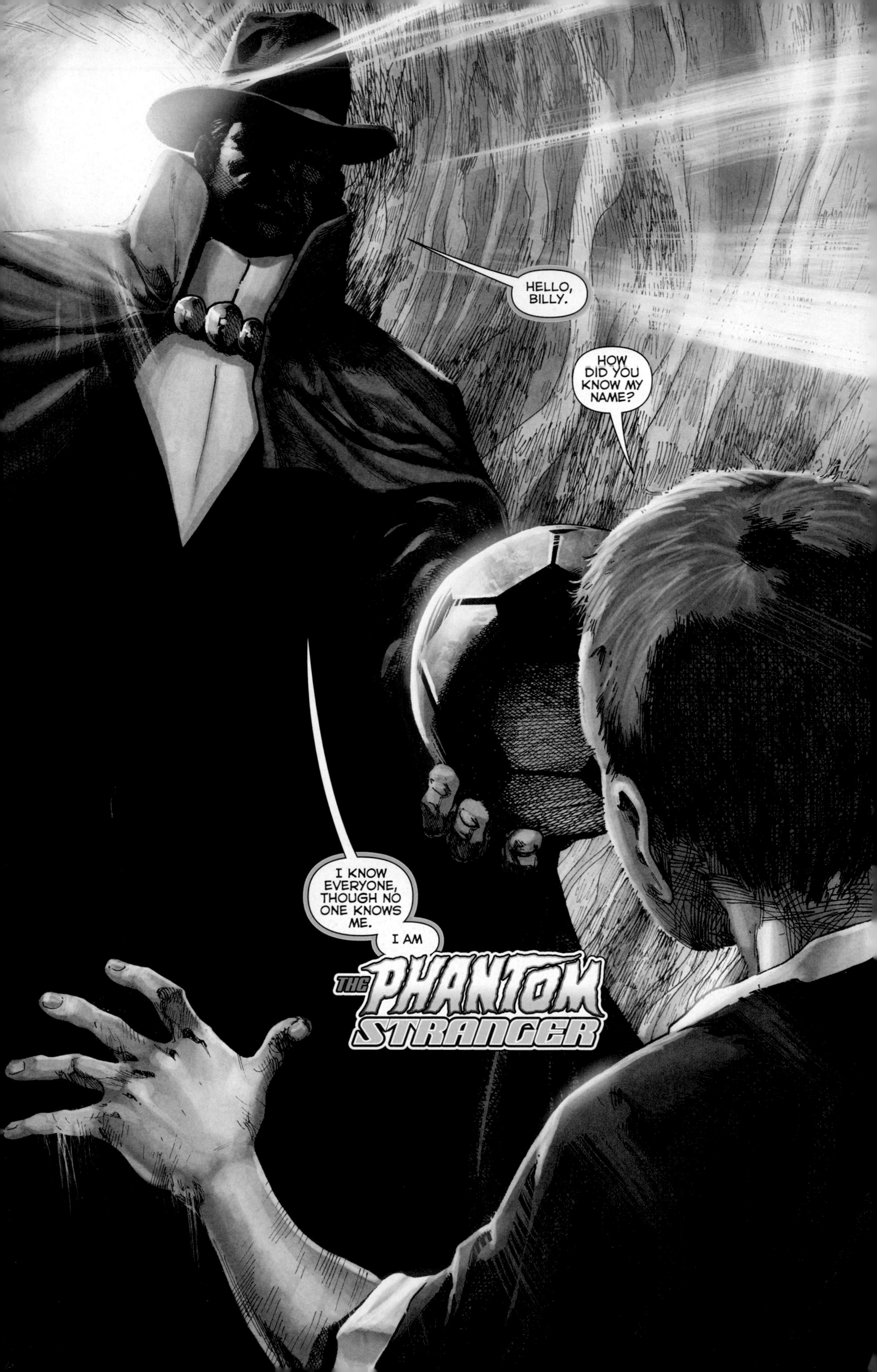
HELLO, BILLY.
HOW DID YOU KNOW MY NAME?
I KNOW EVERYONE, THOUGH NO ONE KNOWS ME.
I AM
THE PHANTOM STRANGER

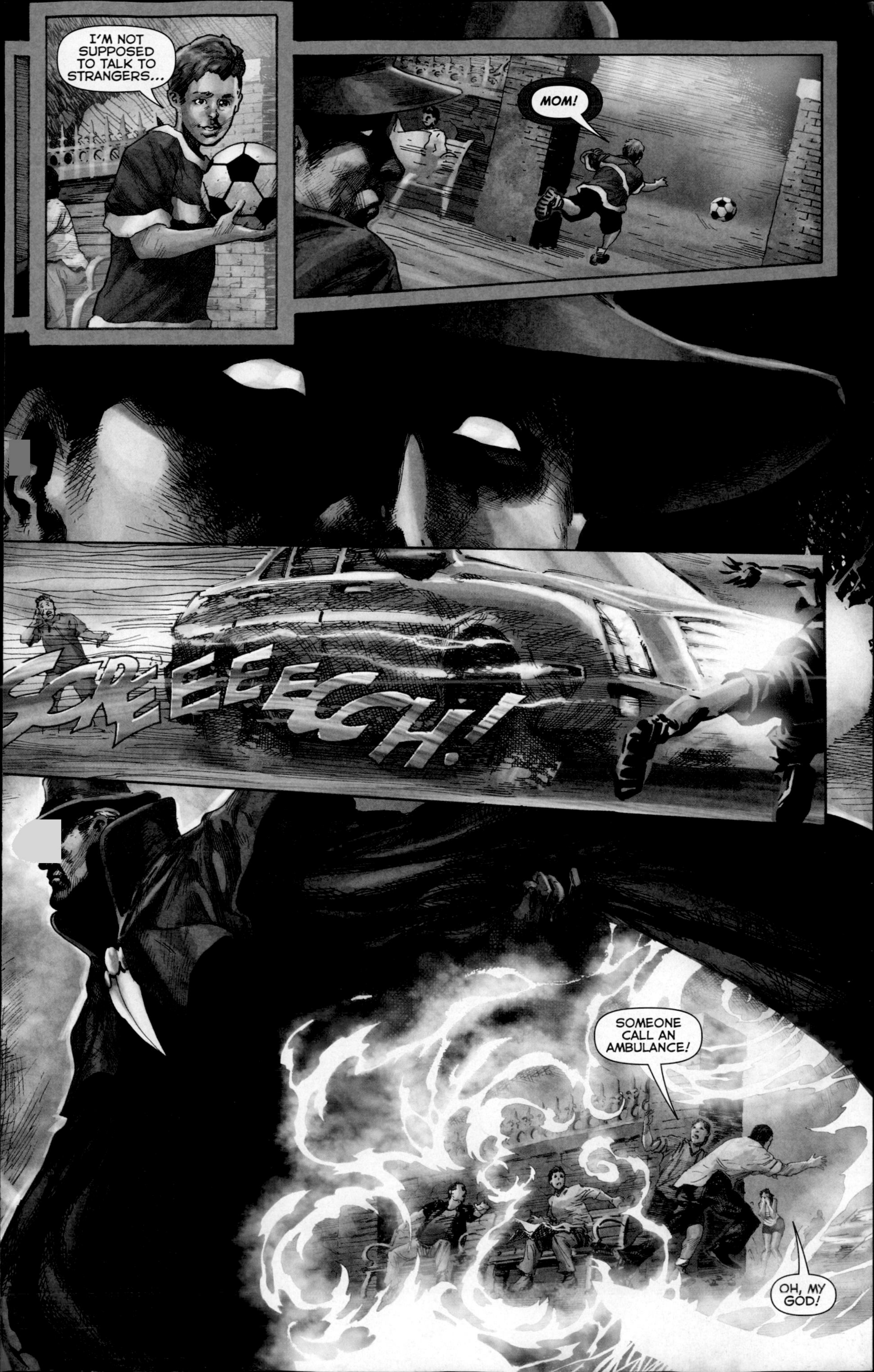
I'M NOT SUPPOSED TO TALK TO STRANGERS...
MOM!
SCREEEECH!
SOMEONE CALL AN AMBULANCE!
OH, MY GOD!

"IT'S TOO LATE."

I FEEL THEIR *LOVE* FOR YOU, BILLY... BUT I FEEL THEIR *GRIEF* TOO.

I CAN TRY TO EASE IT...I CAN TRY TO HELP.

WHO IS THAT GIRL, MOM?

I DON'T KNOW--SO LOWER YOUR VOICE!

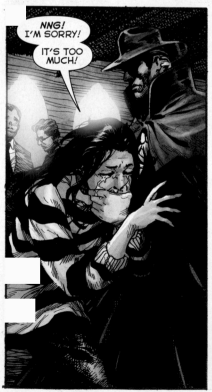

NNG! I'M SORRY!

IT'S TOO MUCH!

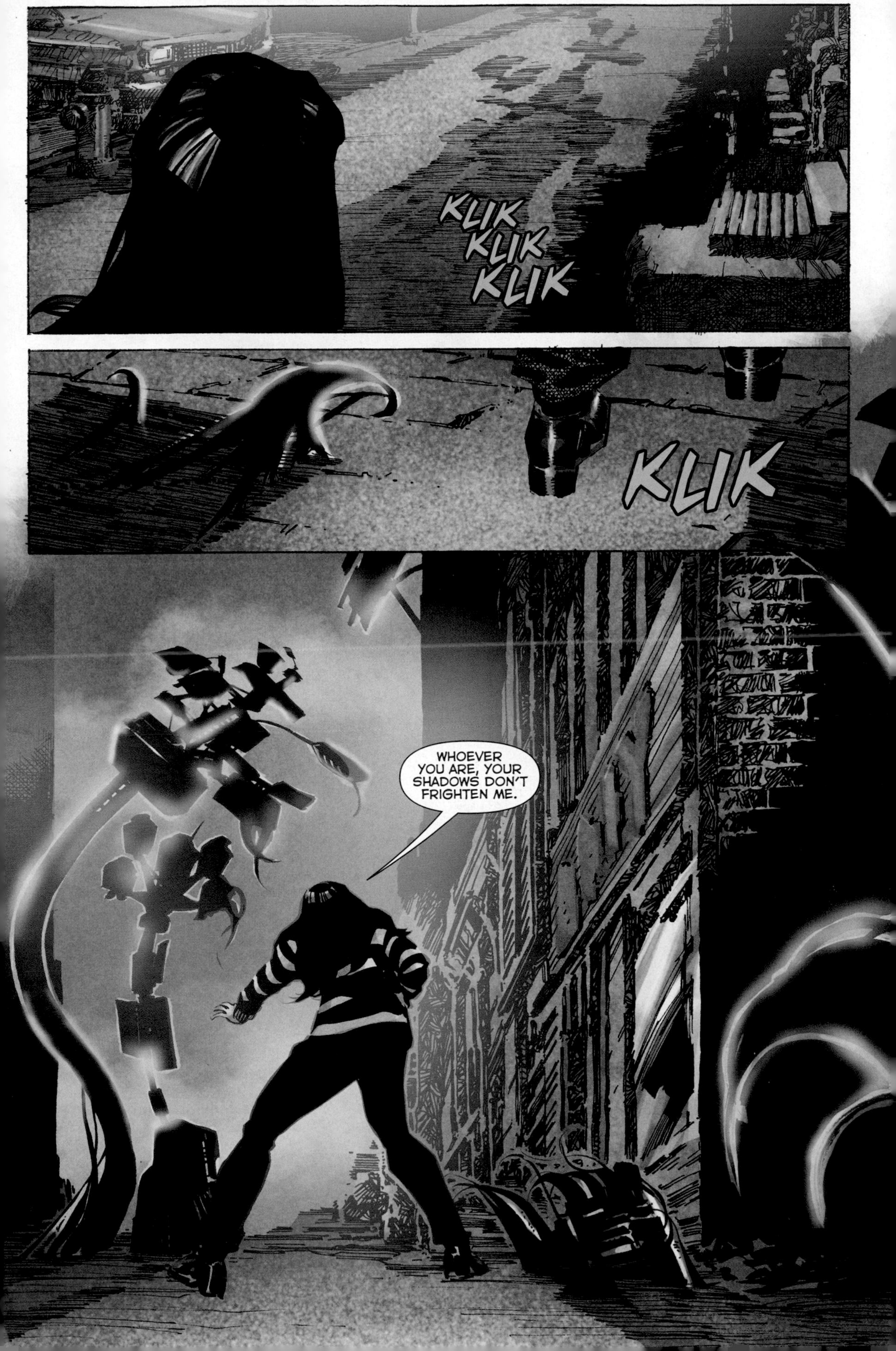
KLIK
KLIK
KLIK
KLIK
WHOEVER YOU ARE, YOUR SHADOWS DON'T FRIGHTEN ME.

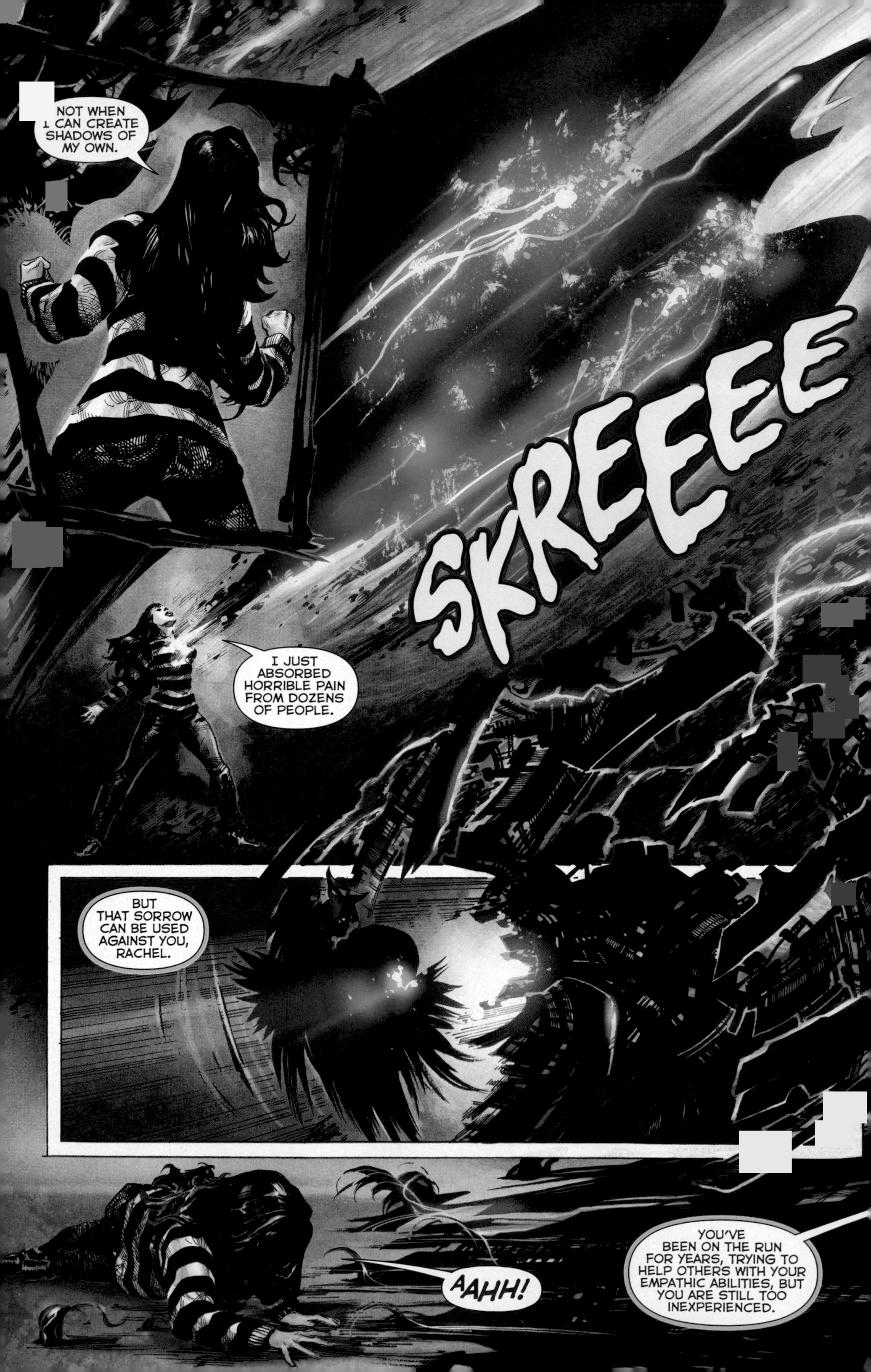
NOT WHEN I CAN CREATE SHADOWS OF MY OWN.
SKREEEE
I JUST ABSORBED HORRIBLE PAIN FROM DOZENS OF PEOPLE.
BUT THAT SORROW CAN BE USED AGAINST YOU, RACHEL.
AAHH!
YOU'VE BEEN ON THE RUN FOR YEARS, TRYING TO HELP OTHERS WITH YOUR EMPATHIC ABILITIES, BUT YOU ARE STILL TOO INEXPERIENCED.

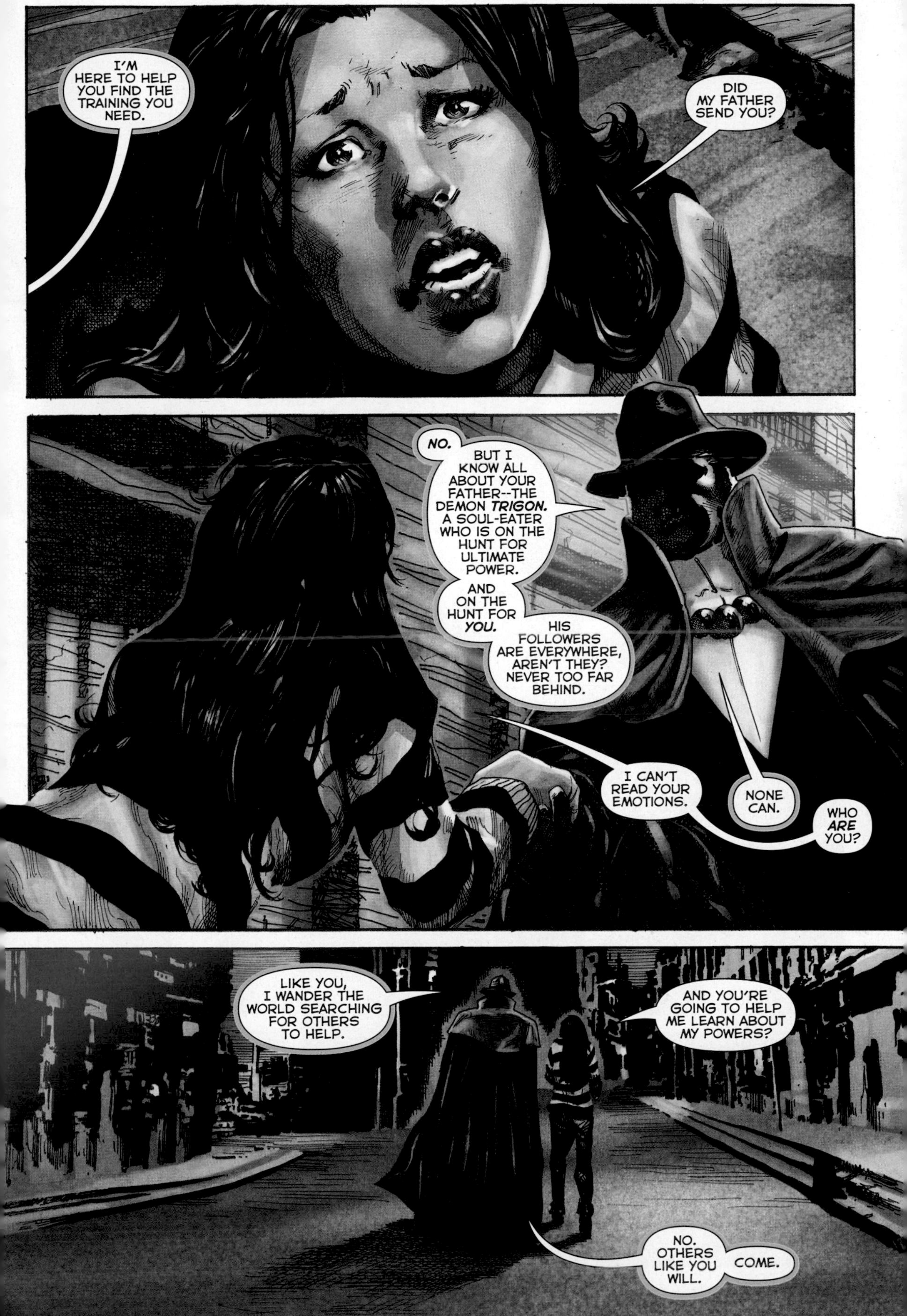
I'M HERE TO HELP YOU FIND THE TRAINING YOU NEED.
DID MY FATHER SEND YOU?
NO.
BUT I KNOW ALL ABOUT YOUR FATHER--THE DEMON TRIGON. A SOUL-EATER WHO IS ON THE HUNT FOR ULTIMATE POWER.
AND ON THE HUNT FOR YOU.
HIS FOLLOWERS ARE EVERYWHERE, AREN'T THEY? NEVER TOO FAR BEHIND.
I CAN'T READ YOUR EMOTIONS.
NONE CAN.
WHO ARE YOU?
LIKE YOU, I WANDER THE WORLD SEARCHING FOR OTHERS TO HELP.
AND YOU'RE GOING TO HELP ME LEARN ABOUT MY POWERS?
NO. OTHERS LIKE YOU WILL.
COME.

YOU'RE REALLY *THAT* STRANGER. I'VE HEARD MY FATHER SPEAK OF YOU.

NOTHING GOOD, I IMAGINE.

IT'S THE ONLY REASON I TRUST YOU.

I UNDERSTAND WHY YOU WOULDN'T.

BUT REGARDLESS, YOU HAVEN'T BEEN ABLE TO TRUST ANYONE, HAVE YOU?

INCLUDING YOURSELF.

MY MOTHER RAISED ME IN A HIDDEN DIMENSION CALLED *AZARATH*. A PLACE OF PEACE AND TRANQUILITY THAT HELPED ME KEEP MY ABILITIES UNDER CONTROL.

BUT THERE ARE TIMES WHEN I STRUGGLE WITH THEM. WHEN I CAN FEEL MY FATHER'S INFLUENCE CREEP INTO MY VERY SOUL...AND IT *FRIGHTENS* ME.

IT SHOULD.

BUT THAT IS WHAT MAKES YOU THE STRONG YOUNG WOMAN YOU ARE.

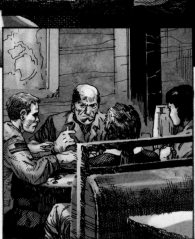

ARE YOU SURE YOU KNOW THE PEOPLE WHO CAN HELP ME?

WAIT... I FEEL...

"...EVIL."

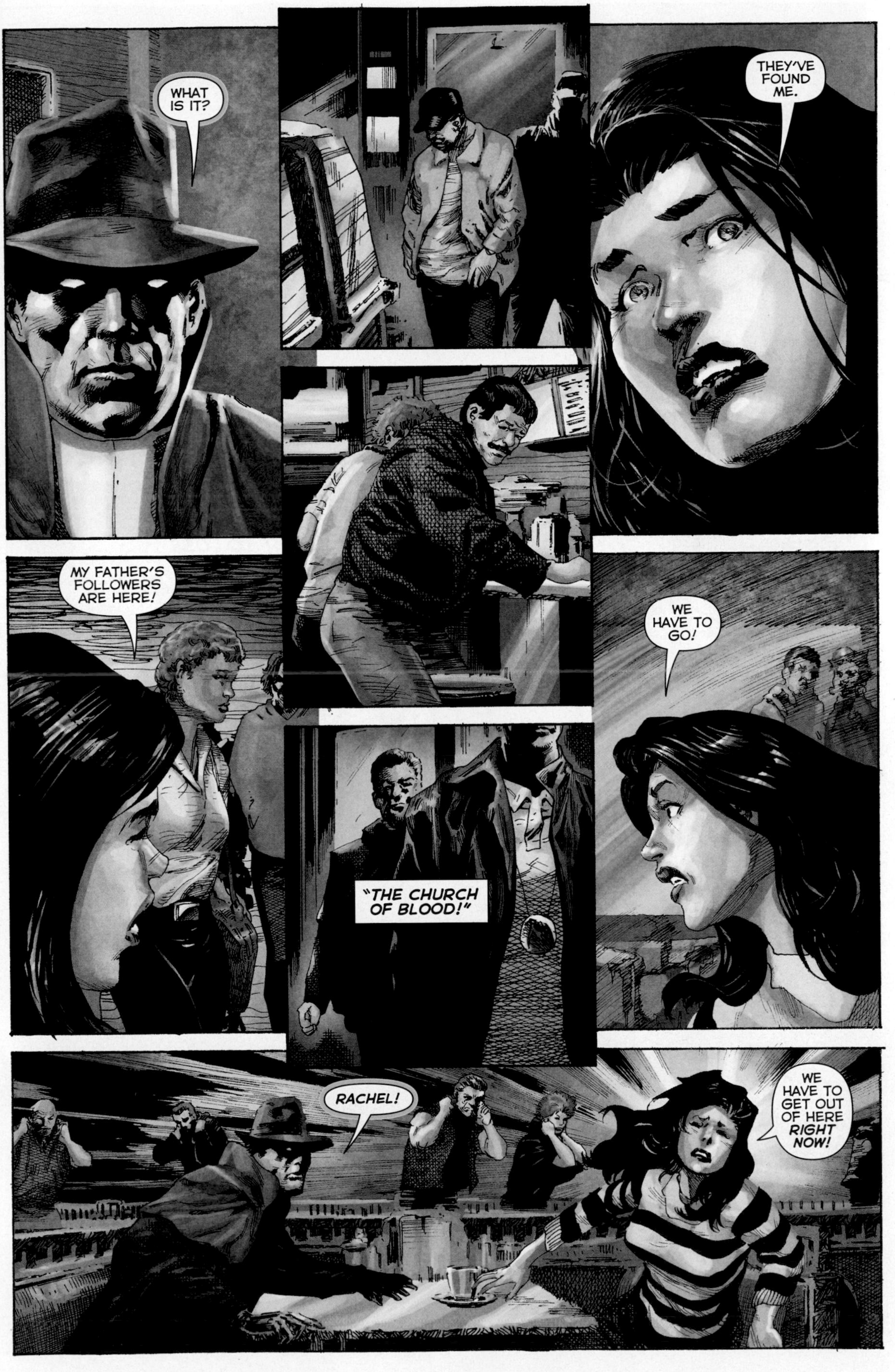
WHAT IS IT?
THEY'VE FOUND ME.
MY FATHER'S FOLLOWERS ARE HERE!
"THE CHURCH OF BLOOD!"
WE HAVE TO GO!
RACHEL!
WE HAVE TO GET OUT OF HERE RIGHT NOW!

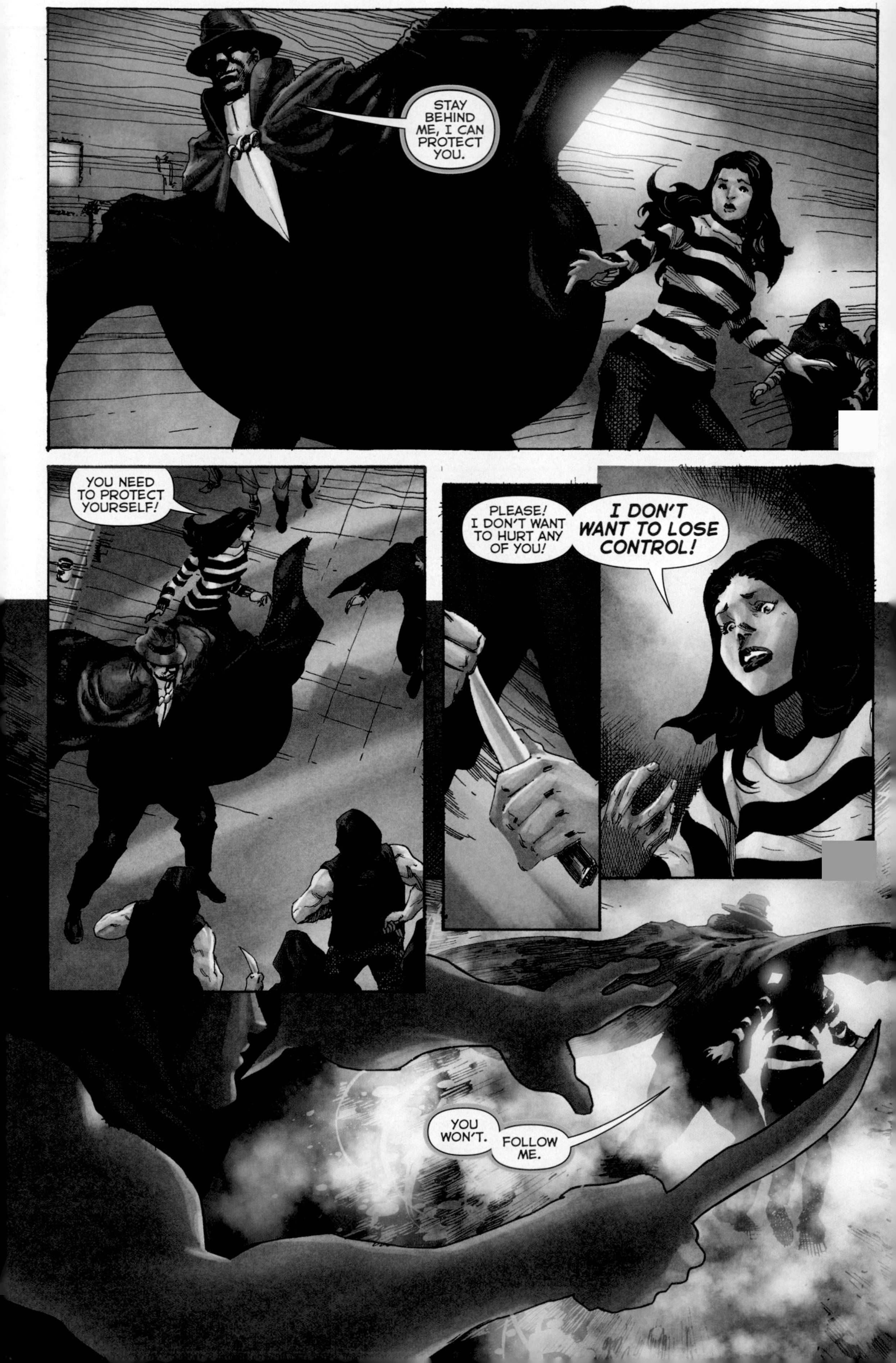
STAY BEHIND ME, I CAN PROTECT YOU.
YOU NEED TO PROTECT YOURSELF!
PLEASE! I DON'T WANT TO HURT ANY OF YOU!
I DON'T WANT TO LOSE CONTROL!
YOU WON'T.
FOLLOW ME.

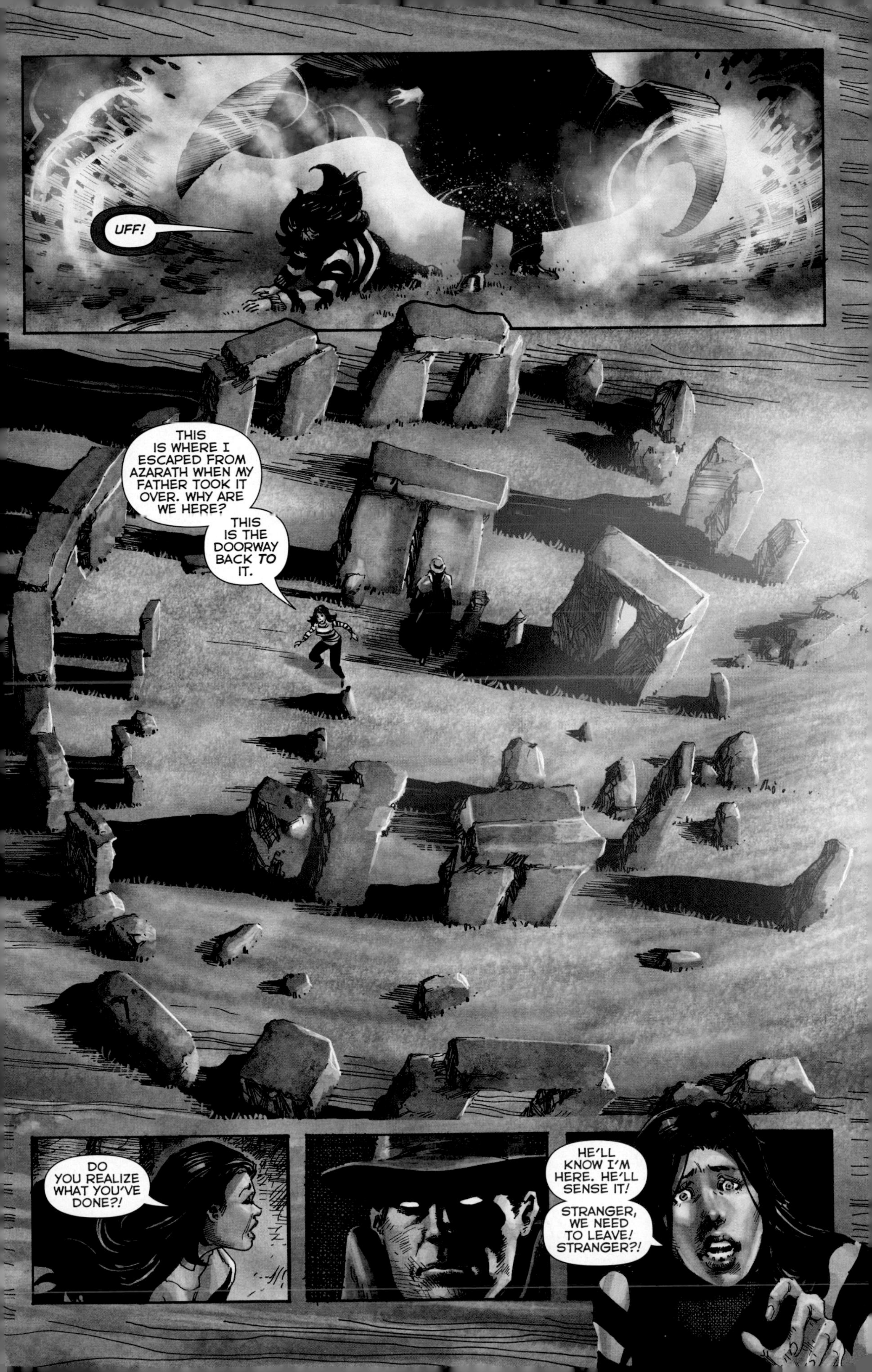
UFF!
THIS IS WHERE I ESCAPED FROM AZARATH WHEN MY FATHER TOOK IT OVER. WHY ARE WE HERE?
THIS IS THE DOORWAY BACK TO IT.
DO YOU REALIZE WHAT YOU'VE DONE?!
HE'LL KNOW I'M HERE. HE'LL SENSE IT!
STRANGER, WE NEED TO LEAVE! STRANGER?!

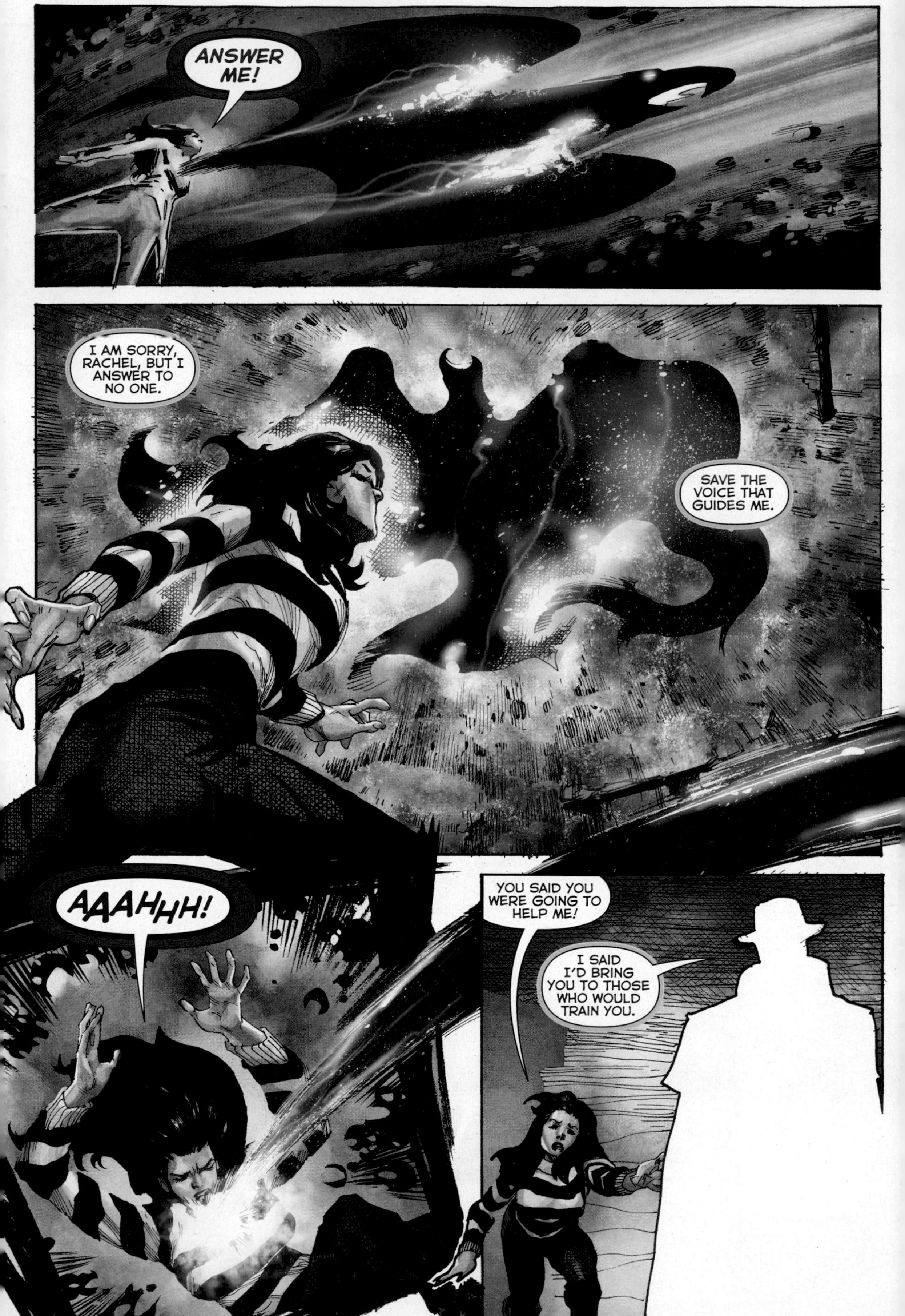
ANSWER ME!
I AM SORRY, RACHEL, BUT I ANSWER TO NO ONE.
SAVE THE VOICE THAT GUIDES ME.
AAAHHH!
YOU SAID YOU WERE GOING TO HELP ME!
I SAID I'D BRING YOU TO THOSE WHO WOULD TRAIN YOU.

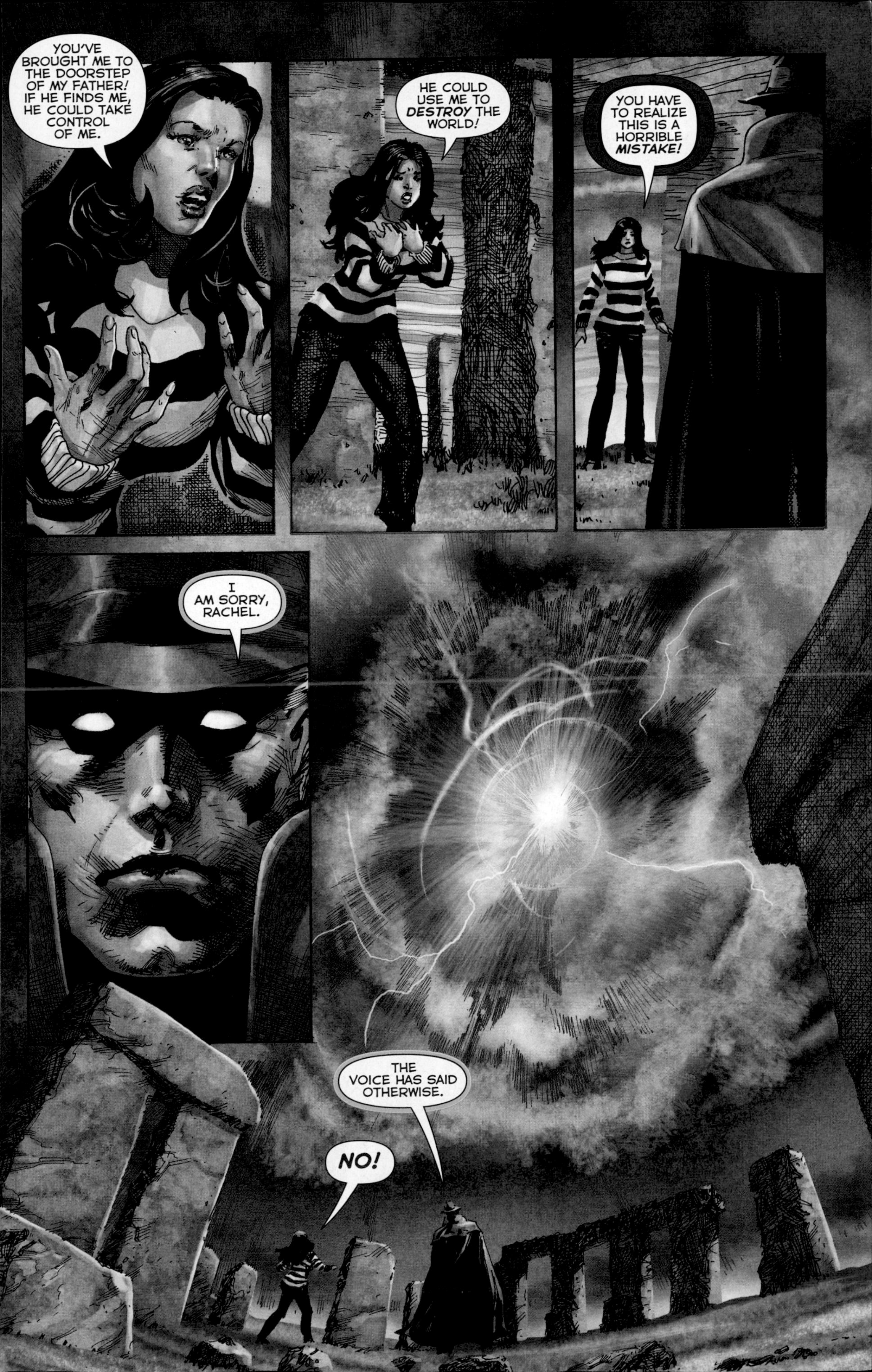

YOU'VE BROUGHT ME TO THE DOORSTEP OF MY FATHER! IF HE FINDS ME, HE COULD TAKE CONTROL OF ME.
HE COULD USE ME TO DESTROY THE WORLD!
YOU HAVE TO REALIZE THIS IS A HORRIBLE MISTAKE!
I AM SORRY, RACHEL.
THE VOICE HAS SAID OTHERWISE.
NO!

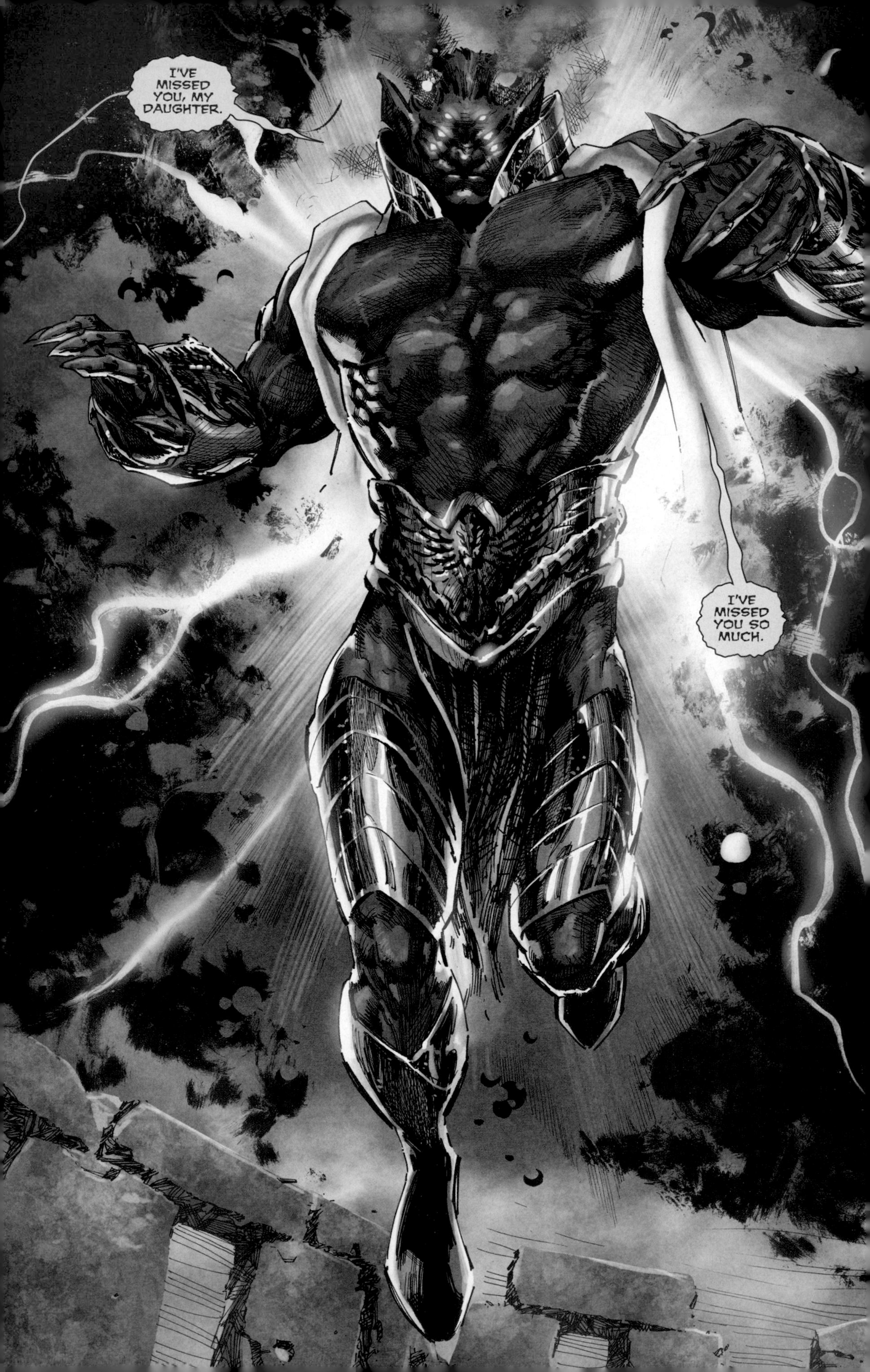
I'VE MISSED YOU, MY DAUGHTER.
I'VE MISSED YOU SO MUCH.

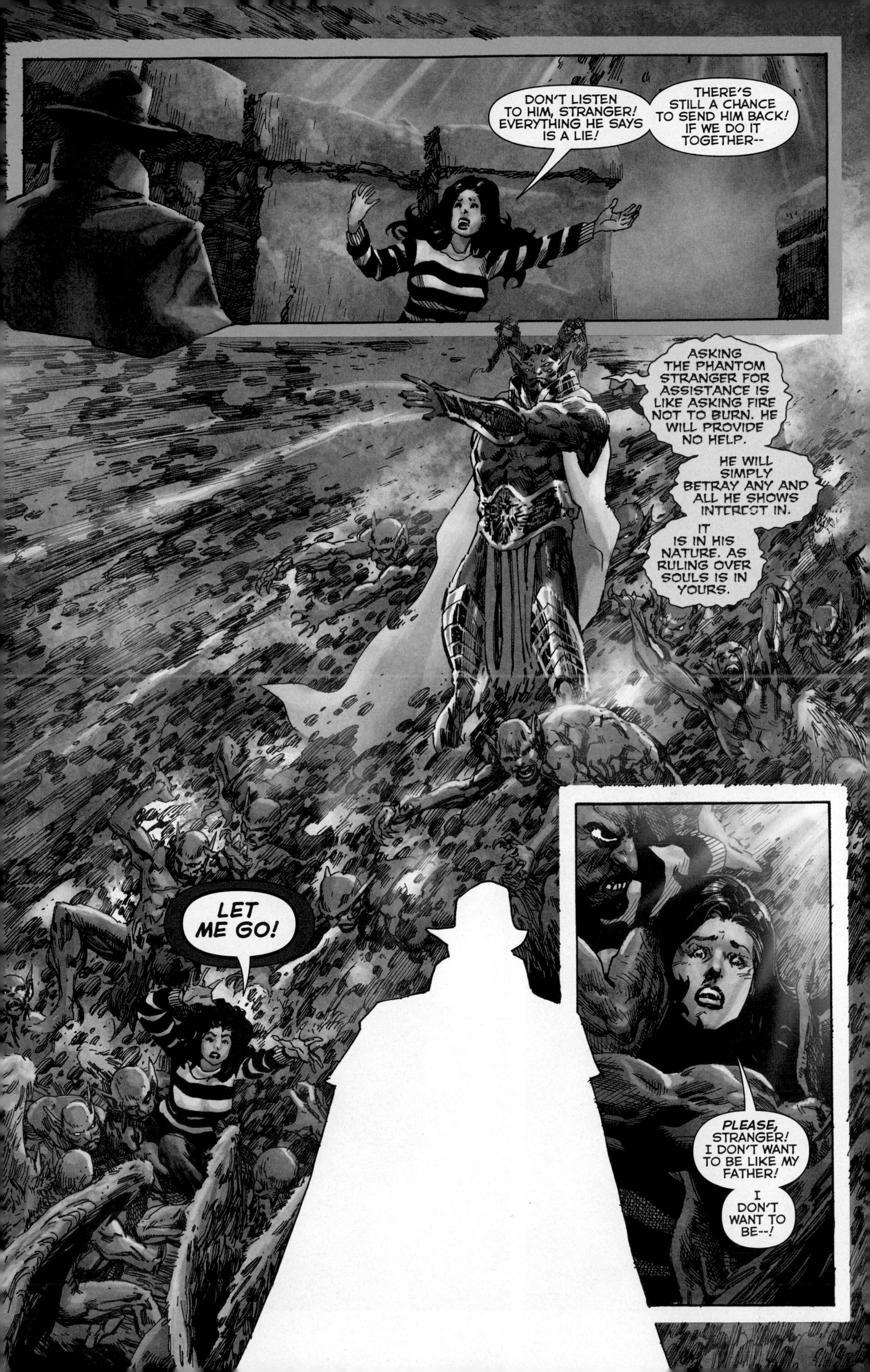

DON'T LISTEN TO HIM, STRANGER! EVERYTHING HE SAYS IS A LIE!
THERE'S STILL A CHANCE TO SEND HIM BACK! IF WE DO IT TOGETHER--
ASKING THE PHANTOM STRANGER FOR ASSISTANCE IS LIKE ASKING FIRE NOT TO BURN. HE WILL PROVIDE NO HELP.
HE WILL SIMPLY BETRAY ANY AND ALL HE SHOWS INTEREST IN.
IT IS IN HIS NATURE. AS RULING OVER SOULS IS IN YOURS.
LET ME GO!
PLEASE, STRANGER! I DON'T WANT TO BE LIKE MY FATHER!
I DON'T WANT TO BE--!

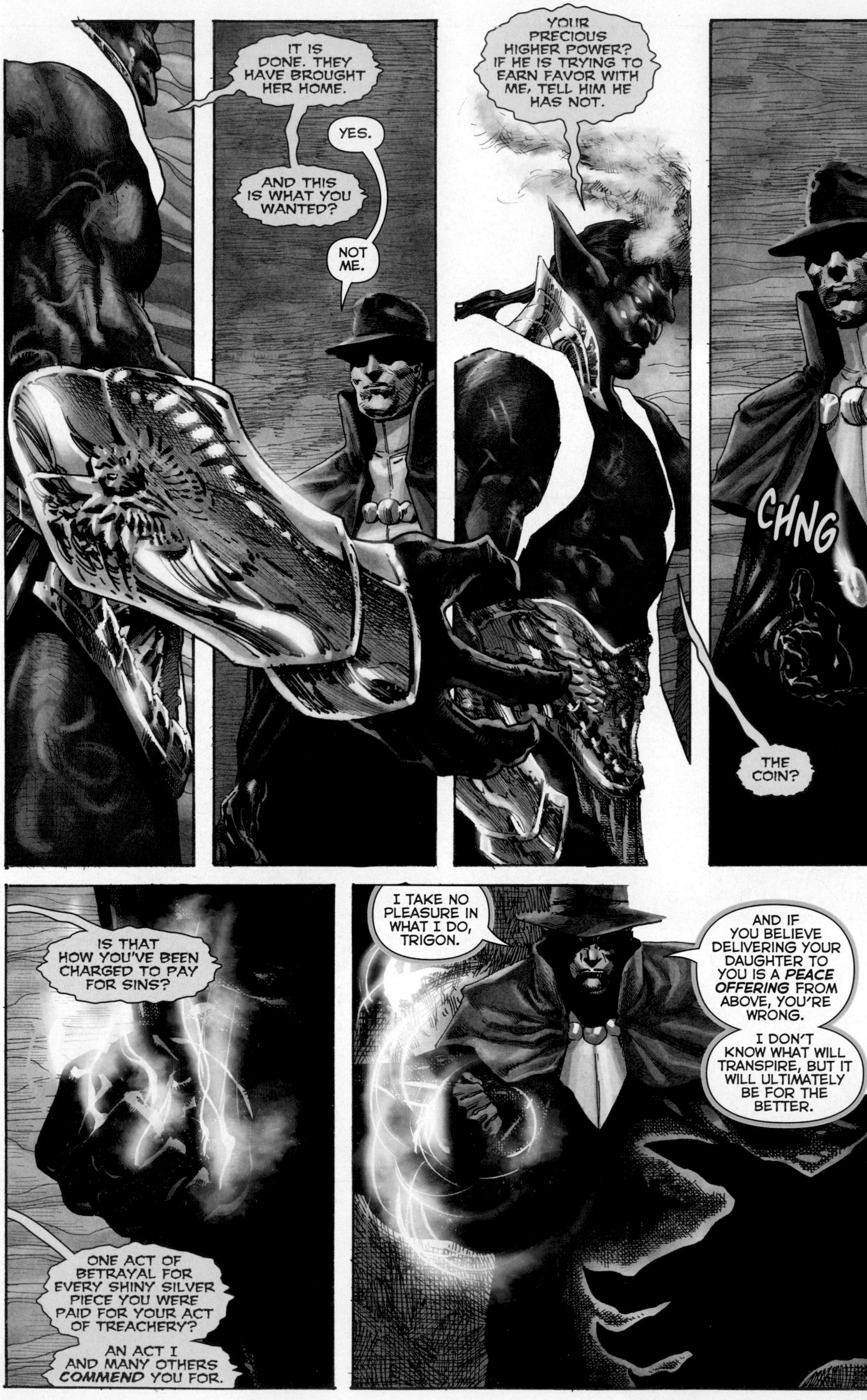
IT IS DONE. THEY HAVE BROUGHT HER HOME.
YES.
AND THIS IS WHAT YOU WANTED?
NOT ME.
YOUR PRECIOUS HIGHER POWER? IF HE IS TRYING TO EARN FAVOR WITH ME, TELL HIM HE HAS NOT.
CHNG
THE COIN?
IS THAT HOW YOU'VE BEEN CHARGED TO PAY FOR SINS?
ONE ACT OF BETRAYAL FOR EVERY SHINY SILVER PIECE YOU WERE PAID FOR YOUR ACT OF TREACHERY?
AN ACT I AND MANY OTHERS COMMEND YOU FOR.
I TAKE NO PLEASURE IN WHAT I DO, TRIGON.
AND IF YOU BELIEVE DELIVERING YOUR DAUGHTER TO YOU IS A PEACE OFFERING FROM ABOVE, YOU'RE WRONG.
I DON'T KNOW WHAT WILL TRANSPIRE, BUT IT WILL ULTIMATELY BE FOR THE BETTER.

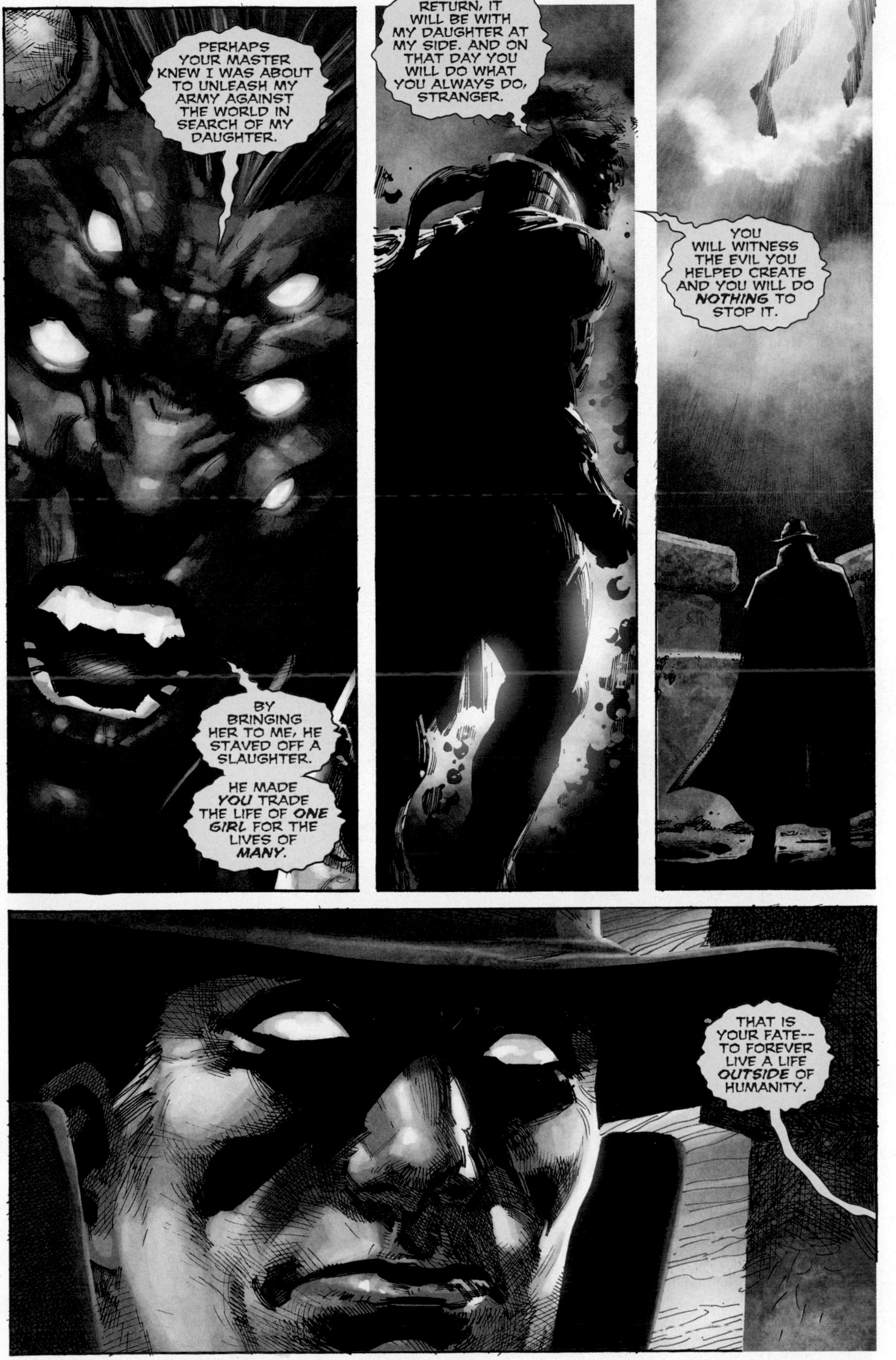
PERHAPS YOUR MASTER KNEW I WAS ABOUT TO UNLEASH MY ARMY AGAINST THE WORLD IN SEARCH OF MY DAUGHTER.
BY BRINGING HER TO ME, HE STAVED OFF A SLAUGHTER.
HE MADE *YOU* TRADE THE LIFE OF *ONE GIRL* FOR THE LIVES OF *MANY*.
WHEN I RETURN, IT WILL BE WITH MY DAUGHTER AT MY SIDE. AND ON THAT DAY YOU WILL DO WHAT YOU ALWAYS DO, STRANGER.
YOU WILL WITNESS THE EVIL YOU HELPED CREATE AND YOU WILL DO *NOTHING* TO STOP IT.
THAT IS YOUR FATE-- TO FOREVER LIVE A LIFE *OUTSIDE* OF HUMANITY.

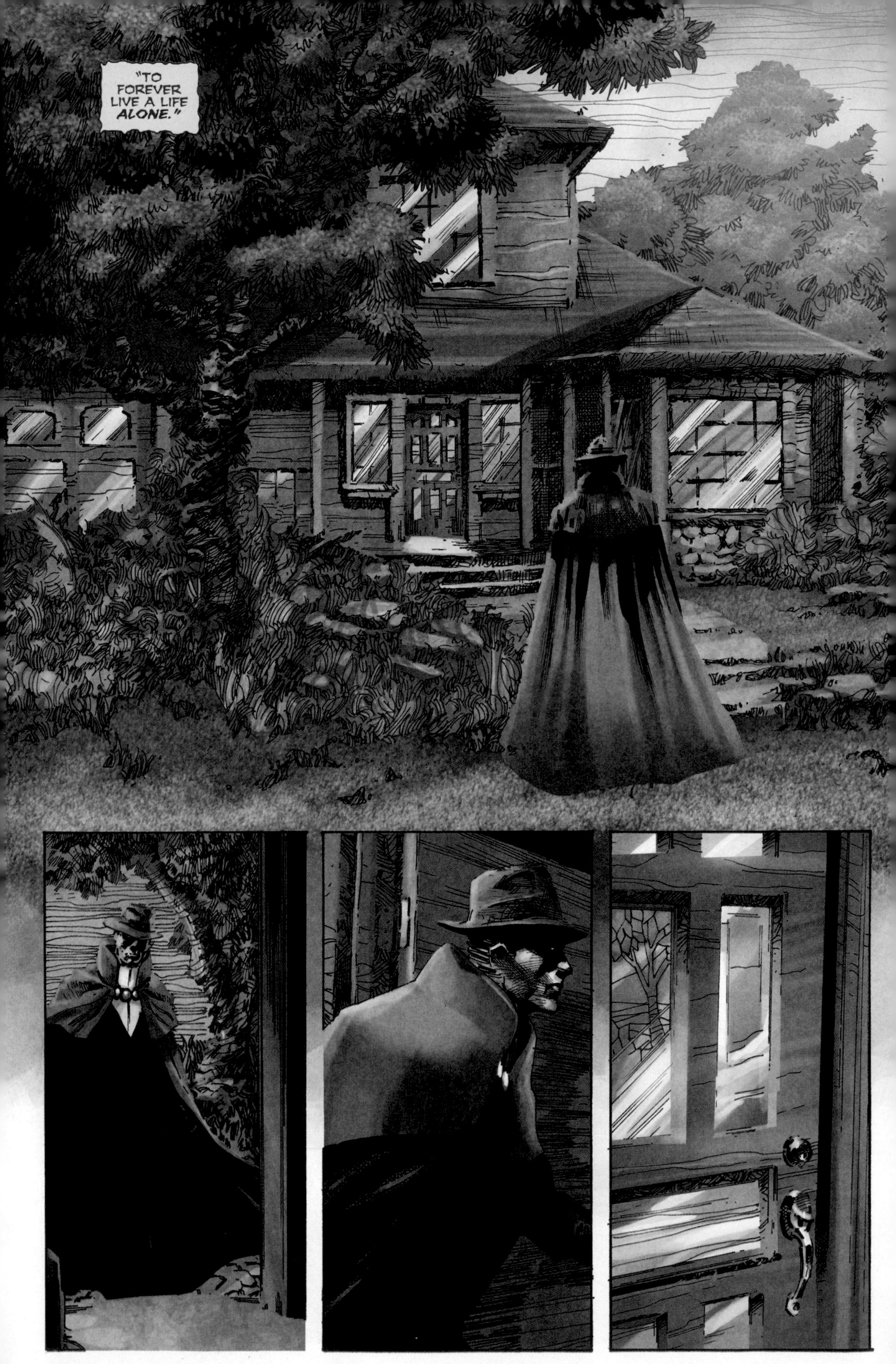
"TO FOREVER LIVE A LIFE ALONE."

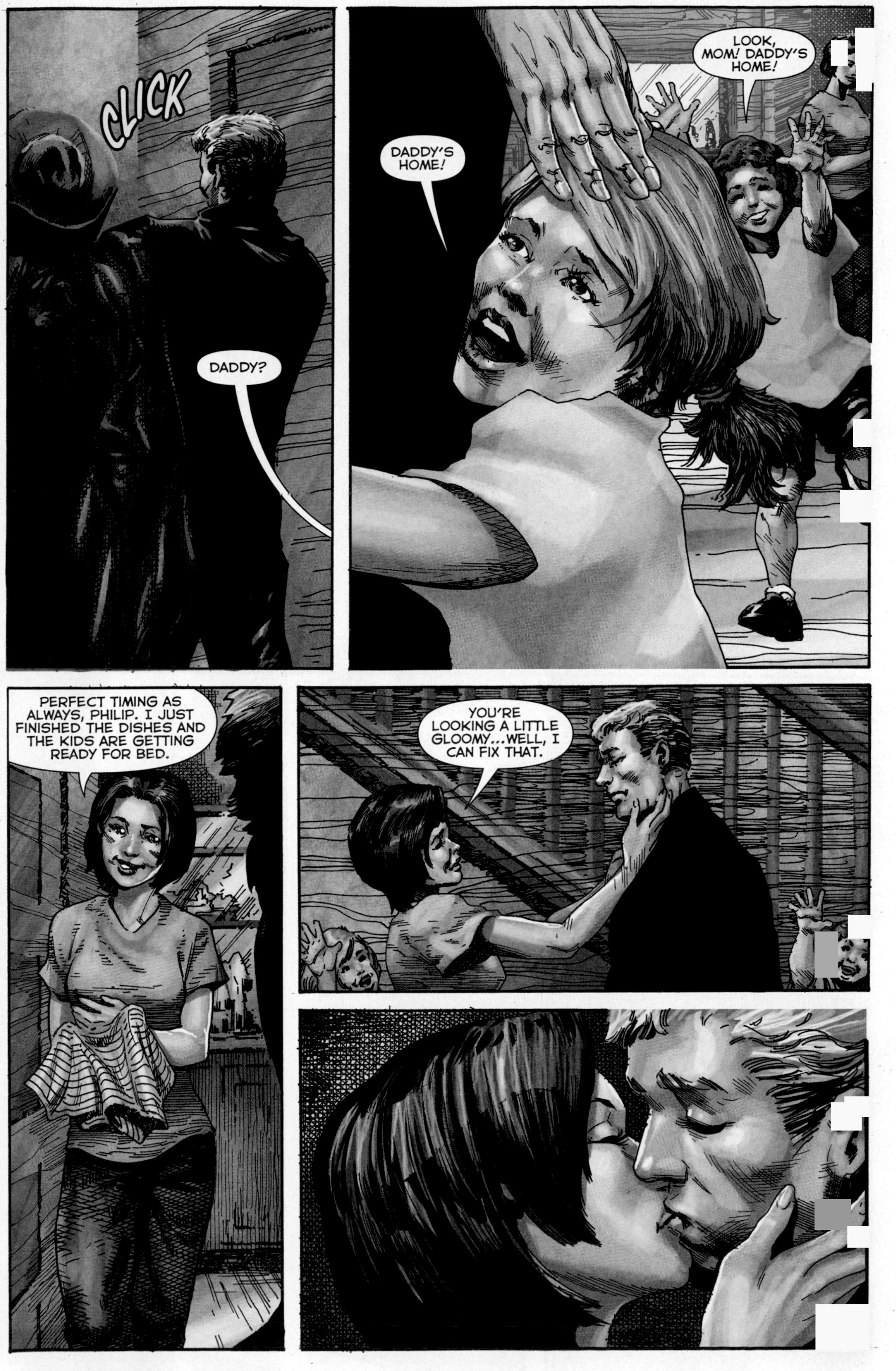
CLICK
DADDY?
DADDY'S HOME!
LOOK, MOM! DADDY'S HOME!
PERFECT TIMING AS ALWAYS, PHILIP. I JUST FINISHED THE DISHES AND THE KIDS ARE GETTING READY FOR BED.
YOU'RE LOOKING A LITTLE GLOOMY...WELL, I CAN FIX THAT.

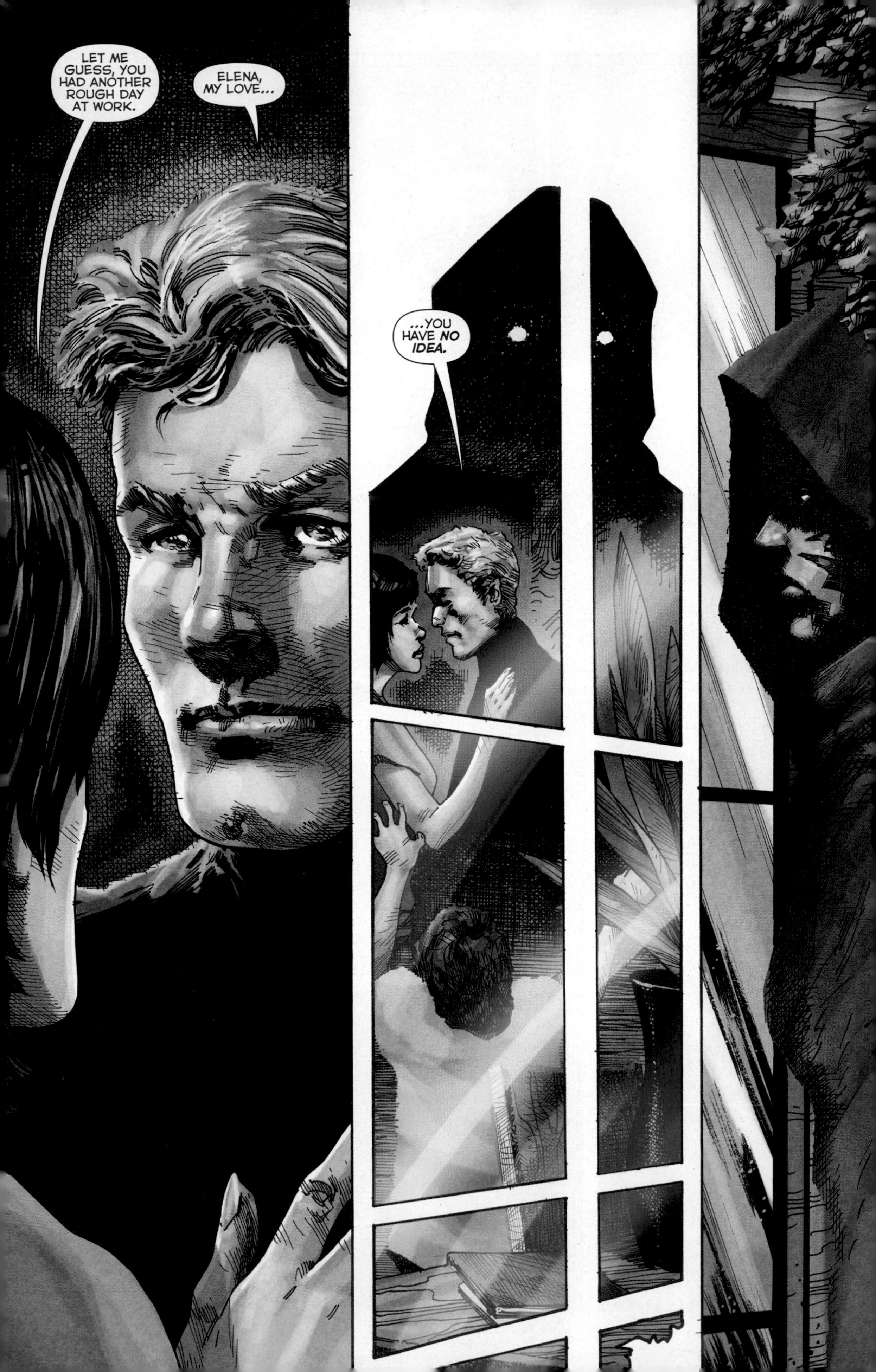
LET ME GUESS, YOU HAD ANOTHER ROUGH DAY AT WORK.
ELENA, MY LOVE...
...YOU HAVE *NO IDEA.*

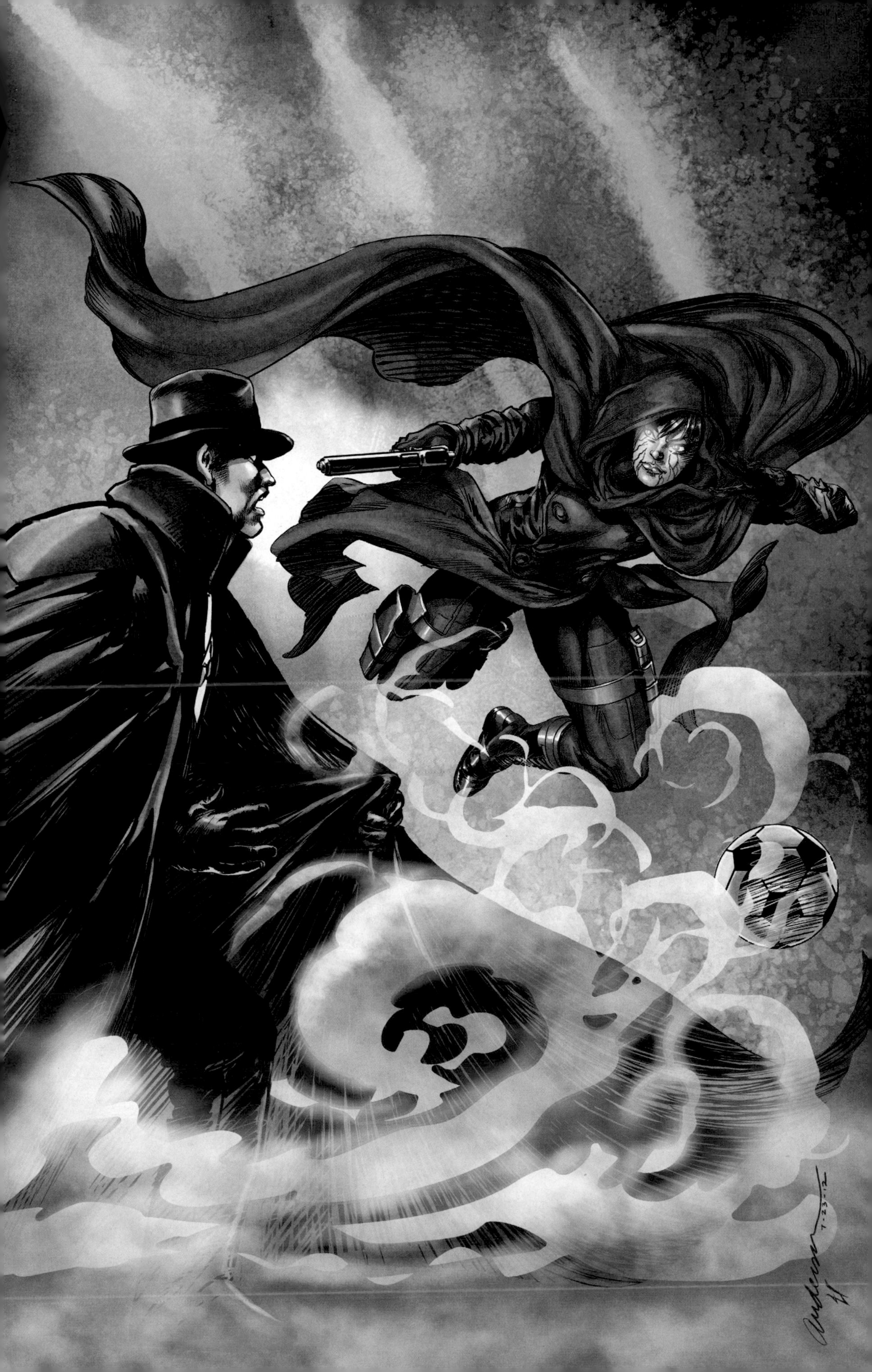

TITLE PHANTOM STRANGER ISSUE # #2 PAGES COVER INTERIORS

Cover by Brent Anderson & Ulises Arreola

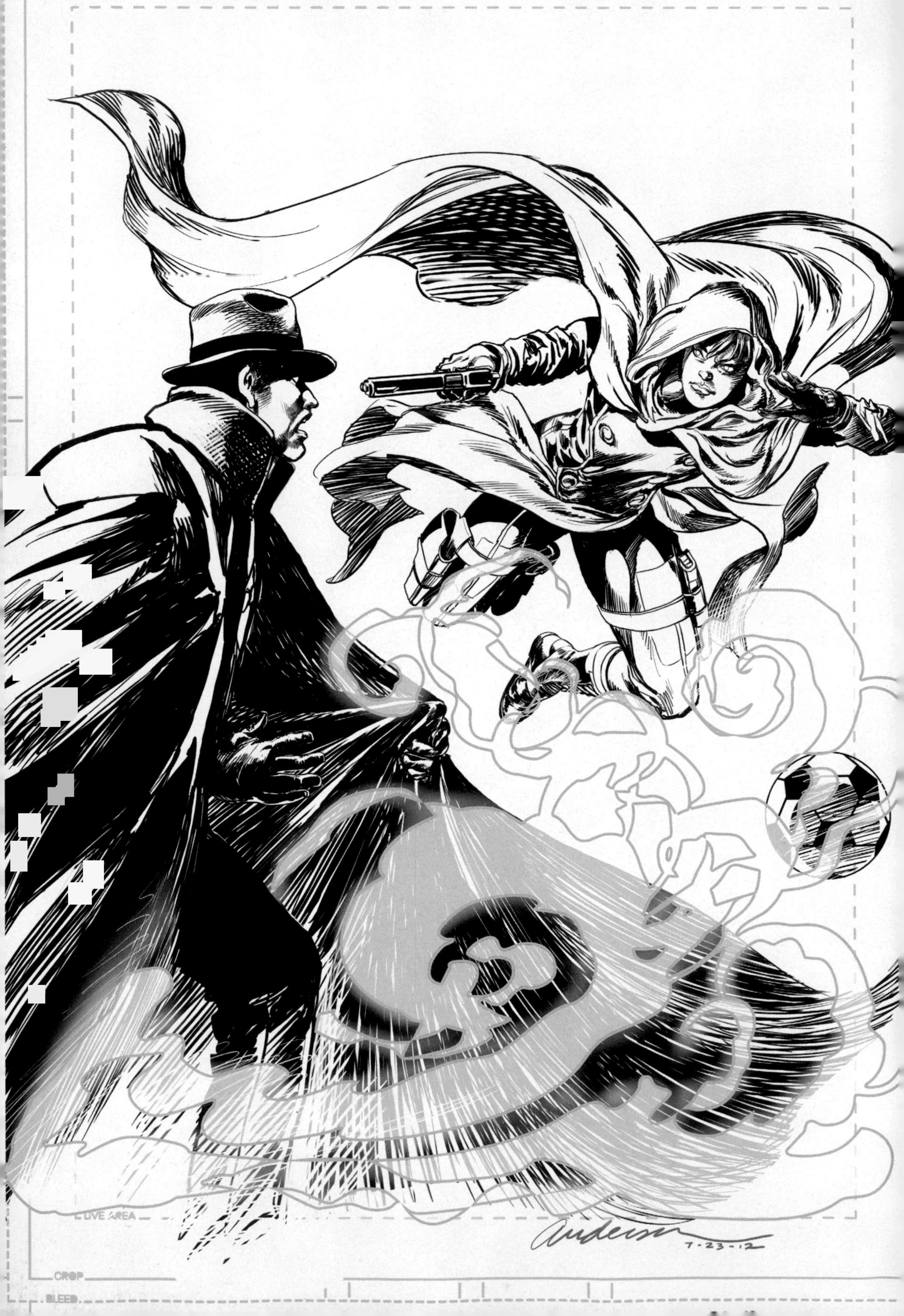
LIVE AREA
anderson
7-23-12
CROP
BLEED

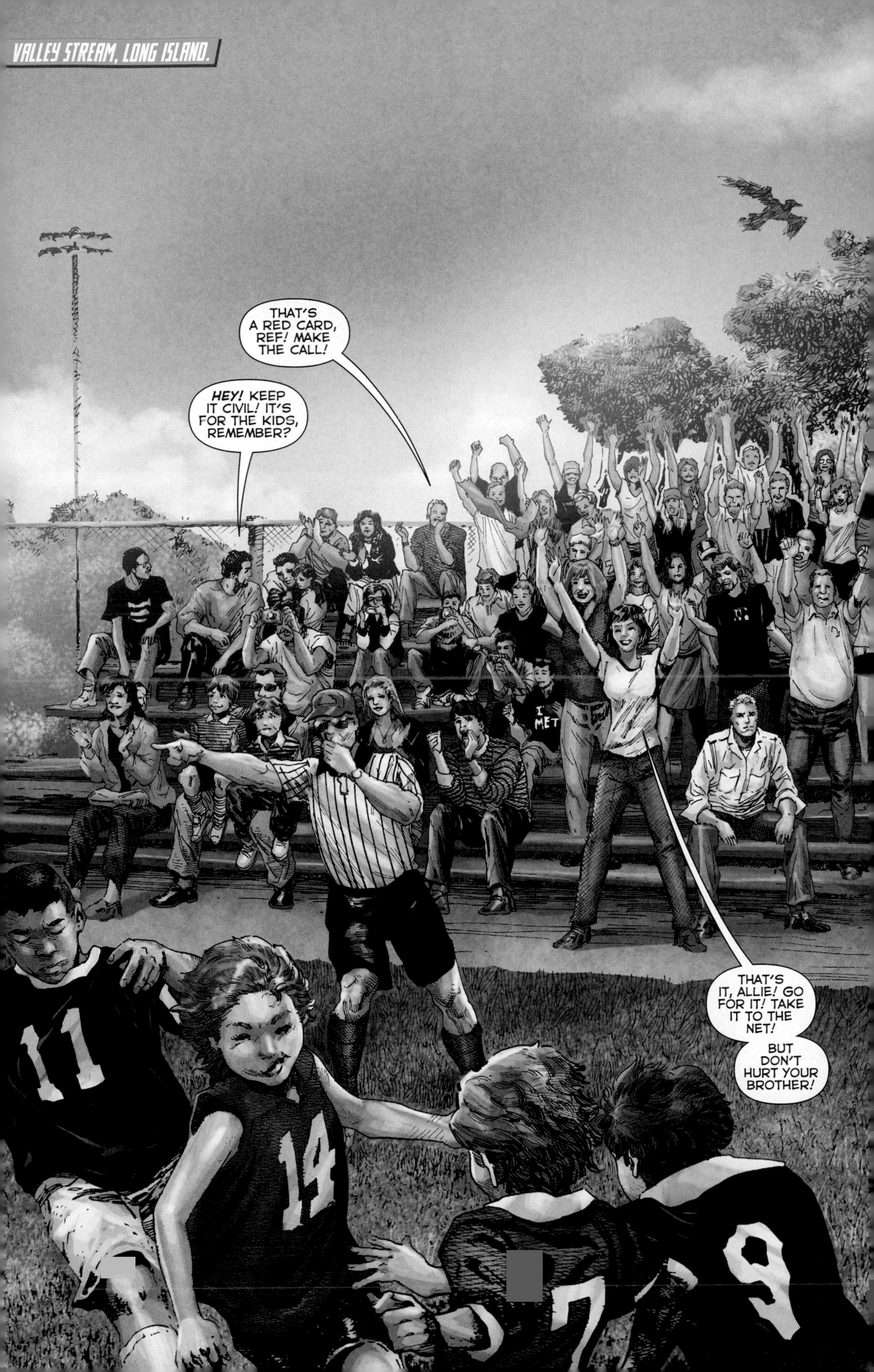
VALLEY STREAM, LONG ISLAND.
HEY! KEEP IT CIVIL! IT'S FOR THE KIDS, REMEMBER?
THAT'S A RED CARD, REF! MAKE THE CALL!
THAT'S IT, ALLIE! GO FOR IT! TAKE IT TO THE NET!
BUT DON'T HURT YOUR BROTHER!

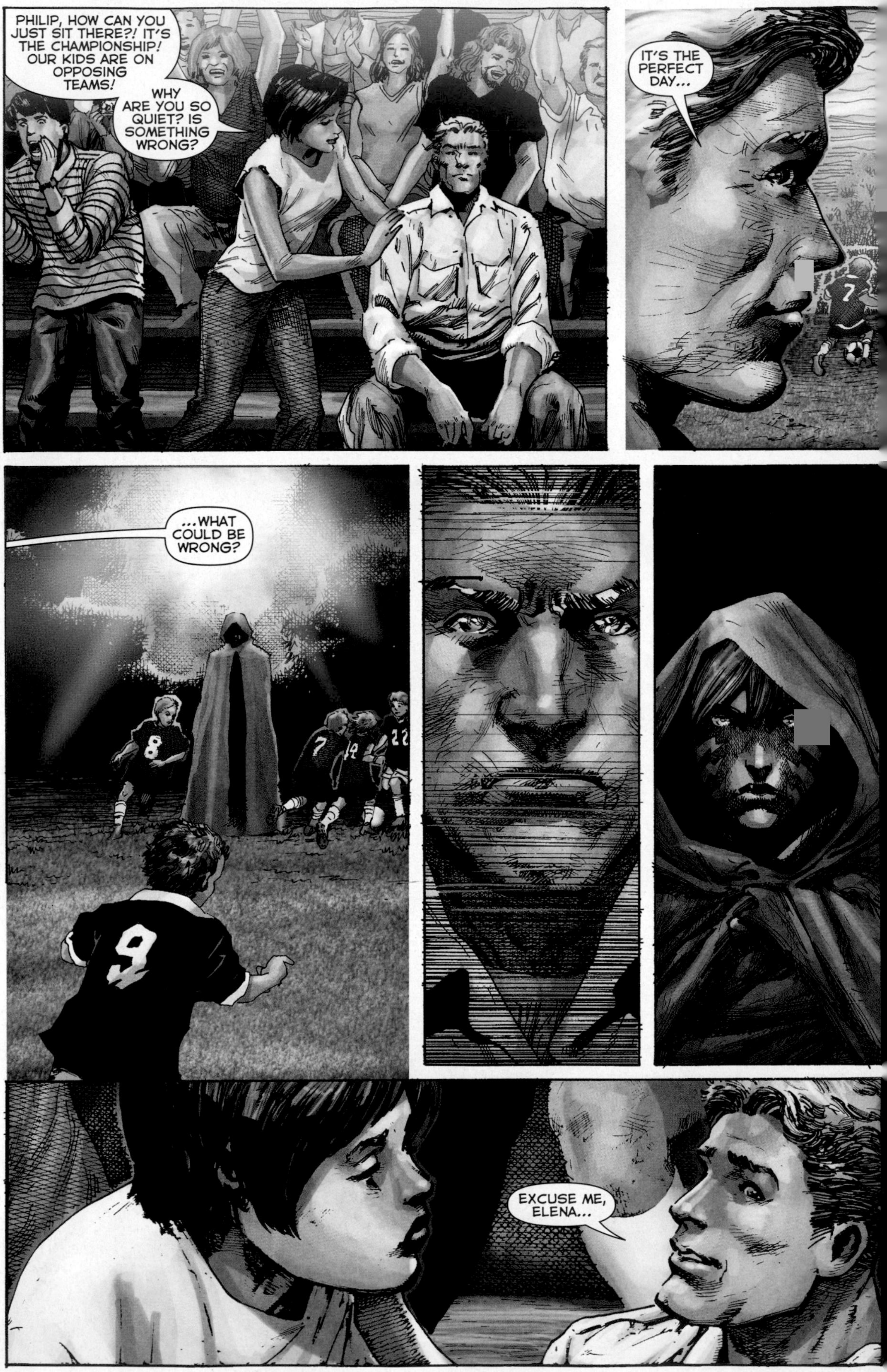
PHILIP, HOW CAN YOU JUST SIT THERE?! IT'S THE CHAMPIONSHIP! OUR KIDS ARE ON OPPOSING TEAMS!
WHY ARE YOU SO QUIET? IS SOMETHING WRONG?
IT'S THE PERFECT DAY...
...WHAT COULD BE WRONG?
EXCUSE ME, ELENA...

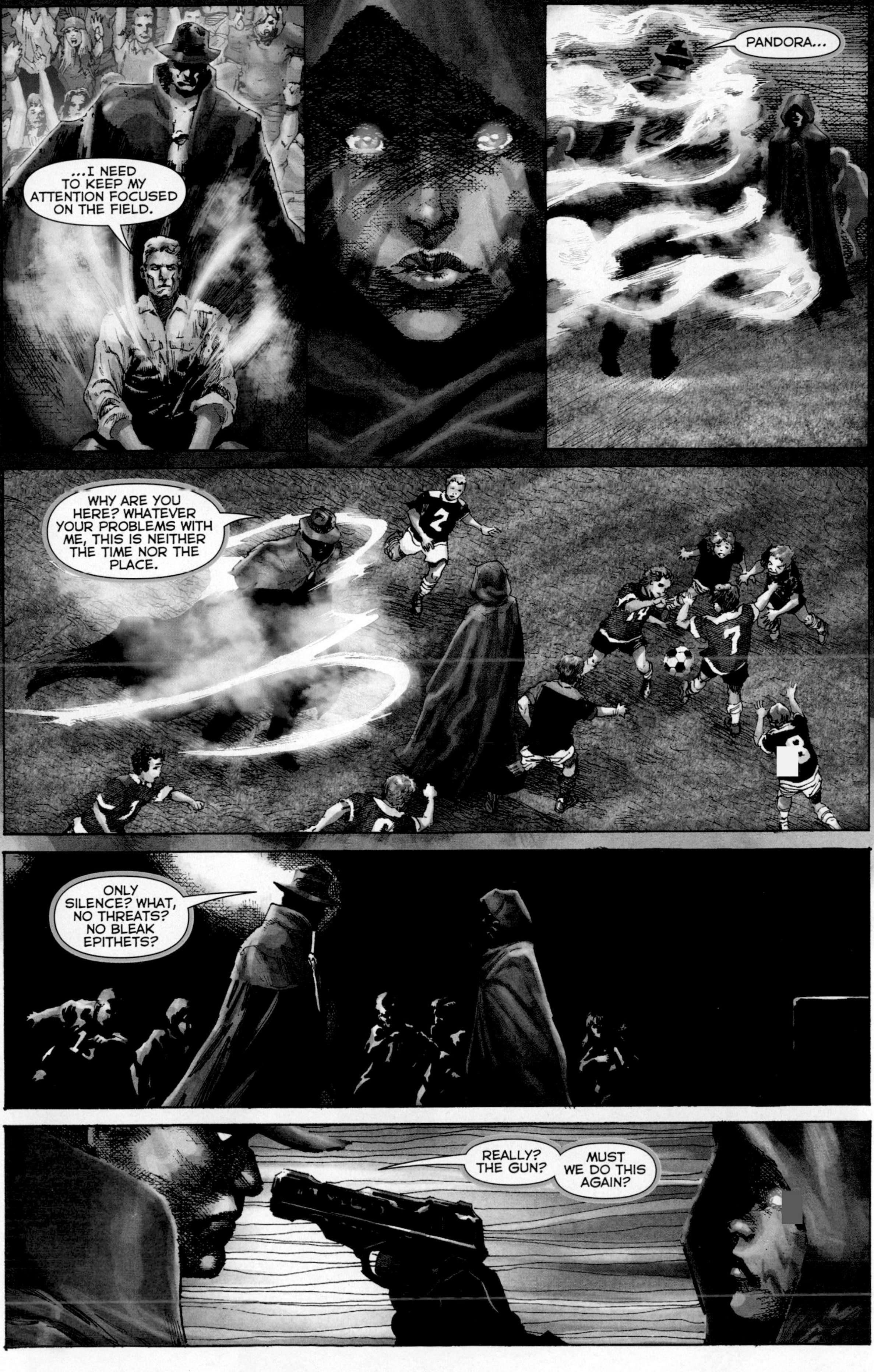
...I NEED TO KEEP MY ATTENTION FOCUSED ON THE FIELD.
PANDORA...
WHY ARE YOU HERE? WHATEVER YOUR PROBLEMS WITH ME, THIS IS NEITHER THE TIME NOR THE PLACE.
ONLY SILENCE? WHAT, NO THREATS? NO BLEAK EPITHETS?
REALLY? THE GUN?
MUST WE DO THIS AGAIN?

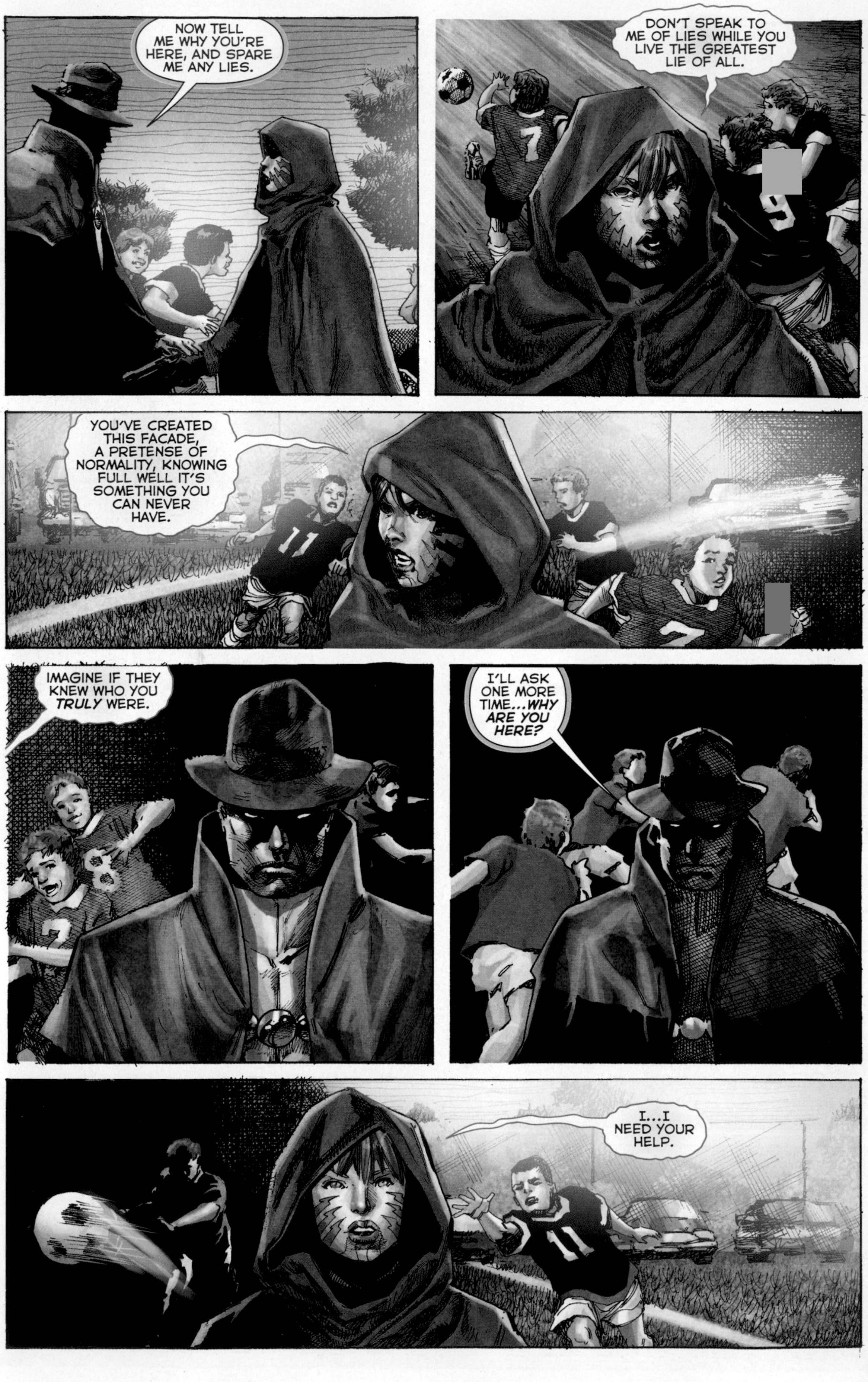
NOW TELL ME WHY YOU'RE HERE, AND SPARE ME ANY LIES.
DON'T SPEAK TO ME OF LIES WHILE YOU LIVE THE GREATEST LIE OF ALL.
YOU'VE CREATED THIS FACADE, A PRETENSE OF NORMALITY, KNOWING FULL WELL IT'S SOMETHING YOU CAN NEVER HAVE.
IMAGINE IF THEY KNEW WHO YOU *TRULY* WERE.
I'LL ASK ONE MORE TIME...*WHY ARE YOU HERE?*
I...I NEED YOUR HELP.

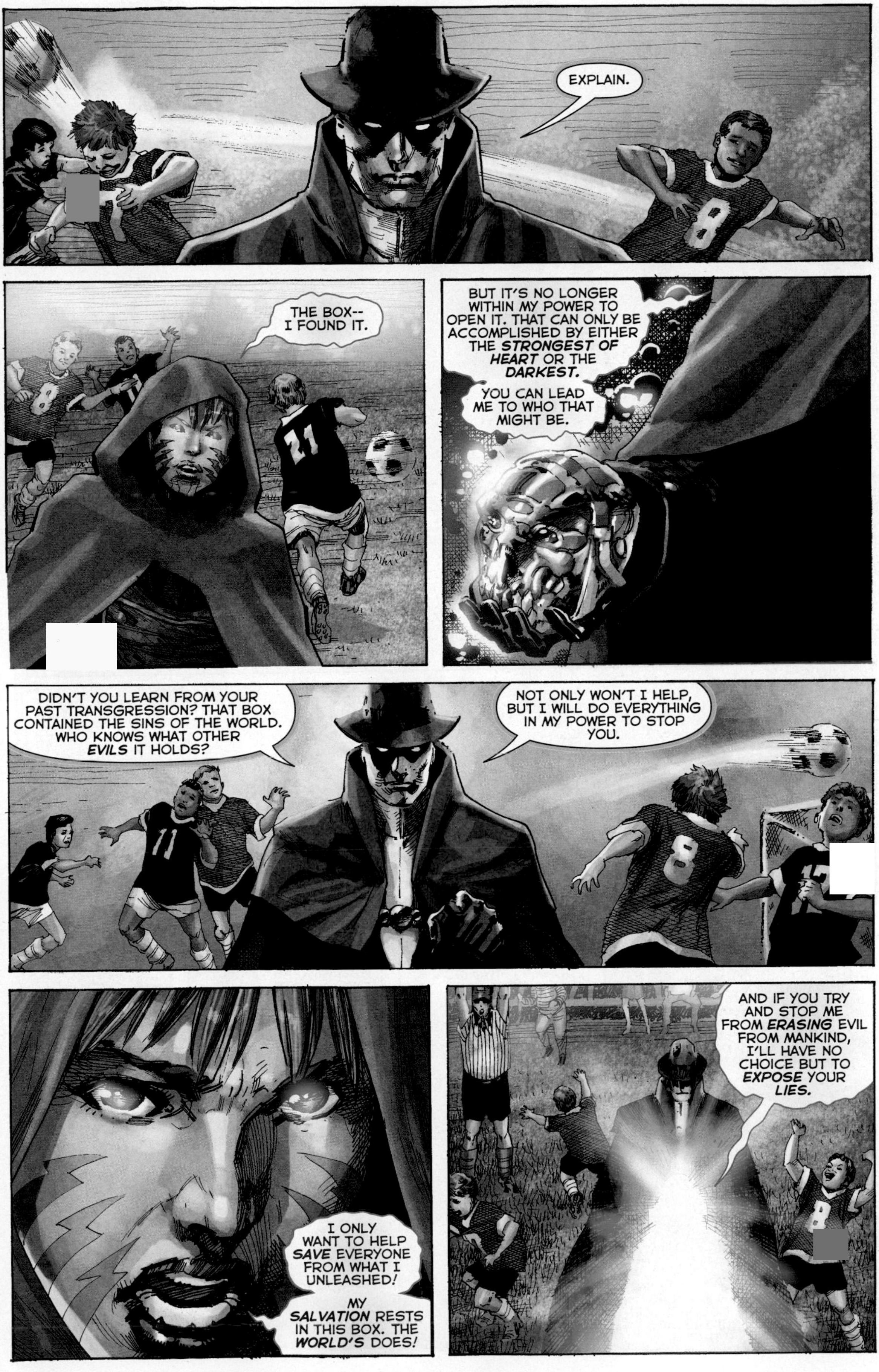
EXPLAIN.
THE BOX-- I FOUND IT.
BUT IT'S NO LONGER WITHIN MY POWER TO OPEN IT. THAT CAN ONLY BE ACCOMPLISHED BY EITHER THE ***STRONGEST OF HEART*** OR THE ***DARKEST.***
YOU CAN LEAD ME TO WHO THAT MIGHT BE.
DIDN'T YOU LEARN FROM YOUR PAST TRANSGRESSION? THAT BOX CONTAINED THE SINS OF THE WORLD. WHO KNOWS WHAT OTHER ***EVILS*** IT HOLDS?
NOT ONLY WON'T I HELP, BUT I WILL DO EVERYTHING IN MY POWER TO STOP YOU.
I ONLY WANT TO HELP ***SAVE*** EVERYONE FROM WHAT I UNLEASHED!
MY ***SALVATION*** RESTS IN THIS BOX. THE ***WORLD'S*** DOES!
AND IF YOU TRY AND STOP ME FROM ***ERASING*** EVIL FROM MANKIND, I'LL HAVE NO CHOICE BUT TO ***EXPOSE*** YOUR ***LIES.***

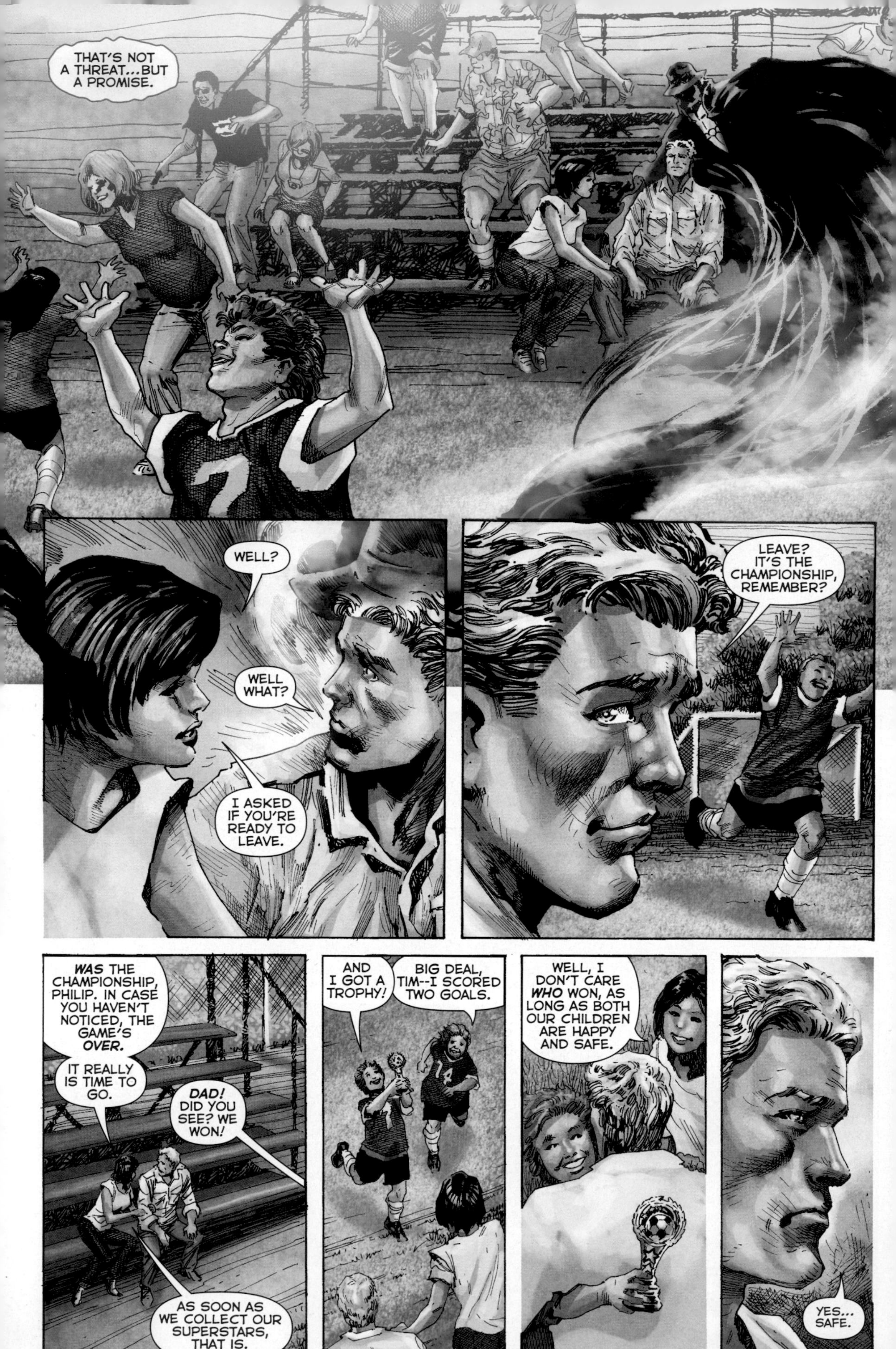
THAT'S NOT A THREAT...BUT A PROMISE.
WELL?
WELL WHAT?
I ASKED IF YOU'RE READY TO LEAVE.
LEAVE? IT'S THE CHAMPIONSHIP, REMEMBER?
WAS THE CHAMPIONSHIP, PHILIP. IN CASE YOU HAVEN'T NOTICED, THE GAME'S *OVER.*
IT REALLY IS TIME TO GO.
DAD! DID YOU SEE? WE WON!
AS SOON AS WE COLLECT OUR SUPERSTARS, THAT IS.
AND I GOT A TROPHY!
BIG DEAL, TIM--I SCORED TWO GOALS.
WELL, I DON'T CARE *WHO* WON, AS LONG AS BOTH OUR CHILDREN ARE HAPPY AND SAFE.
YES... SAFE.

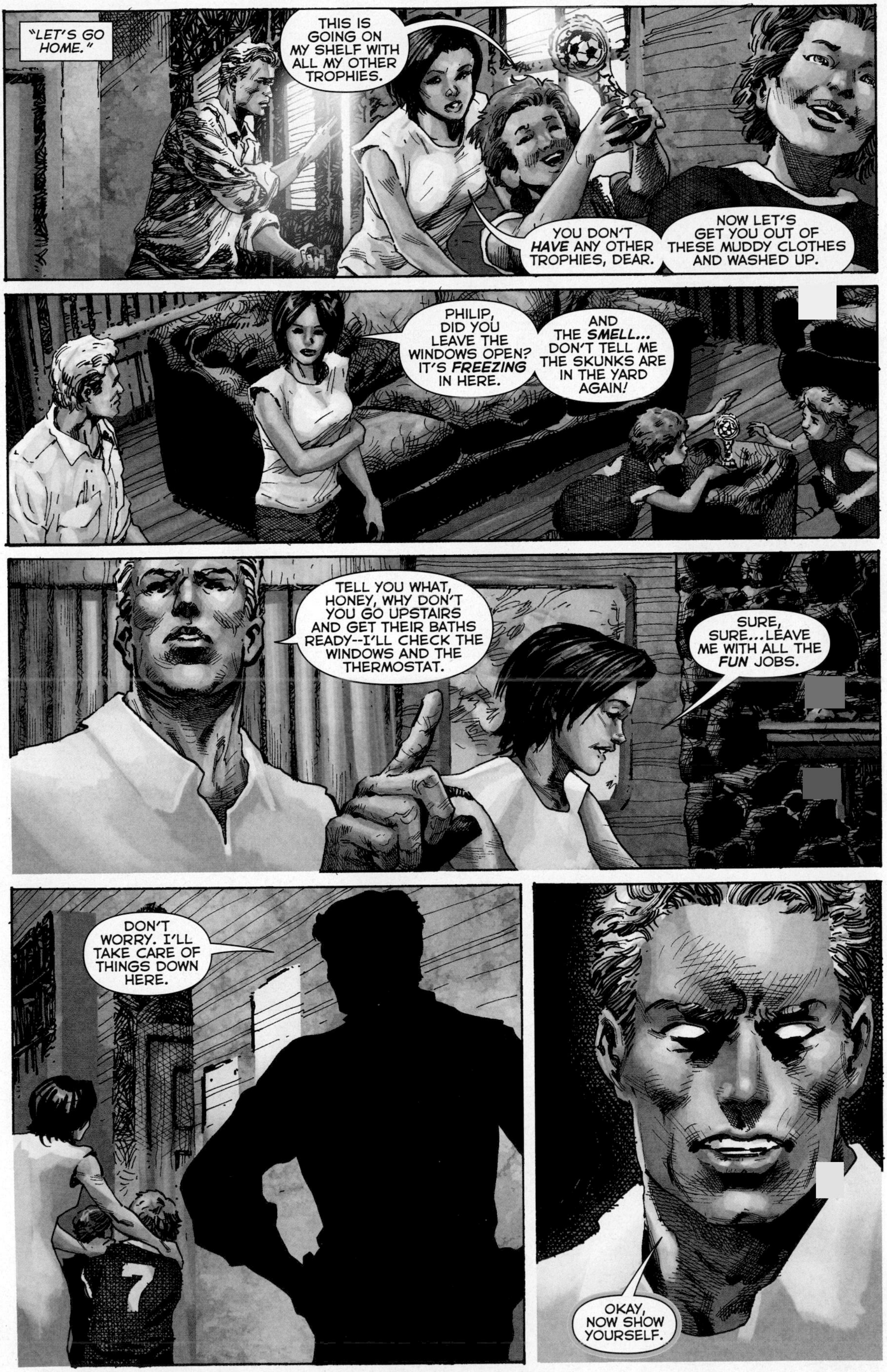
"LET'S GO HOME."
THIS IS GOING ON MY SHELF WITH ALL MY OTHER TROPHIES.
YOU DON'T HAVE ANY OTHER TROPHIES, DEAR.
NOW LET'S GET YOU OUT OF THESE MUDDY CLOTHES AND WASHED UP.
PHILIP, DID YOU LEAVE THE WINDOWS OPEN? IT'S FREEZING IN HERE.
AND THE SMELL... DON'T TELL ME THE SKUNKS ARE IN THE YARD AGAIN!
TELL YOU WHAT, HONEY, WHY DON'T YOU GO UPSTAIRS AND GET THEIR BATHS READY--I'LL CHECK THE WINDOWS AND THE THERMOSTAT.
SURE, SURE...LEAVE ME WITH ALL THE FUN JOBS.
DON'T WORRY. I'LL TAKE CARE OF THINGS DOWN HERE.
OKAY, NOW SHOW YOURSELF.

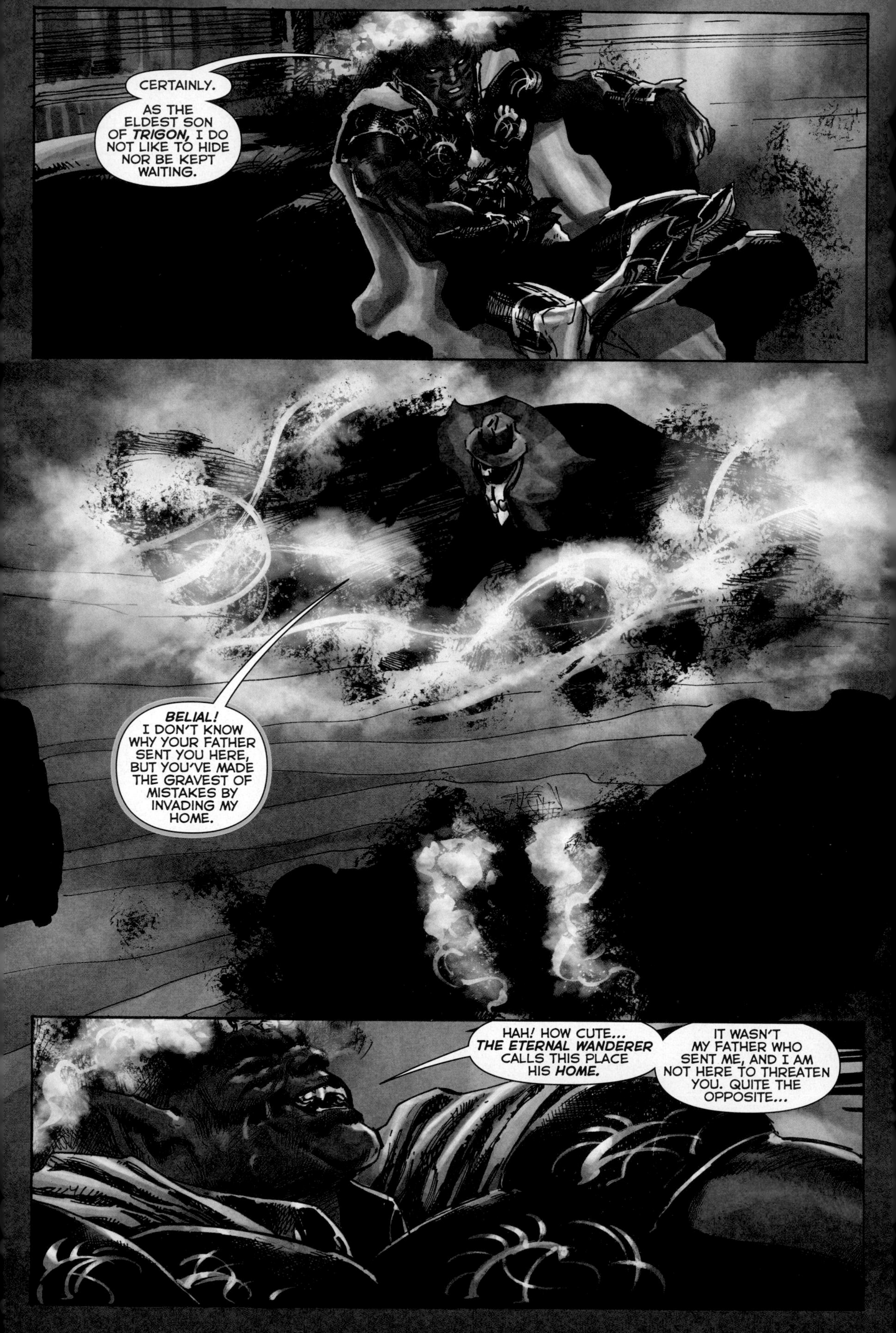
CERTAINLY.
AS THE ELDEST SON OF TRIGON, I DO NOT LIKE TO HIDE NOR BE KEPT WAITING.
BELIAL! I DON'T KNOW WHY YOUR FATHER SENT YOU HERE, BUT YOU'VE MADE THE GRAVEST OF MISTAKES BY INVADING MY HOME.
HAH! HOW CUTE... THE ETERNAL WANDERER CALLS THIS PLACE HIS HOME.
IT WASN'T MY FATHER WHO SENT ME, AND I AM NOT HERE TO THREATEN YOU. QUITE THE OPPOSITE...

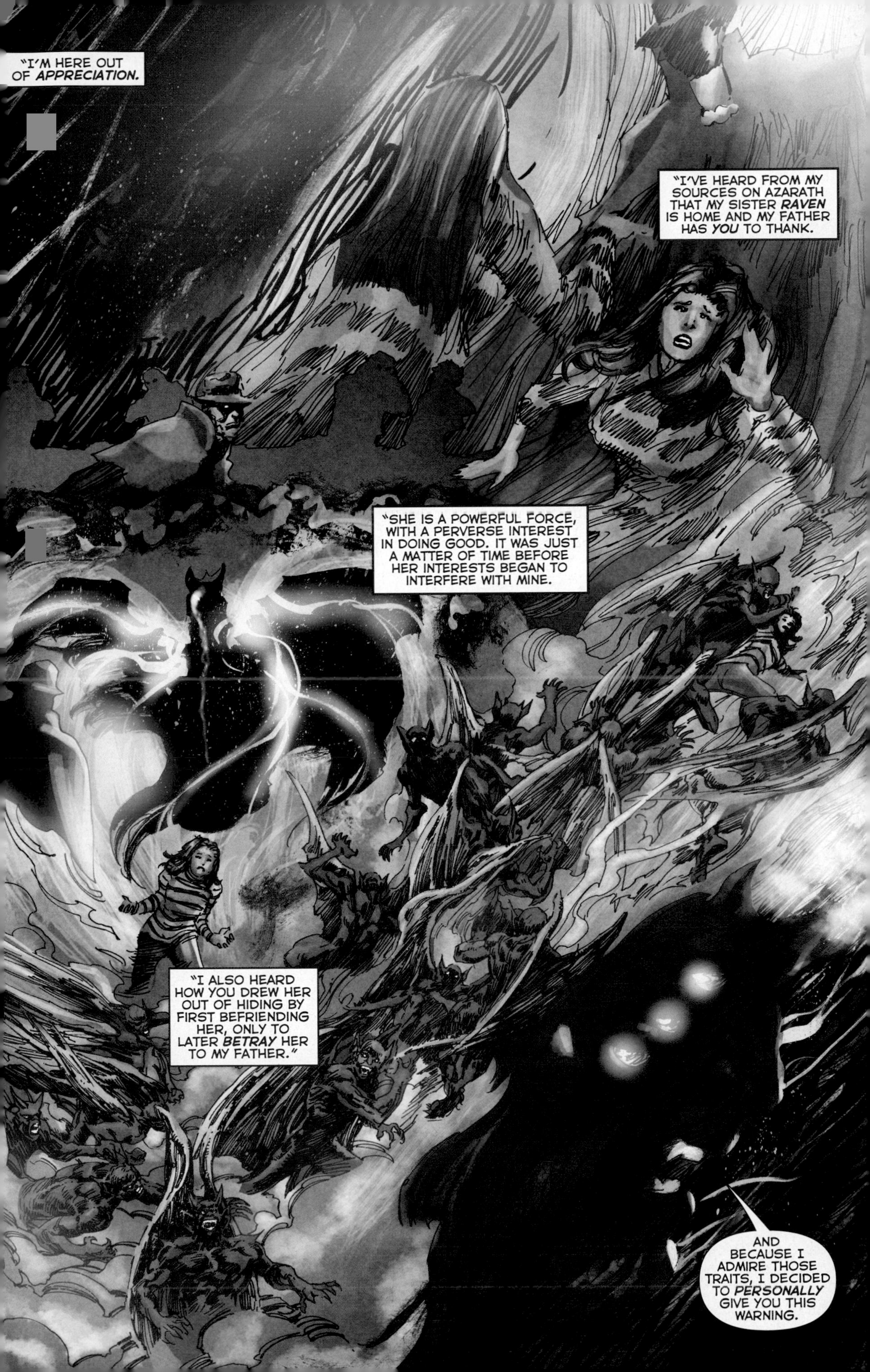
"I'M HERE OUT OF *APPRECIATION.*
"I'VE HEARD FROM MY SOURCES ON AZARATH THAT MY SISTER *RAVEN* IS HOME AND MY FATHER HAS *YOU* TO THANK.
"SHE IS A POWERFUL FORCE, WITH A PERVERSE INTEREST IN DOING GOOD. IT WAS JUST A MATTER OF TIME BEFORE HER INTERESTS BEGAN TO INTERFERE WITH MINE.
"I ALSO HEARD HOW YOU DREW HER OUT OF HIDING BY FIRST BEFRIENDING HER, ONLY TO LATER *BETRAY* HER TO MY FATHER."
AND BECAUSE I ADMIRE THOSE TRAITS, I DECIDED TO *PERSONALLY* GIVE YOU THIS WARNING.

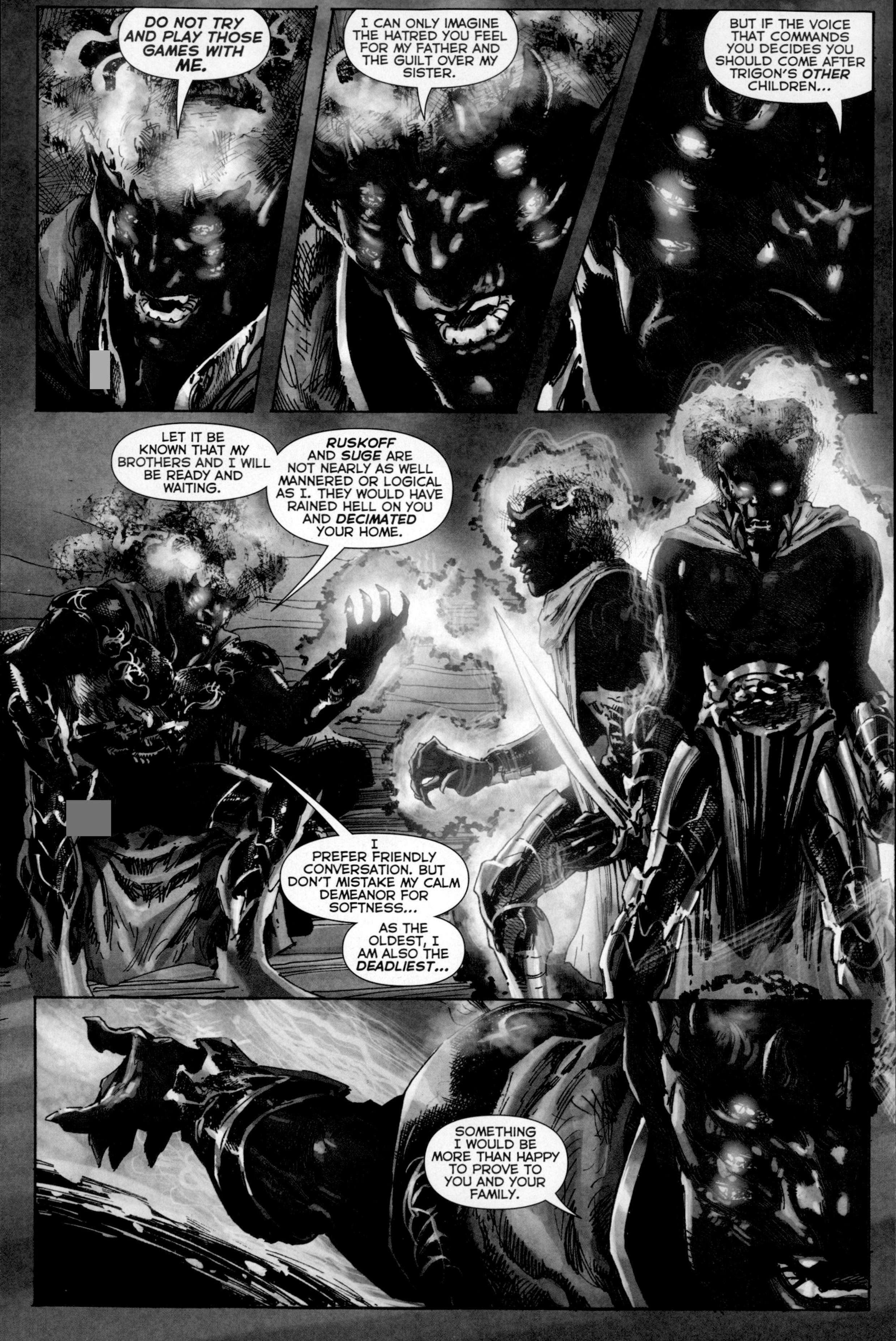
DO NOT TRY AND PLAY THOSE GAMES WITH ME.
I CAN ONLY IMAGINE THE HATRED YOU FEEL FOR MY FATHER AND THE GUILT OVER MY SISTER.
BUT IF THE VOICE THAT COMMANDS YOU DECIDES YOU SHOULD COME AFTER TRIGON'S OTHER CHILDREN...
LET IT BE KNOWN THAT MY BROTHERS AND I WILL BE READY AND WAITING.
RUSKOFF AND SUGE ARE NOT NEARLY AS WELL MANNERED OR LOGICAL AS I. THEY WOULD HAVE RAINED HELL ON YOU AND DECIMATED YOUR HOME.
I PREFER FRIENDLY CONVERSATION. BUT DON'T MISTAKE MY CALM DEMEANOR FOR SOFTNESS...
AS THE OLDEST, I AM ALSO THE DEADLIEST...
SOMETHING I WOULD BE MORE THAN HAPPY TO PROVE TO YOU AND YOUR FAMILY.

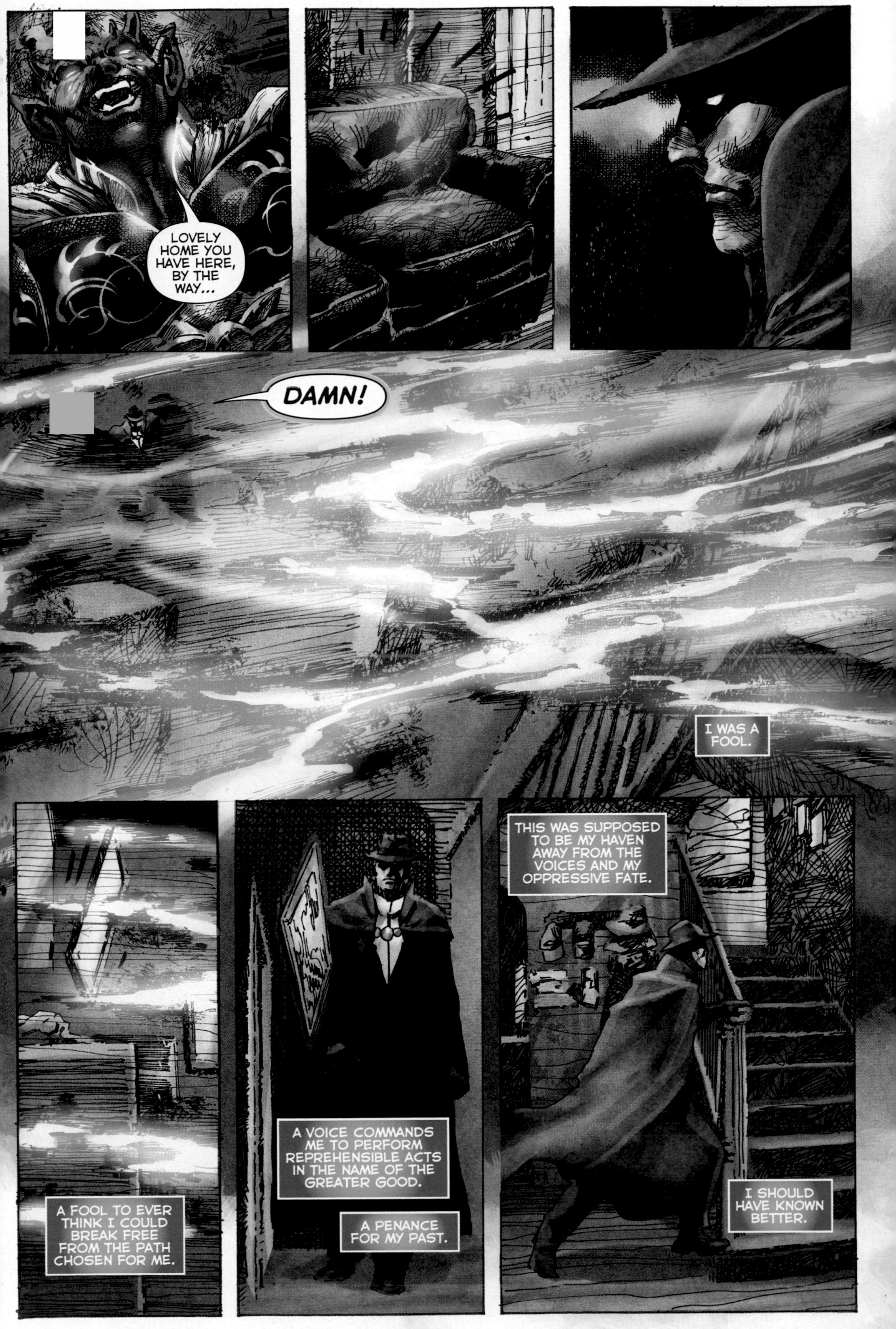

LOVELY HOME YOU HAVE HERE, BY THE WAY...
DAMN!
I WAS A FOOL.
A FOOL TO EVER THINK I COULD BREAK FREE FROM THE PATH CHOSEN FOR ME.
A VOICE COMMANDS ME TO PERFORM REPREHENSIBLE ACTS IN THE NAME OF THE GREATER GOOD.
A PENANCE FOR MY PAST.
THIS WAS SUPPOSED TO BE MY HAVEN AWAY FROM THE VOICES AND MY OPPRESSIVE FATE.
I SHOULD HAVE KNOWN BETTER.

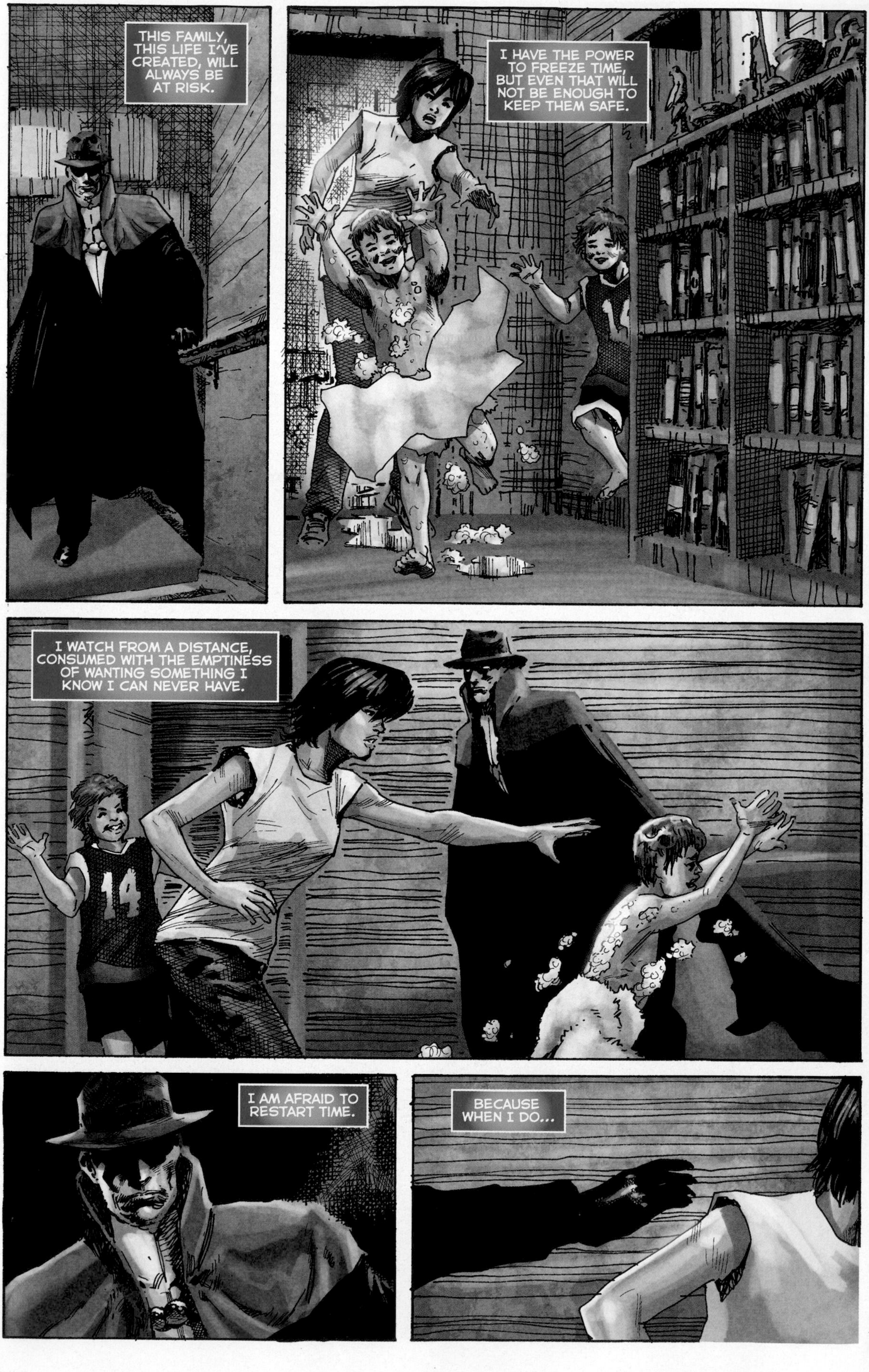
THIS FAMILY, THIS LIFE I'VE CREATED, WILL ALWAYS BE AT RISK.
I HAVE THE POWER TO FREEZE TIME, BUT EVEN THAT WILL NOT BE ENOUGH TO KEEP THEM SAFE.
I WATCH FROM A DISTANCE, CONSUMED WITH THE EMPTINESS OF WANTING SOMETHING I KNOW I CAN NEVER HAVE.
14
I AM AFRAID TO RESTART TIME.
BECAUSE WHEN I DO...

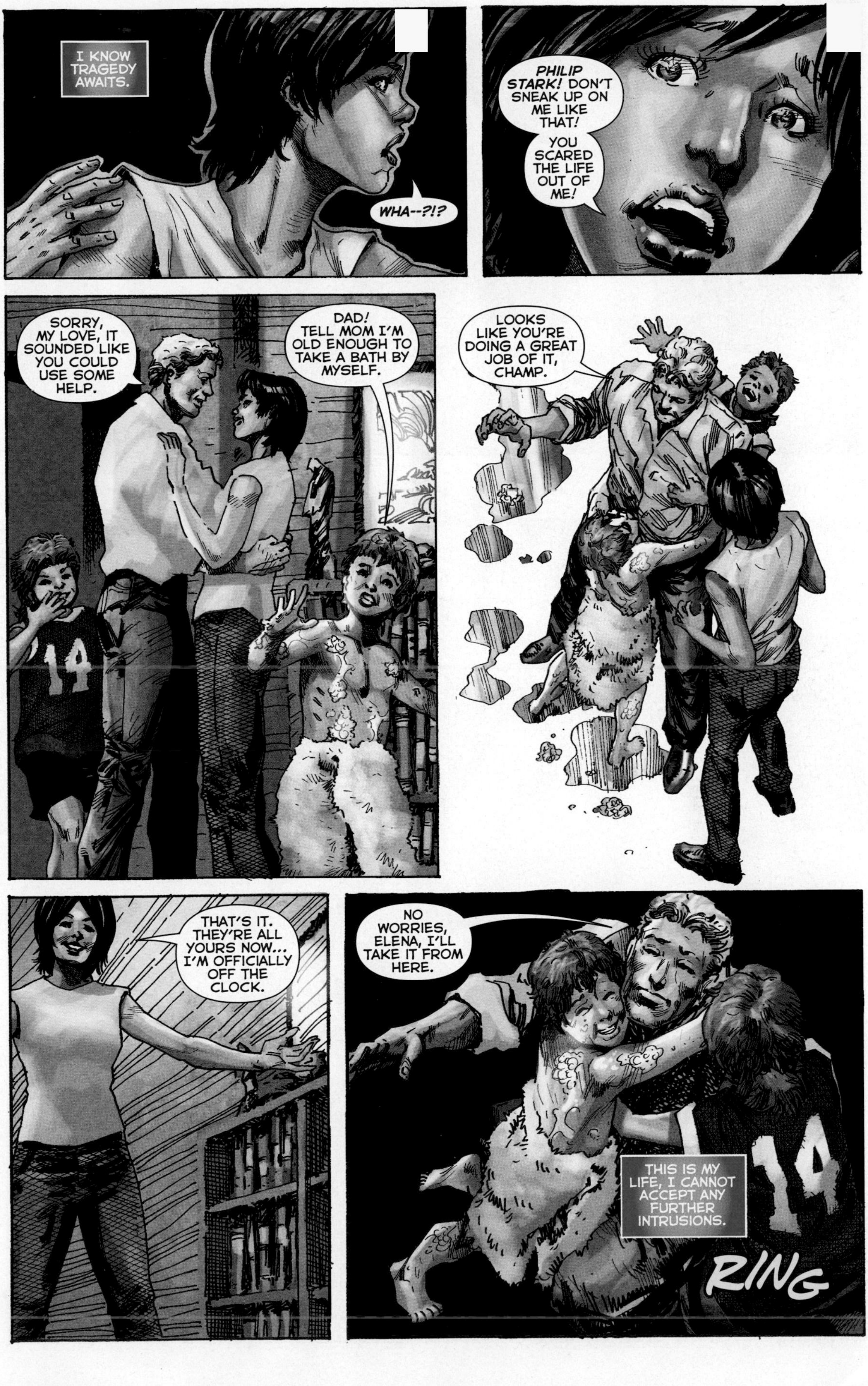
I KNOW TRAGEDY AWAITS.
WHA--?!?
PHILIP STARK! DON'T SNEAK UP ON ME LIKE THAT!
YOU SCARED THE LIFE OUT OF ME!
SORRY, MY LOVE, IT SOUNDED LIKE YOU COULD USE SOME HELP.
DAD! TELL MOM I'M OLD ENOUGH TO TAKE A BATH BY MYSELF.
LOOKS LIKE YOU'RE DOING A GREAT JOB OF IT, CHAMP.
THAT'S IT. THEY'RE ALL YOURS NOW... I'M OFFICIALLY OFF THE CLOCK.
NO WORRIES, ELENA, I'LL TAKE IT FROM HERE.
THIS IS MY LIFE, I CANNOT ACCEPT ANY FURTHER INTRUSIONS.
RING

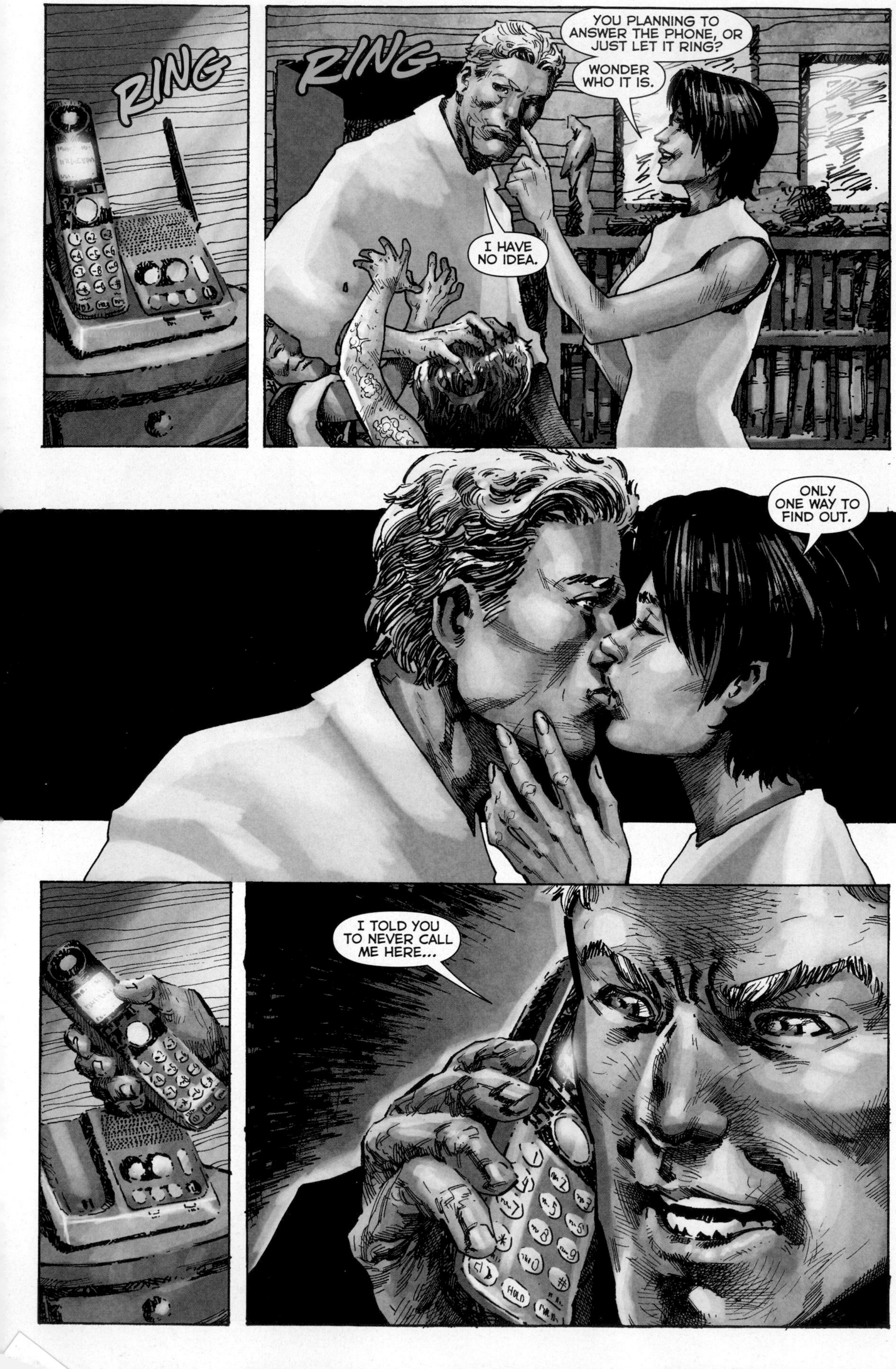
RING
RING
YOU PLANNING TO ANSWER THE PHONE, OR JUST LET IT RING?
WONDER WHO IT IS.
I HAVE NO IDEA.
ONLY ONE WAY TO FIND OUT.
I TOLD YOU TO NEVER CALL ME HERE...

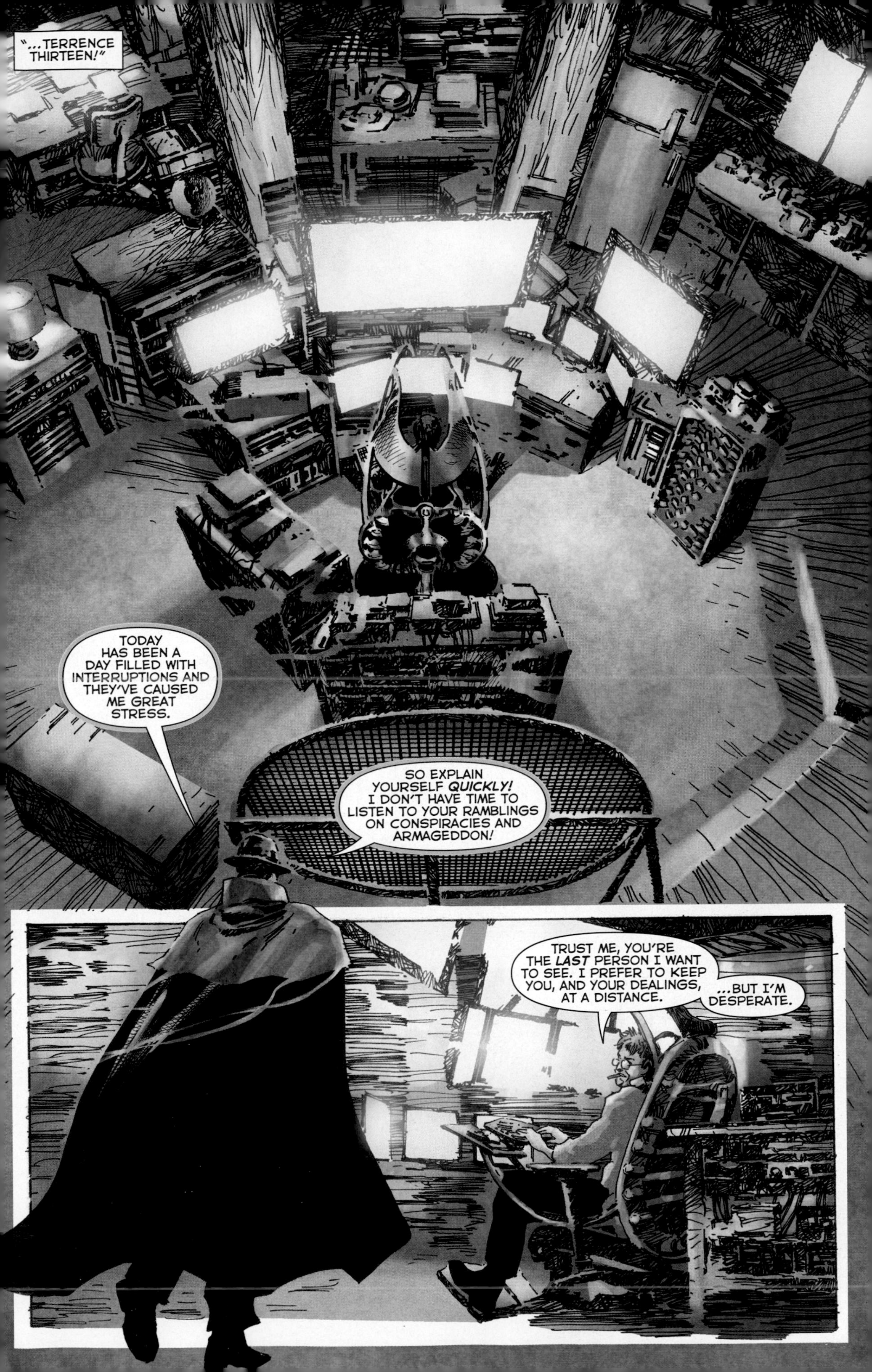
"...TERRENCE THIRTEEN!"
TODAY HAS BEEN A DAY FILLED WITH INTERRUPTIONS AND THEY'VE CAUSED ME GREAT STRESS.
SO EXPLAIN YOURSELF QUICKLY! I DON'T HAVE TIME TO LISTEN TO YOUR RAMBLINGS ON CONSPIRACIES AND ARMAGEDDON!
TRUST ME, YOU'RE THE LAST PERSON I WANT TO SEE. I PREFER TO KEEP YOU, AND YOUR DEALINGS, AT A DISTANCE.
...BUT I'M DESPERATE.

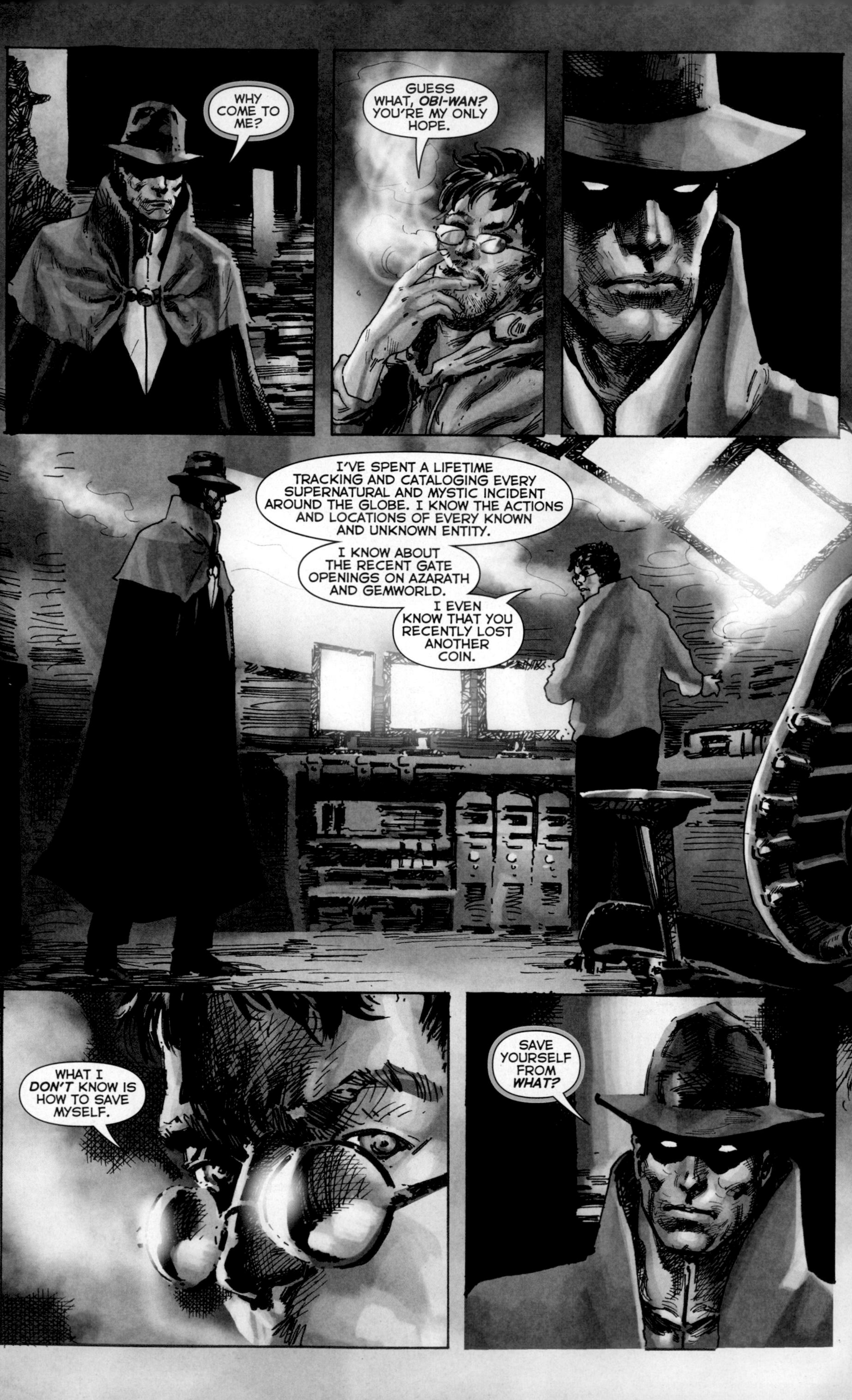
WHY COME TO ME?
GUESS WHAT, OBI-WAN? YOU'RE MY ONLY HOPE.
I'VE SPENT A LIFETIME TRACKING AND CATALOGING EVERY SUPERNATURAL AND MYSTIC INCIDENT AROUND THE GLOBE. I KNOW THE ACTIONS AND LOCATIONS OF EVERY KNOWN AND UNKNOWN ENTITY.
I KNOW ABOUT THE RECENT GATE OPENINGS ON AZARATH AND GEMWORLD.
I EVEN KNOW THAT YOU RECENTLY LOST ANOTHER COIN.
WHAT I DON'T KNOW IS HOW TO SAVE MYSELF.
SAVE YOURSELF FROM WHAT?

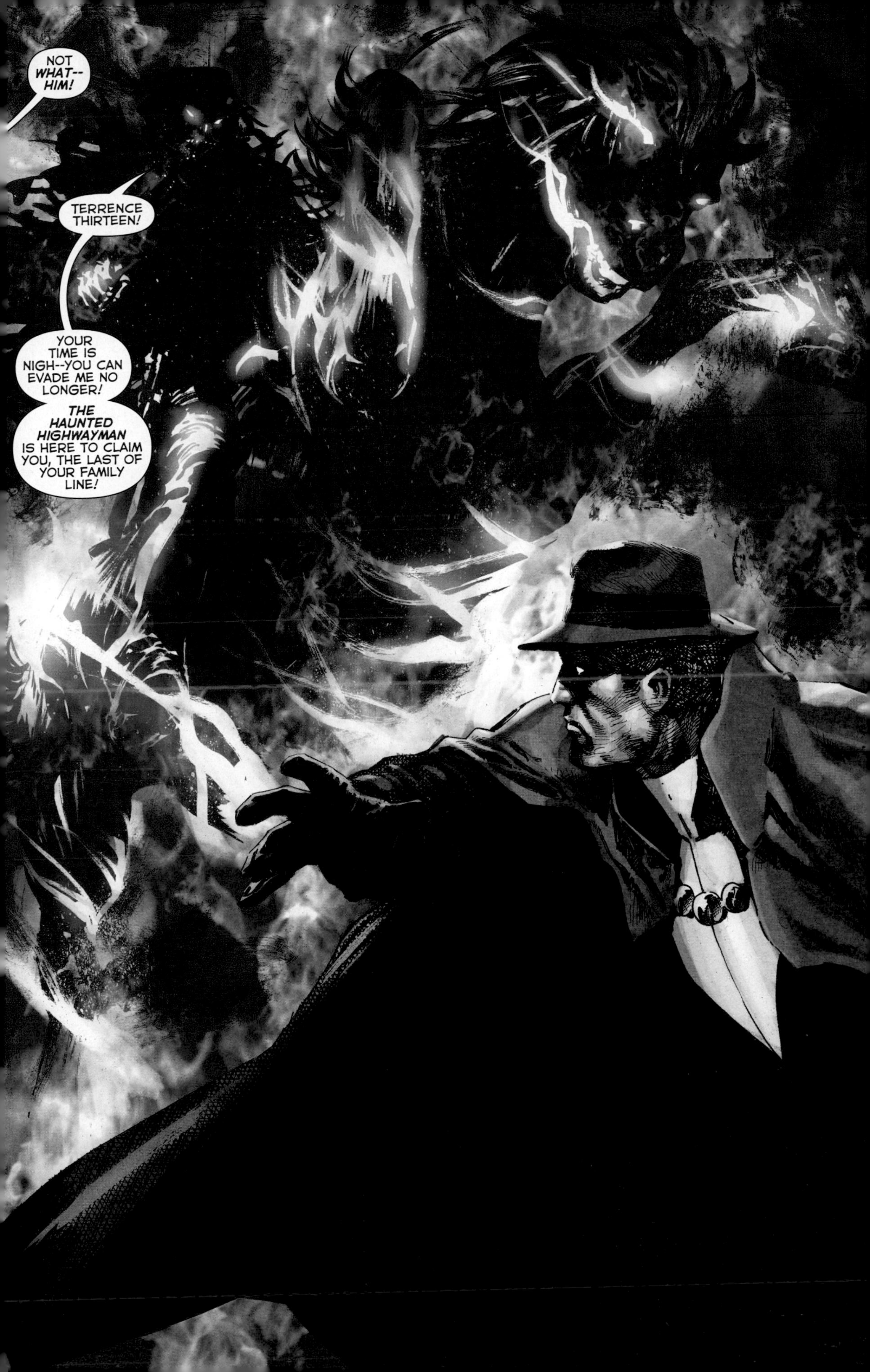
NOT *WHAT*-- *HIM!*
TERRENCE THIRTEEN!
YOUR TIME IS NIGH--YOU CAN EVADE ME NO LONGER!
THE HAUNTED HIGHWAYMAN IS HERE TO CLAIM YOU, THE LAST OF YOUR FAMILY LINE!

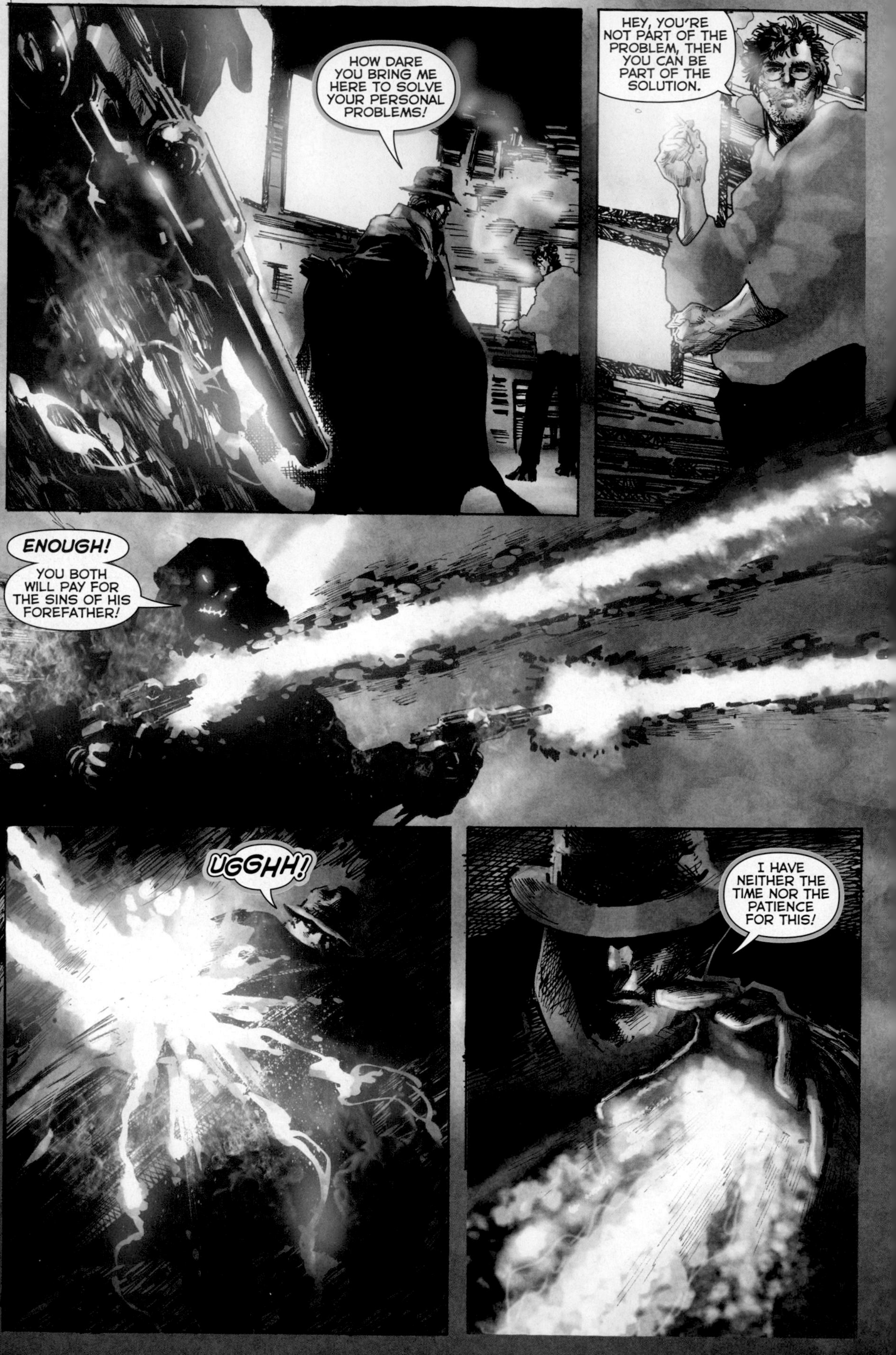
HOW DARE YOU BRING ME HERE TO SOLVE YOUR PERSONAL PROBLEMS!
HEY, YOU'RE NOT PART OF THE PROBLEM, THEN YOU CAN BE PART OF THE SOLUTION.
ENOUGH!
YOU BOTH WILL PAY FOR THE SINS OF HIS FOREFATHER!
UGGHH!
I HAVE NEITHER THE TIME NOR THE PATIENCE FOR THIS!

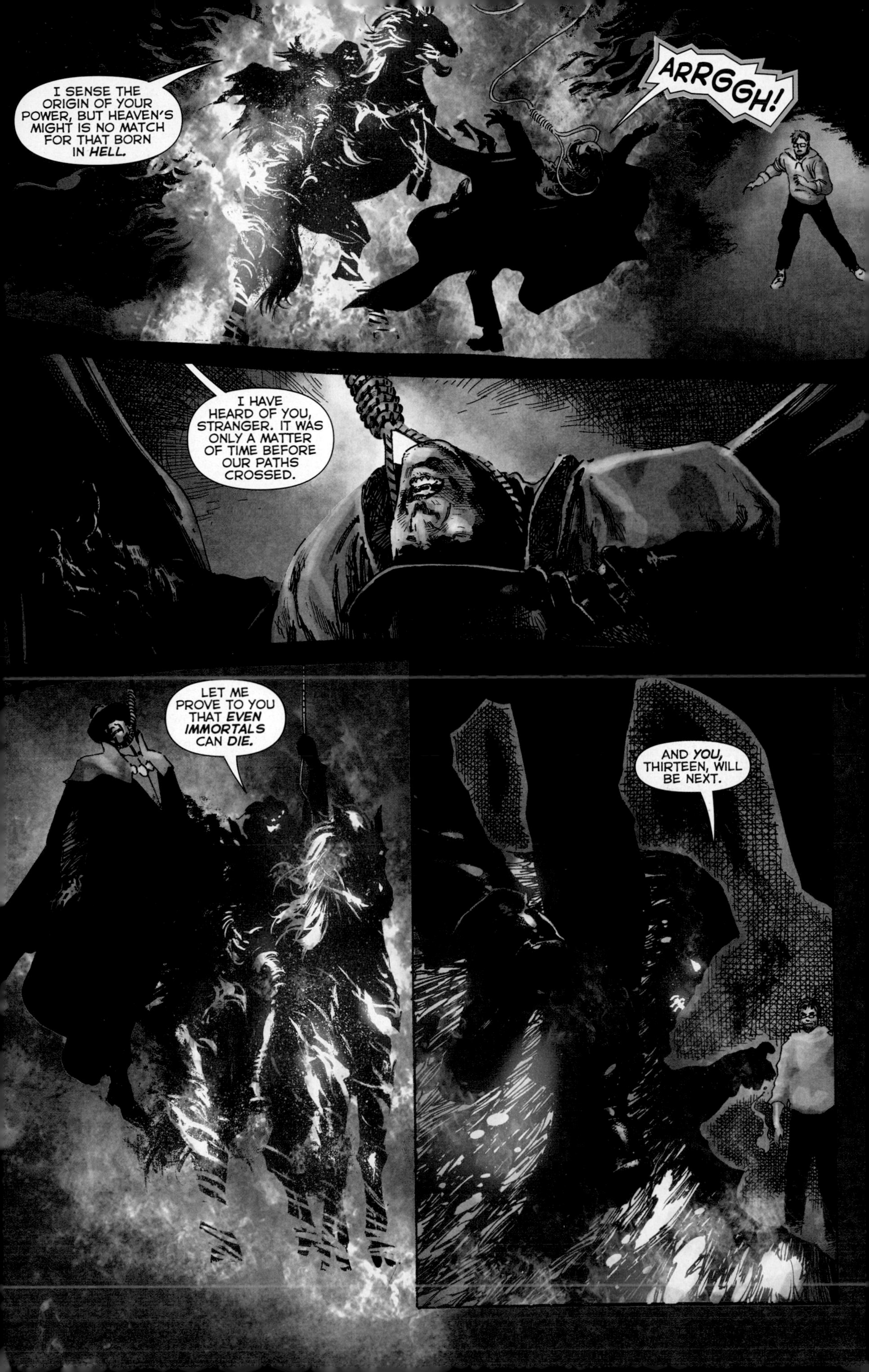
I SENSE THE ORIGIN OF YOUR POWER, BUT HEAVEN'S MIGHT IS NO MATCH FOR THAT BORN IN *HELL.*
ARRGGH!
I HAVE HEARD OF YOU, STRANGER. IT WAS ONLY A MATTER OF TIME BEFORE OUR PATHS CROSSED.
LET ME PROVE TO YOU THAT *EVEN IMMORTALS* CAN *DIE.*
AND *YOU,* THIRTEEN, WILL BE NEXT.

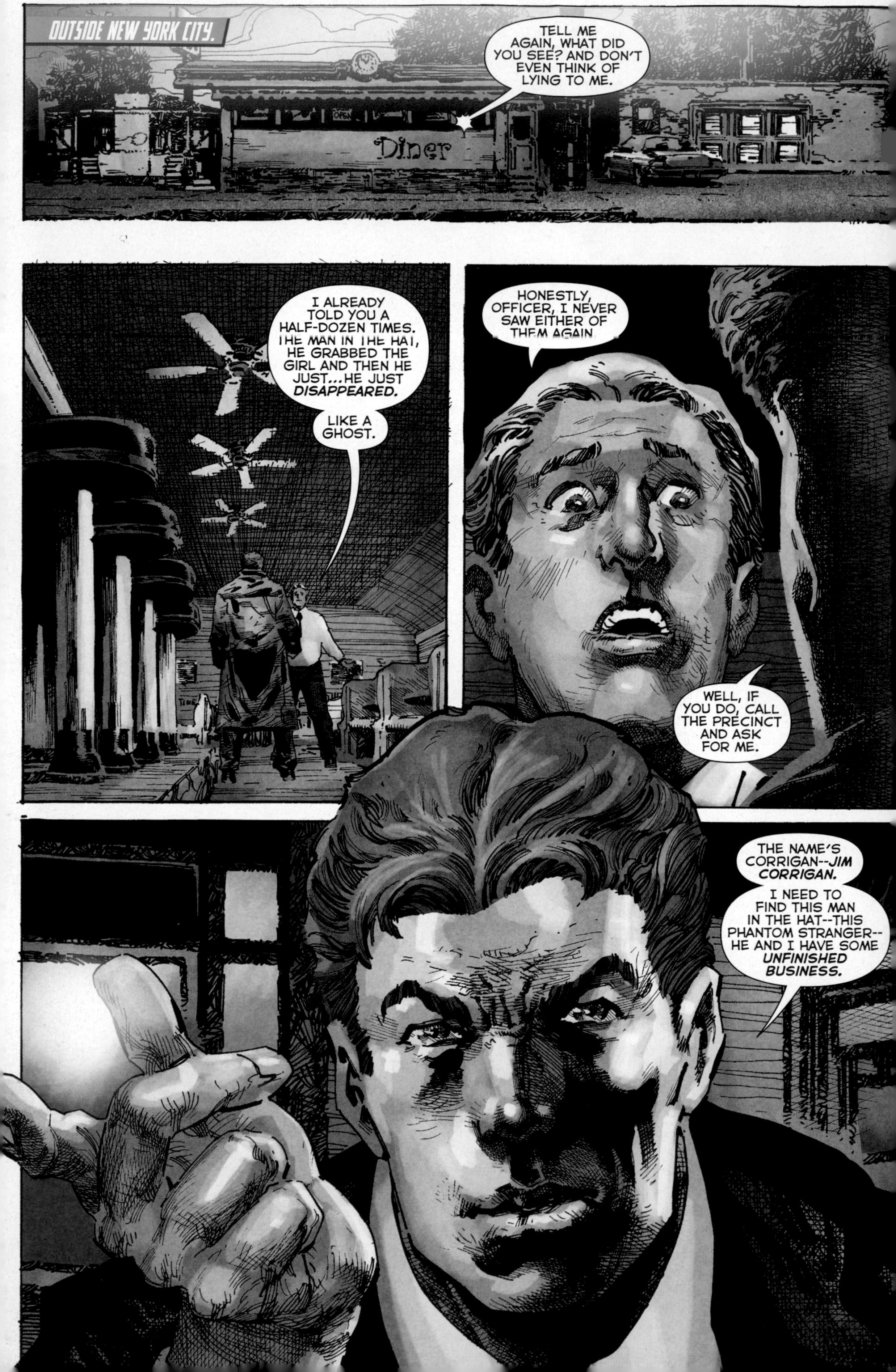
OUTSIDE NEW YORK CITY.
TELL ME AGAIN, WHAT DID YOU SEE? AND DON'T EVEN THINK OF LYING TO ME.
Diner
I ALREADY TOLD YOU A HALF-DOZEN TIMES. THE MAN IN THE HAT, HE GRABBED THE GIRL AND THEN HE JUST...HE JUST *DISAPPEARED.*
LIKE A GHOST.
HONESTLY, OFFICER, I NEVER SAW EITHER OF THEM AGAIN.
WELL, IF YOU DO, CALL THE PRECINCT AND ASK FOR ME.
THE NAME'S CORRIGAN--*JIM CORRIGAN.*
I NEED TO FIND THIS MAN IN THE HAT--THIS PHANTOM STRANGER--HE AND I HAVE SOME *UNFINISHED BUSINESS.*

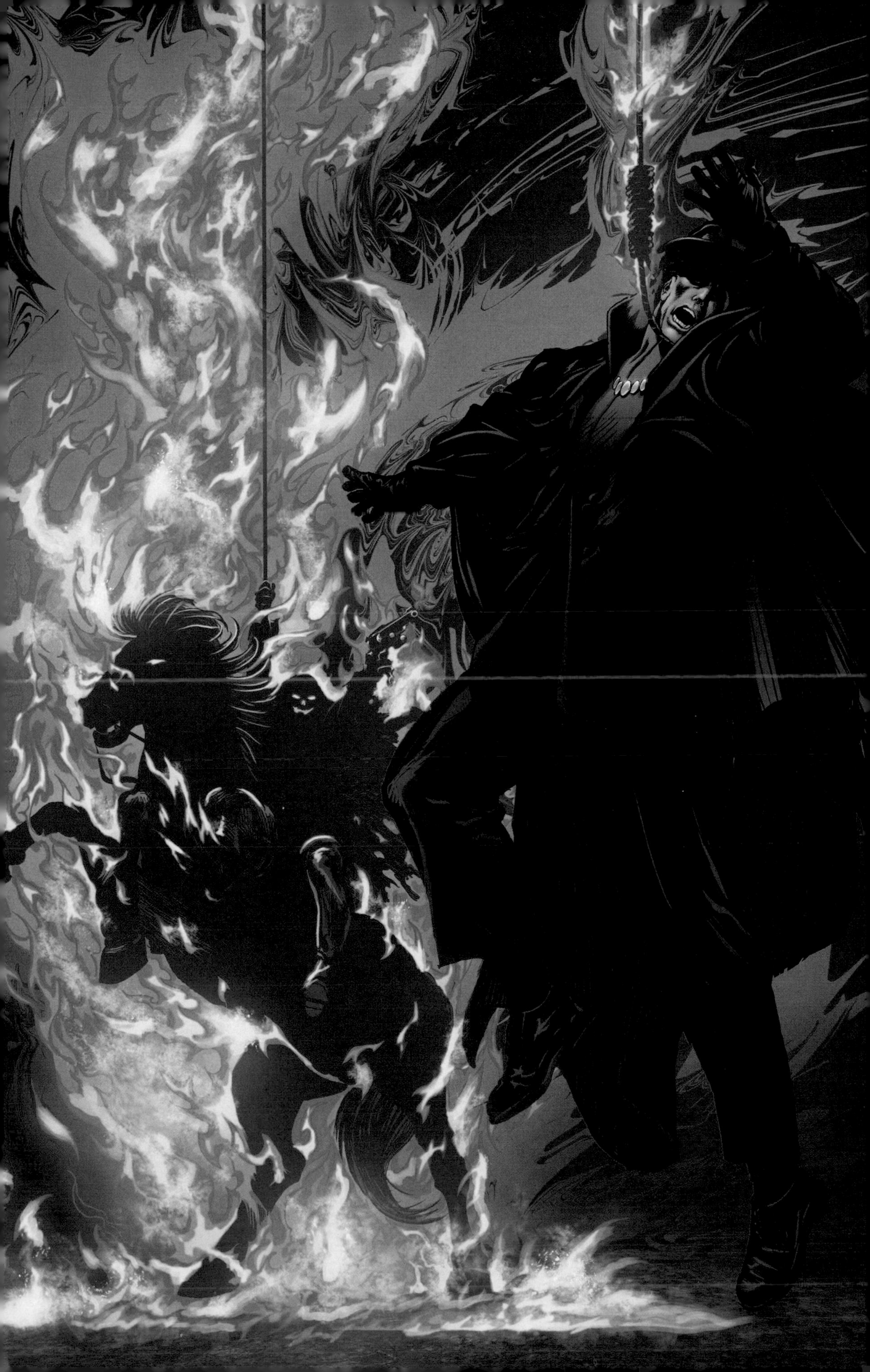

Cover by Brent Anderson & Ulises Arreola

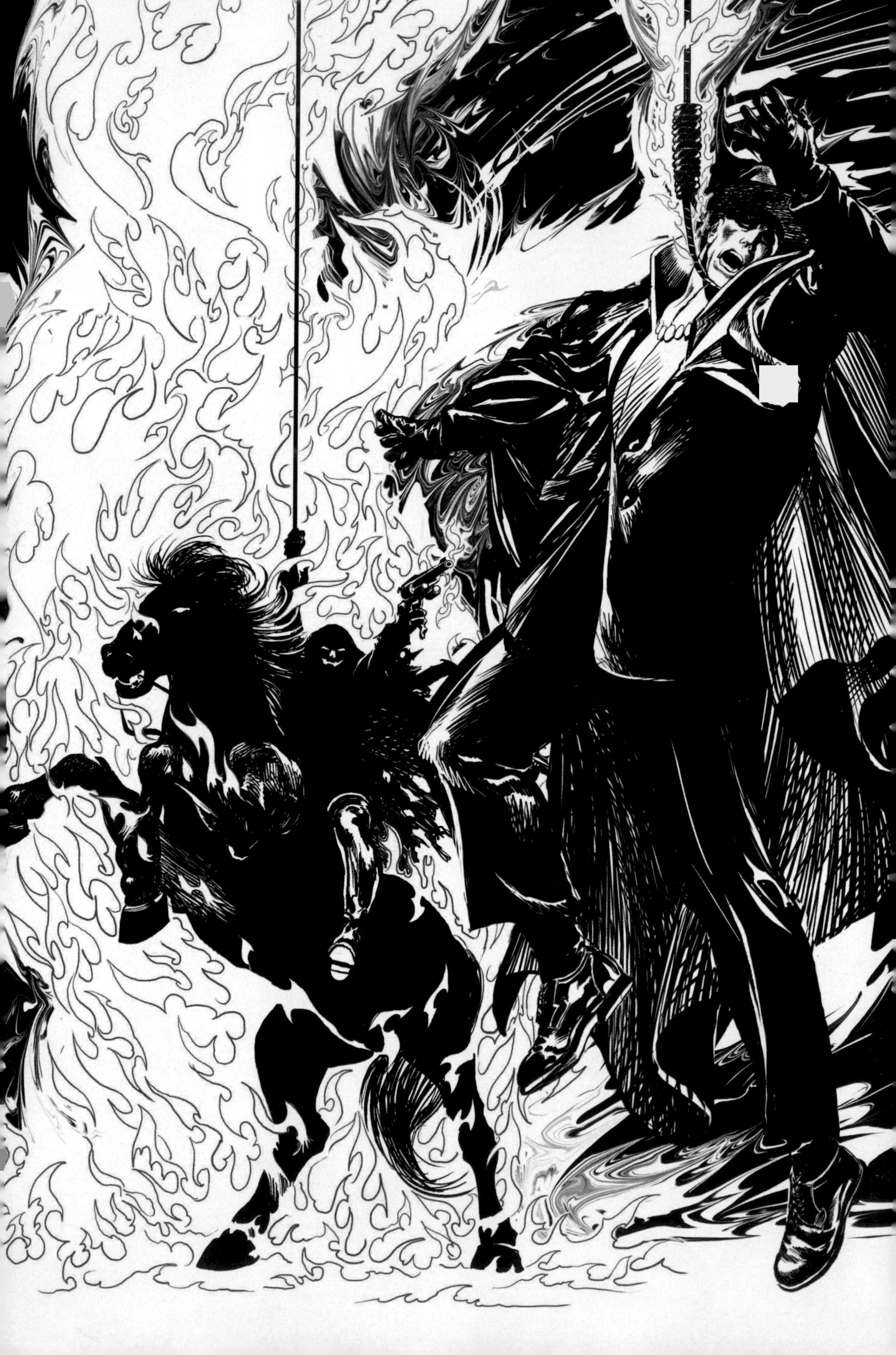

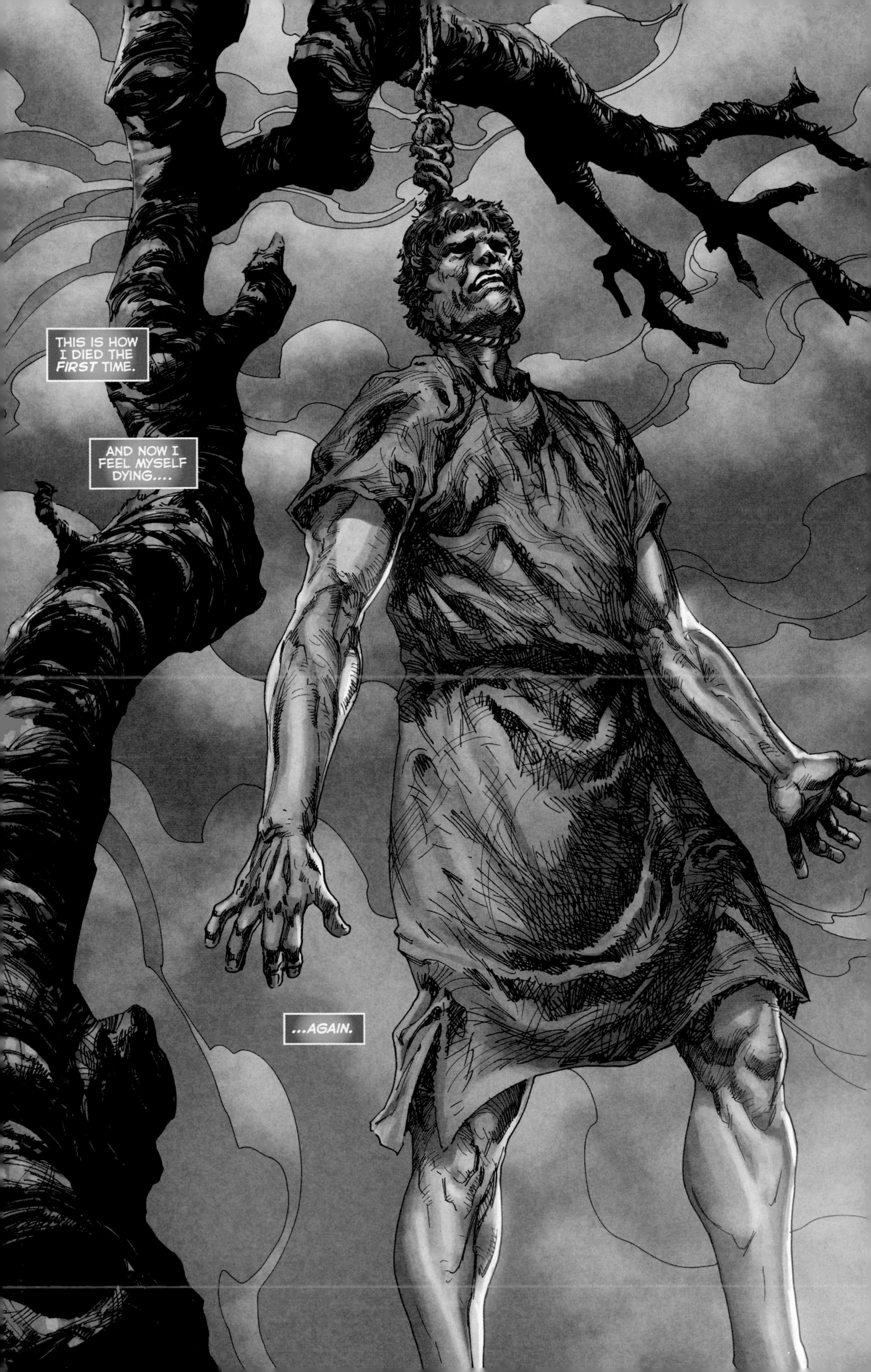
THIS IS HOW I DIED THE *FIRST* TIME.
AND NOW I FEEL MYSELF DYING....
...AGAIN.

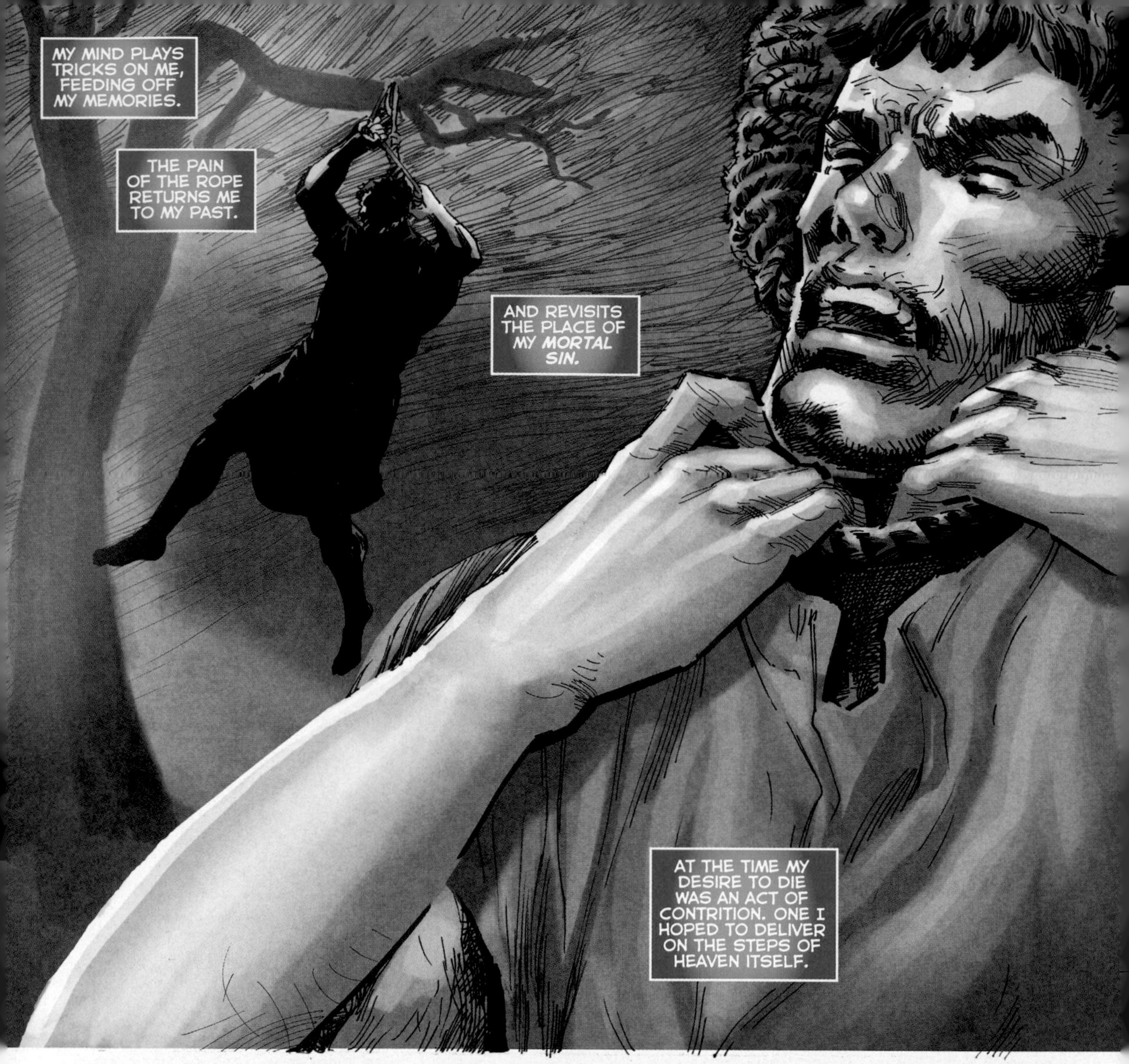
MY MIND PLAYS TRICKS ON ME, FEEDING OFF MY MEMORIES.
THE PAIN OF THE ROPE RETURNS ME TO MY PAST.
AND REVISITS THE PLACE OF MY *MORTAL SIN.*
AT THE TIME MY DESIRE TO DIE WAS AN ACT OF CONTRITION. ONE I HOPED TO DELIVER ON THE STEPS OF HEAVEN ITSELF.

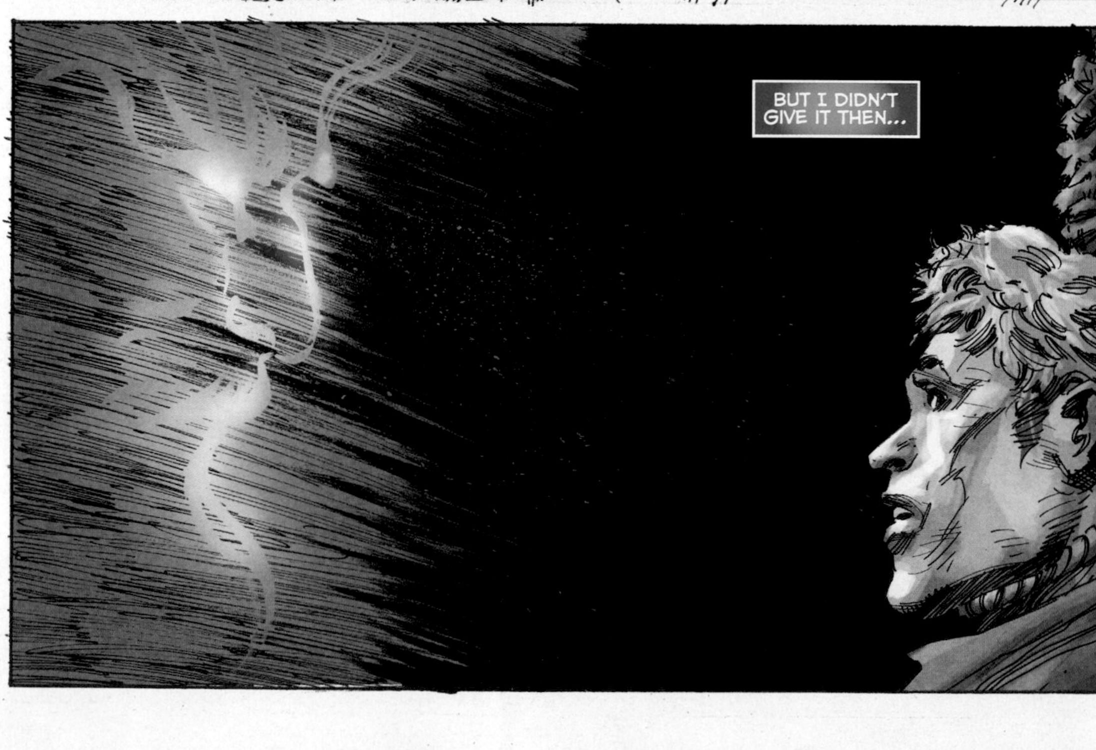
BUT I DIDN'T GIVE IT THEN...

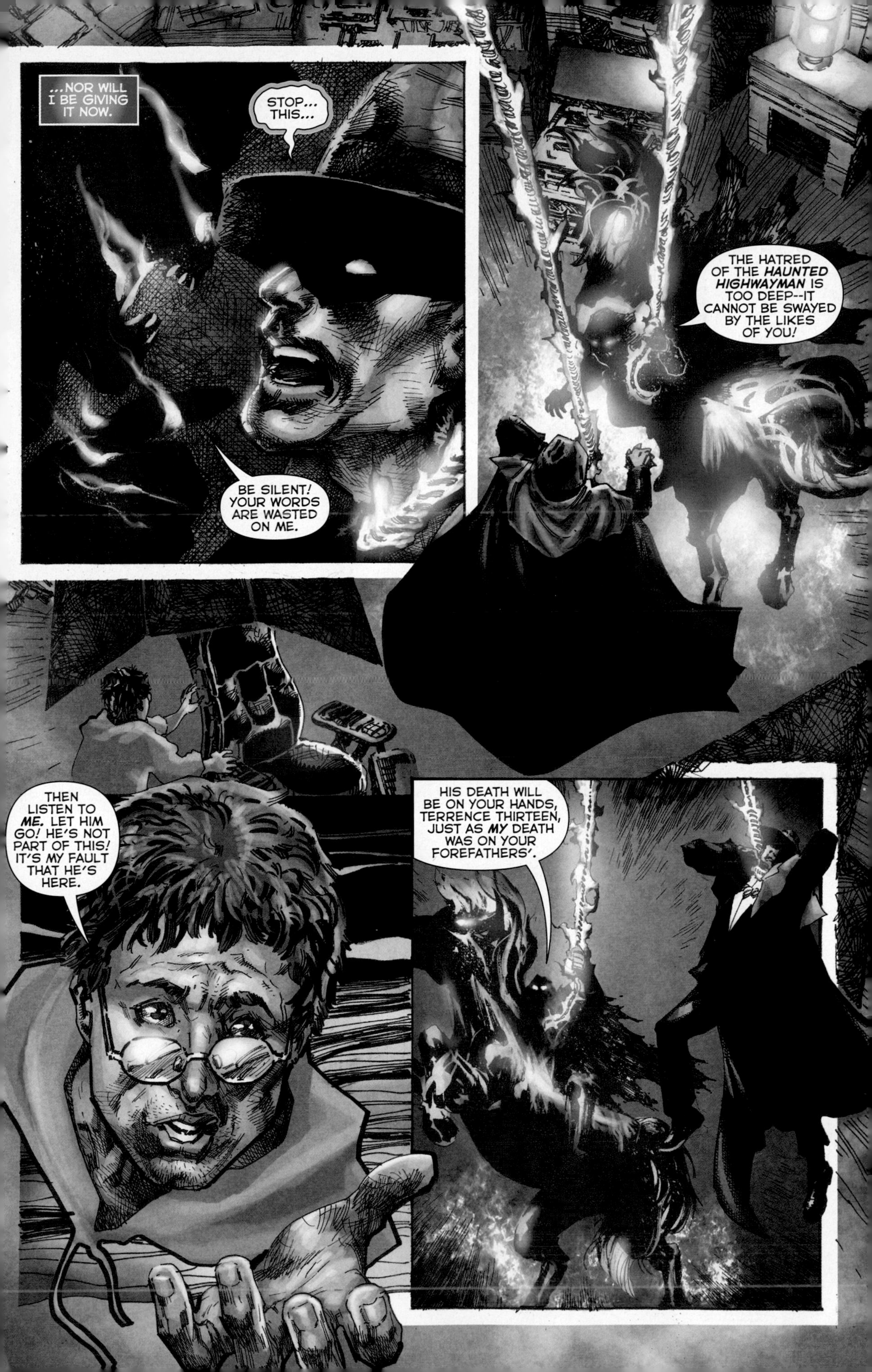
...NOR WILL I BE GIVING IT NOW.
STOP... THIS...
BE SILENT! YOUR WORDS ARE WASTED ON ME.
THE HATRED OF THE HAUNTED HIGHWAYMAN IS TOO DEEP--IT CANNOT BE SWAYED BY THE LIKES OF YOU!
THEN LISTEN TO ME. LET HIM GO! HE'S NOT PART OF THIS! IT'S MY FAULT THAT HE'S HERE.
HIS DEATH WILL BE ON YOUR HANDS, TERRENCE THIRTEEN, JUST AS MY DEATH WAS ON YOUR FOREFATHERS'.

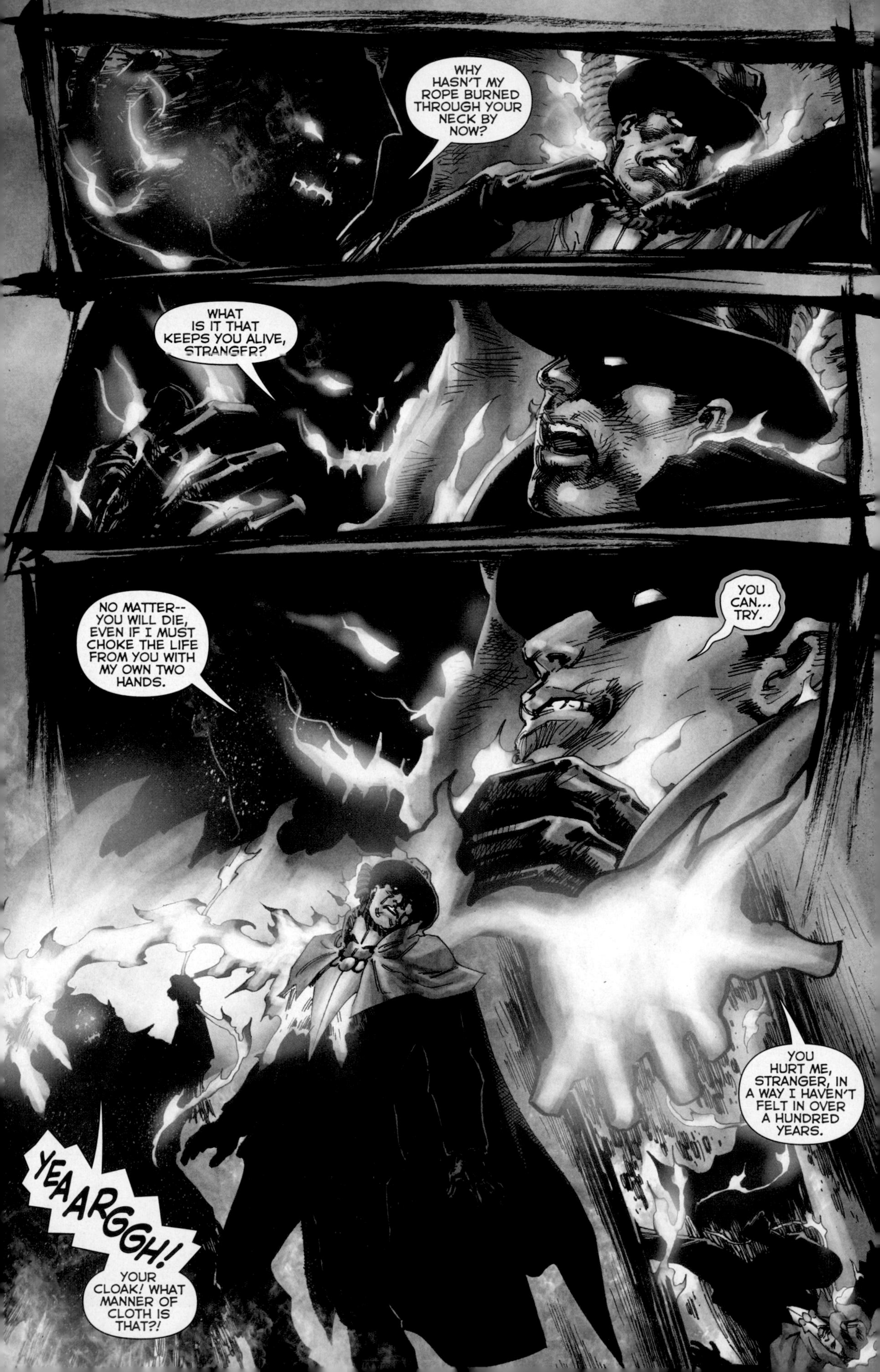
WHY HASN'T MY ROPE BURNED THROUGH YOUR NECK BY NOW?
WHAT IS IT THAT KEEPS YOU ALIVE, STRANGER?
NO MATTER-- YOU WILL DIE, EVEN IF I MUST CHOKE THE LIFE FROM YOU WITH MY OWN TWO HANDS.
YOU CAN... TRY.
YOU HURT ME, STRANGER, IN A WAY I HAVEN'T FELT IN OVER A HUNDRED YEARS.
YEAARGGH!
YOUR CLOAK! WHAT MANNER OF CLOTH IS THAT?!

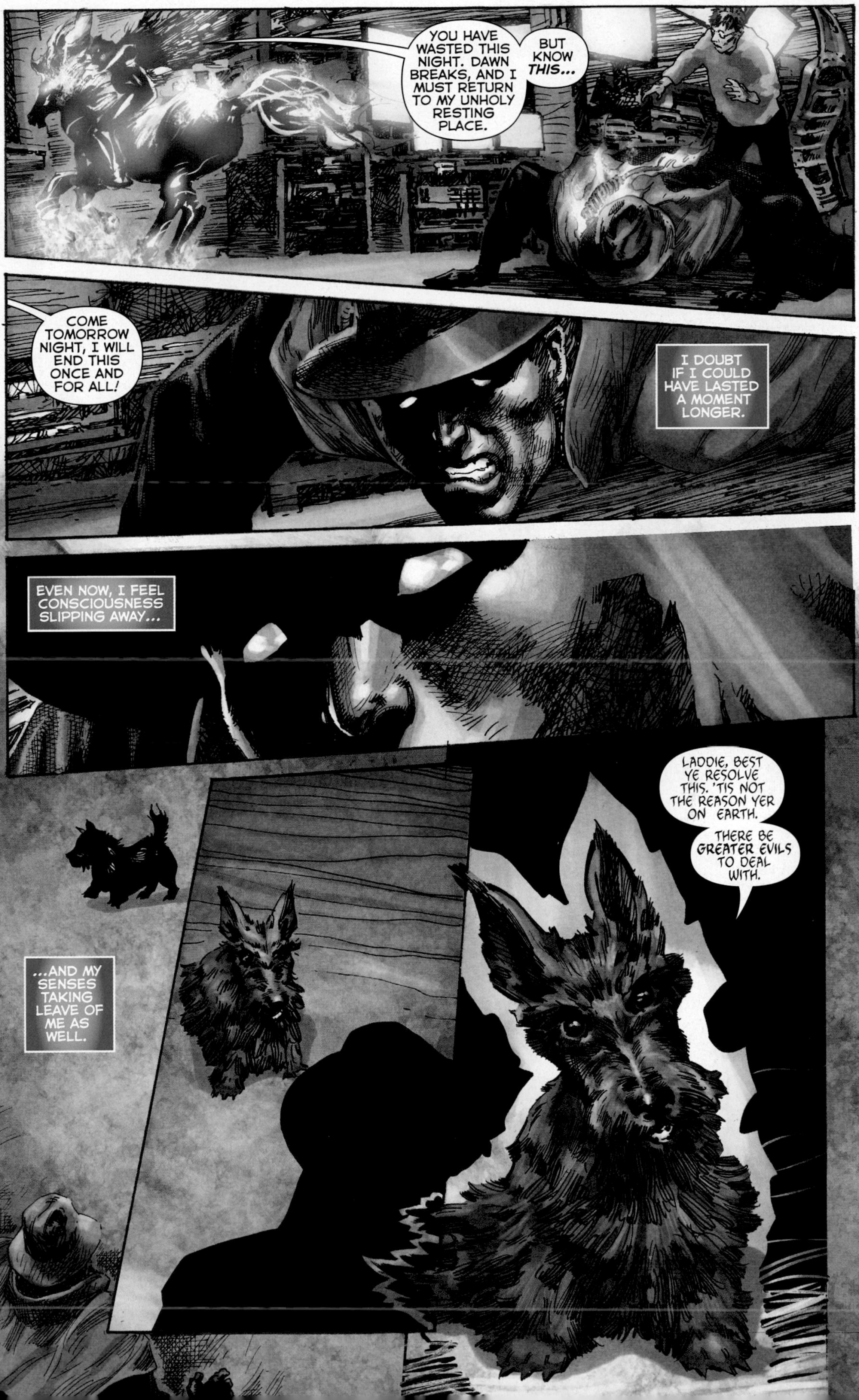
YOU HAVE WASTED THIS NIGHT. DAWN BREAKS, AND I MUST RETURN TO MY UNHOLY RESTING PLACE.
BUT KNOW *THIS...*
COME TOMORROW NIGHT, I WILL END THIS ONCE AND FOR ALL!
I DOUBT IF I COULD HAVE LASTED A MOMENT LONGER.
EVEN NOW, I FEEL CONSCIOUSNESS SLIPPING AWAY...
LADDIE, BEST YE RESOLVE THIS. 'TIS NOT THE REASON YER ON EARTH.
THERE BE **GREATER EVILS** TO DEAL WITH.
...AND MY SENSES TAKING LEAVE OF ME AS WELL.

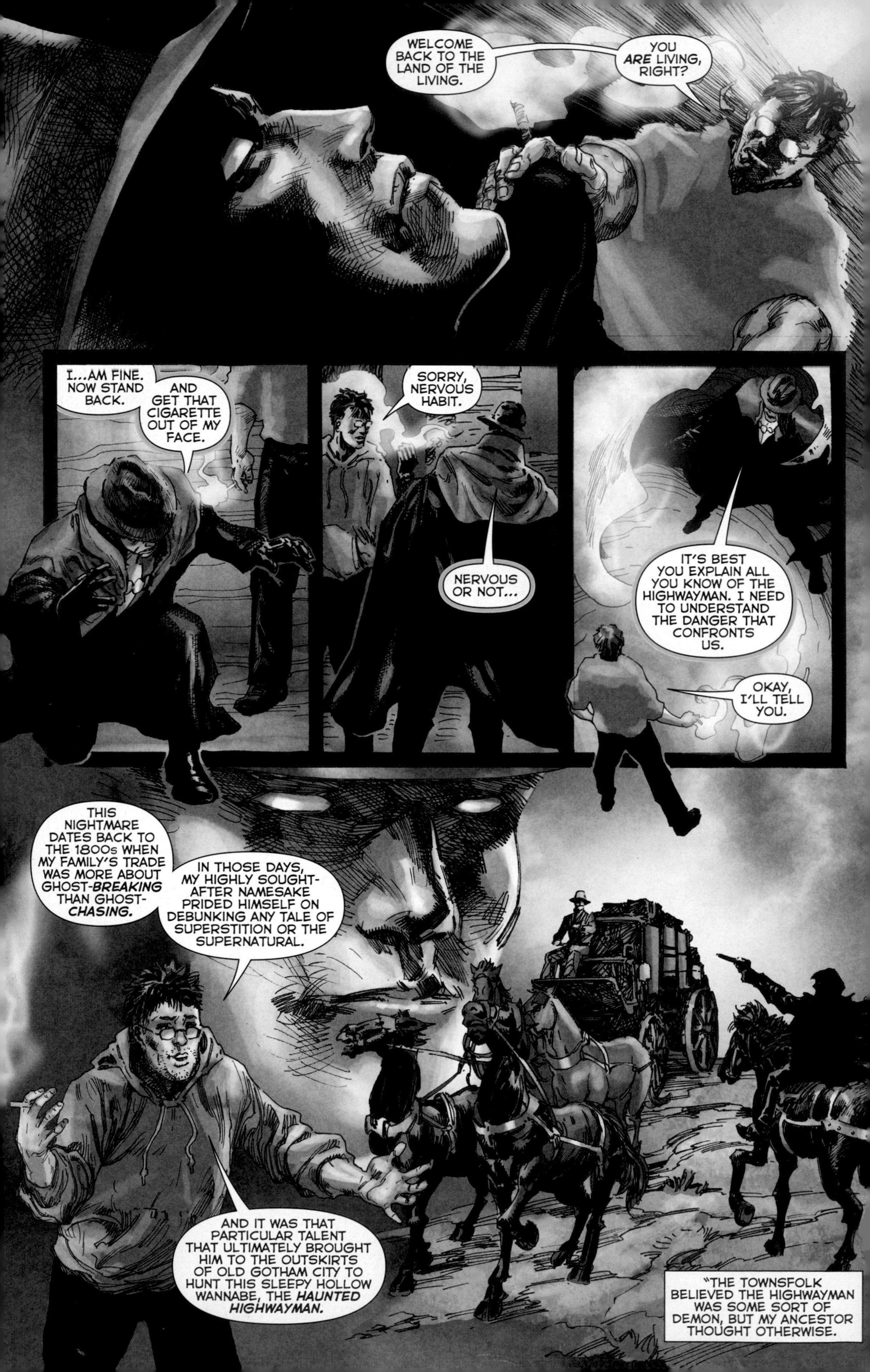
WELCOME BACK TO THE LAND OF THE LIVING.
YOU *ARE* LIVING, RIGHT?
I...AM FINE. NOW STAND BACK.
AND GET THAT CIGARETTE OUT OF MY FACE.
SORRY, NERVOUS HABIT.
NERVOUS OR NOT...
IT'S BEST YOU EXPLAIN ALL YOU KNOW OF THE HIGHWAYMAN. I NEED TO UNDERSTAND THE DANGER THAT CONFRONTS US.
OKAY, I'LL TELL YOU.
THIS NIGHTMARE DATES BACK TO THE 1800s WHEN MY FAMILY'S TRADE WAS MORE ABOUT GHOST-*BREAKING* THAN GHOST-*CHASING.*
IN THOSE DAYS, MY HIGHLY SOUGHT-AFTER NAMESAKE PRIDED HIMSELF ON DEBUNKING ANY TALE OF SUPERSTITION OR THE SUPERNATURAL.
AND IT WAS THAT PARTICULAR TALENT THAT ULTIMATELY BROUGHT HIM TO THE OUTSKIRTS OF OLD GOTHAM CITY TO HUNT THIS SLEEPY HOLLOW WANNABE, THE *HAUNTED HIGHWAYMAN.*
"THE TOWNSFOLK BELIEVED THE HIGHWAYMAN WAS SOME SORT OF DEMON, BUT MY ANCESTOR THOUGHT OTHERWISE.

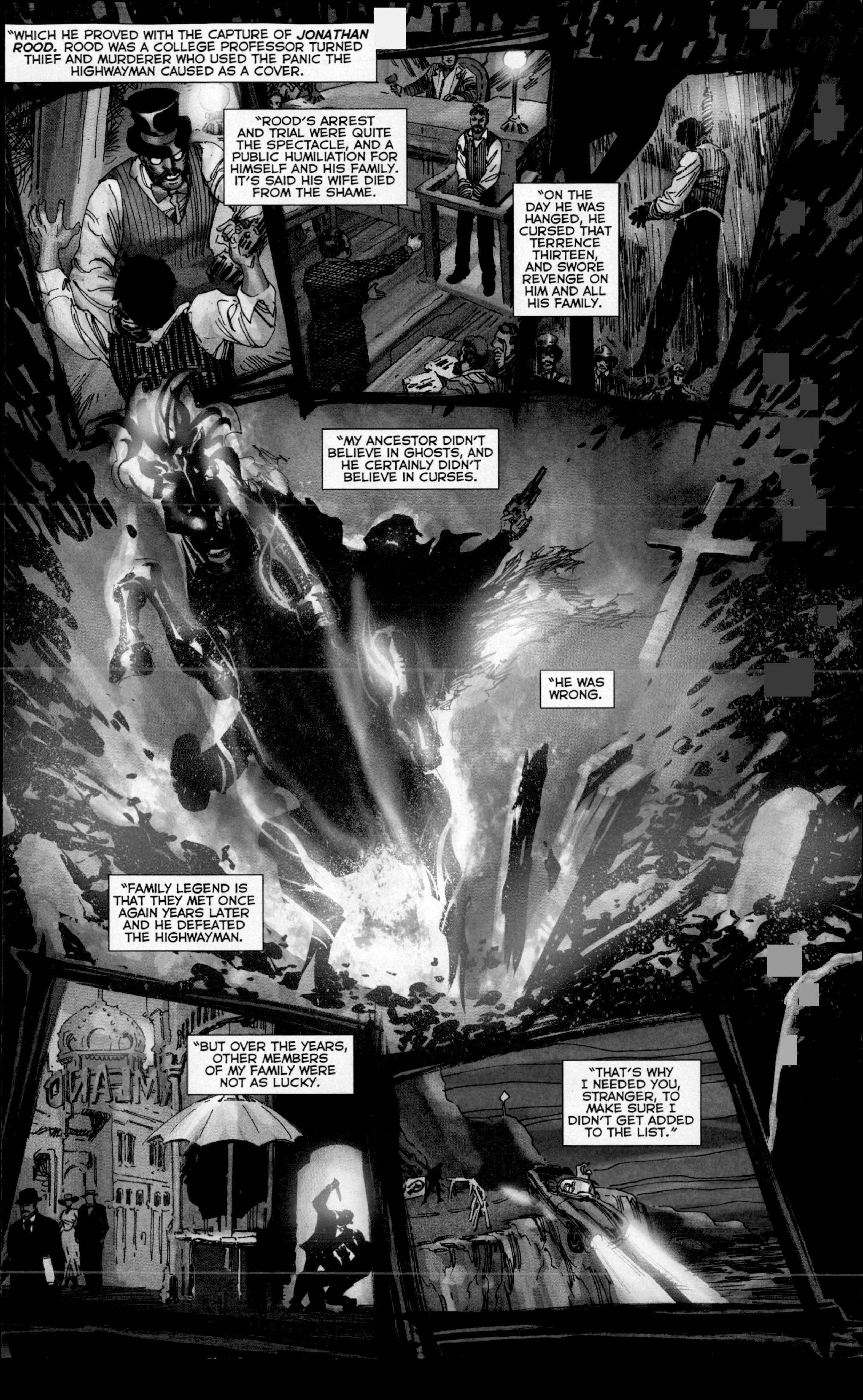

"WHICH HE PROVED WITH THE CAPTURE OF *JONATHAN ROOD.* ROOD WAS A COLLEGE PROFESSOR TURNED THIEF AND MURDERER WHO USED THE PANIC THE HIGHWAYMAN CAUSED AS A COVER.
"ROOD'S ARREST AND TRIAL WERE QUITE THE SPECTACLE, AND A PUBLIC HUMILIATION FOR HIMSELF AND HIS FAMILY. IT'S SAID HIS WIFE DIED FROM THE SHAME.
"ON THE DAY HE WAS HANGED, HE CURSED THAT TERRENCE THIRTEEN, AND SWORE REVENGE ON HIM AND ALL HIS FAMILY.
"MY ANCESTOR DIDN'T BELIEVE IN GHOSTS, AND HE CERTAINLY DIDN'T BELIEVE IN CURSES.
"HE WAS WRONG.
"FAMILY LEGEND IS THAT THEY MET ONCE AGAIN YEARS LATER AND HE DEFEATED THE HIGHWAYMAN.
"BUT OVER THE YEARS, OTHER MEMBERS OF MY FAMILY WERE NOT AS LUCKY.
"THAT'S WHY I NEEDED YOU, STRANGER, TO MAKE SURE I DIDN'T GET ADDED TO THE LIST."

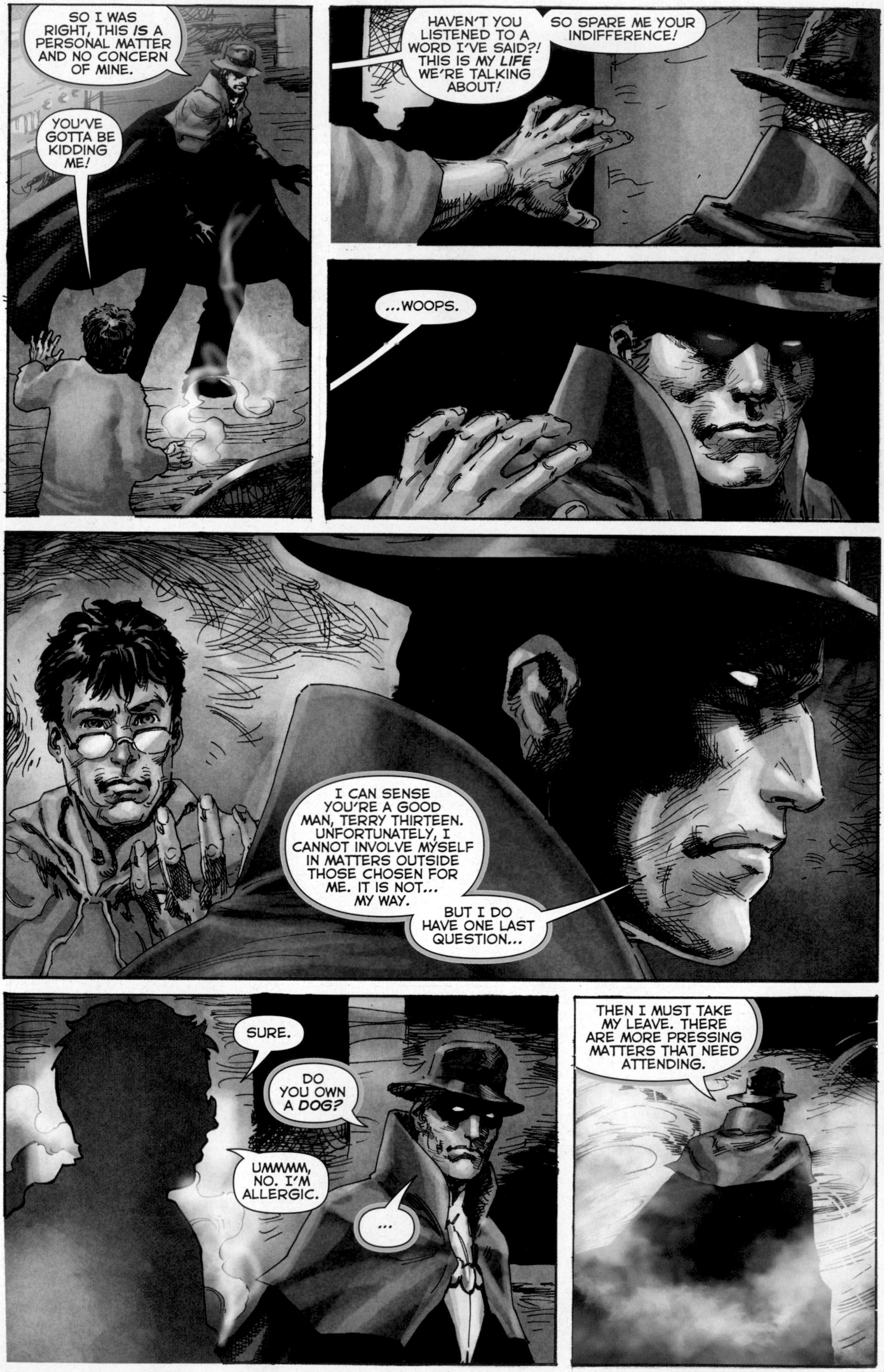
SO I WAS RIGHT, THIS *IS* A PERSONAL MATTER AND NO CONCERN OF MINE.
YOU'VE GOTTA BE KIDDING ME!
HAVEN'T YOU LISTENED TO A WORD I'VE SAID?! THIS IS MY *LIFE* WE'RE TALKING ABOUT!
SO SPARE ME YOUR INDIFFERENCE!
...WOOPS.
I CAN SENSE YOU'RE A GOOD MAN, TERRY THIRTEEN. UNFORTUNATELY, I CANNOT INVOLVE MYSELF IN MATTERS OUTSIDE THOSE CHOSEN FOR ME. IT IS NOT... MY WAY.
BUT I DO HAVE ONE LAST QUESTION...
SURE.
DO YOU OWN A *DOG?*
UMMMM, NO. I'M ALLERGIC.
...
THEN I MUST TAKE MY LEAVE. THERE ARE MORE PRESSING MATTERS THAT NEED ATTENDING.

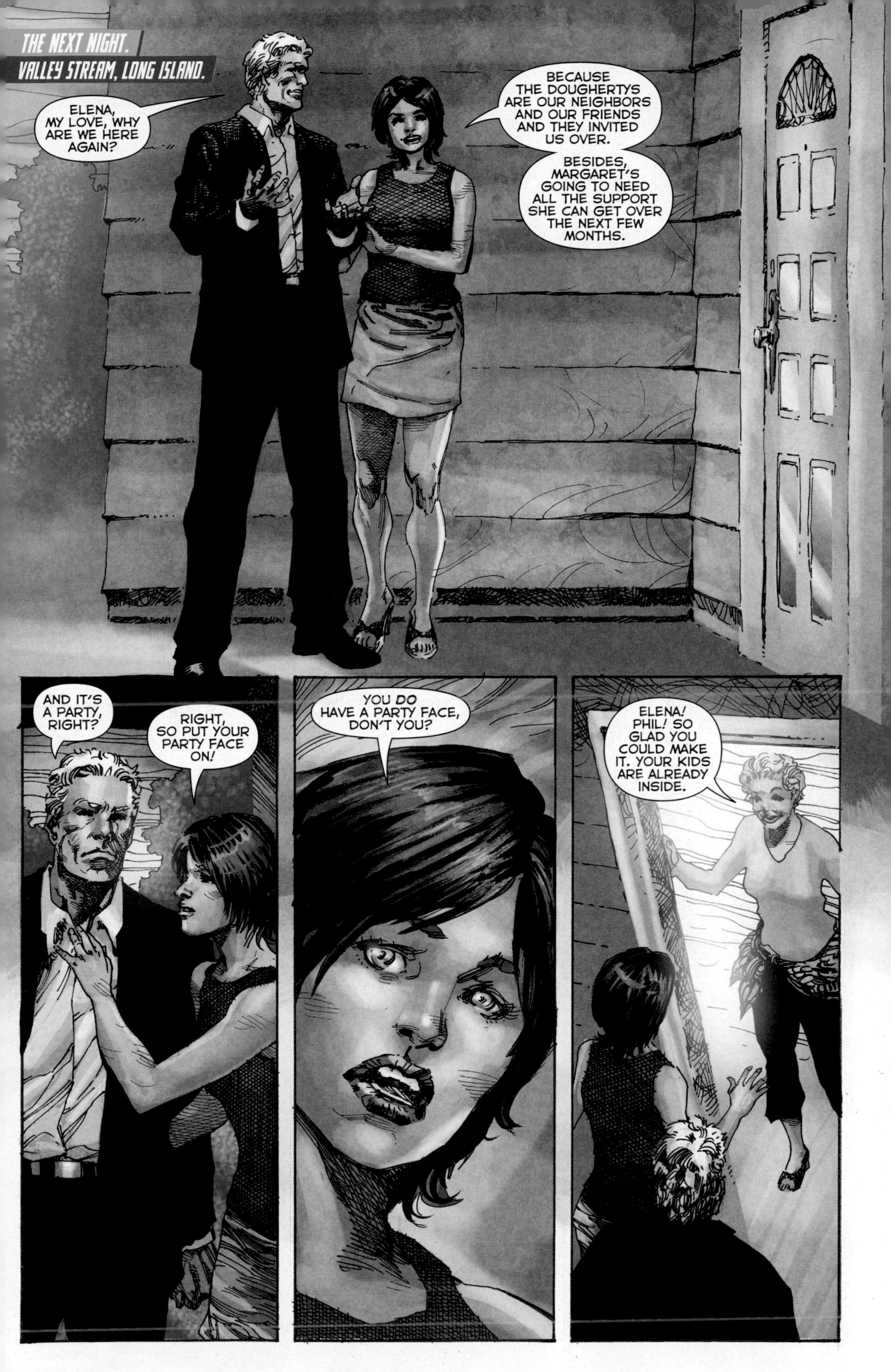
THE NEXT NIGHT.
VALLEY STREAM, LONG ISLAND.
ELENA, MY LOVE, WHY ARE WE HERE AGAIN?
BECAUSE THE DOUGHERTYS ARE OUR NEIGHBORS AND OUR FRIENDS AND THEY INVITED US OVER.
BESIDES, MARGARET'S GOING TO NEED ALL THE SUPPORT SHE CAN GET OVER THE NEXT FEW MONTHS.
AND IT'S A PARTY, RIGHT?
RIGHT, SO PUT YOUR PARTY FACE ON!
YOU DO HAVE A PARTY FACE, DON'T YOU?
ELENA! PHIL! SO GLAD YOU COULD MAKE IT. YOUR KIDS ARE ALREADY INSIDE.

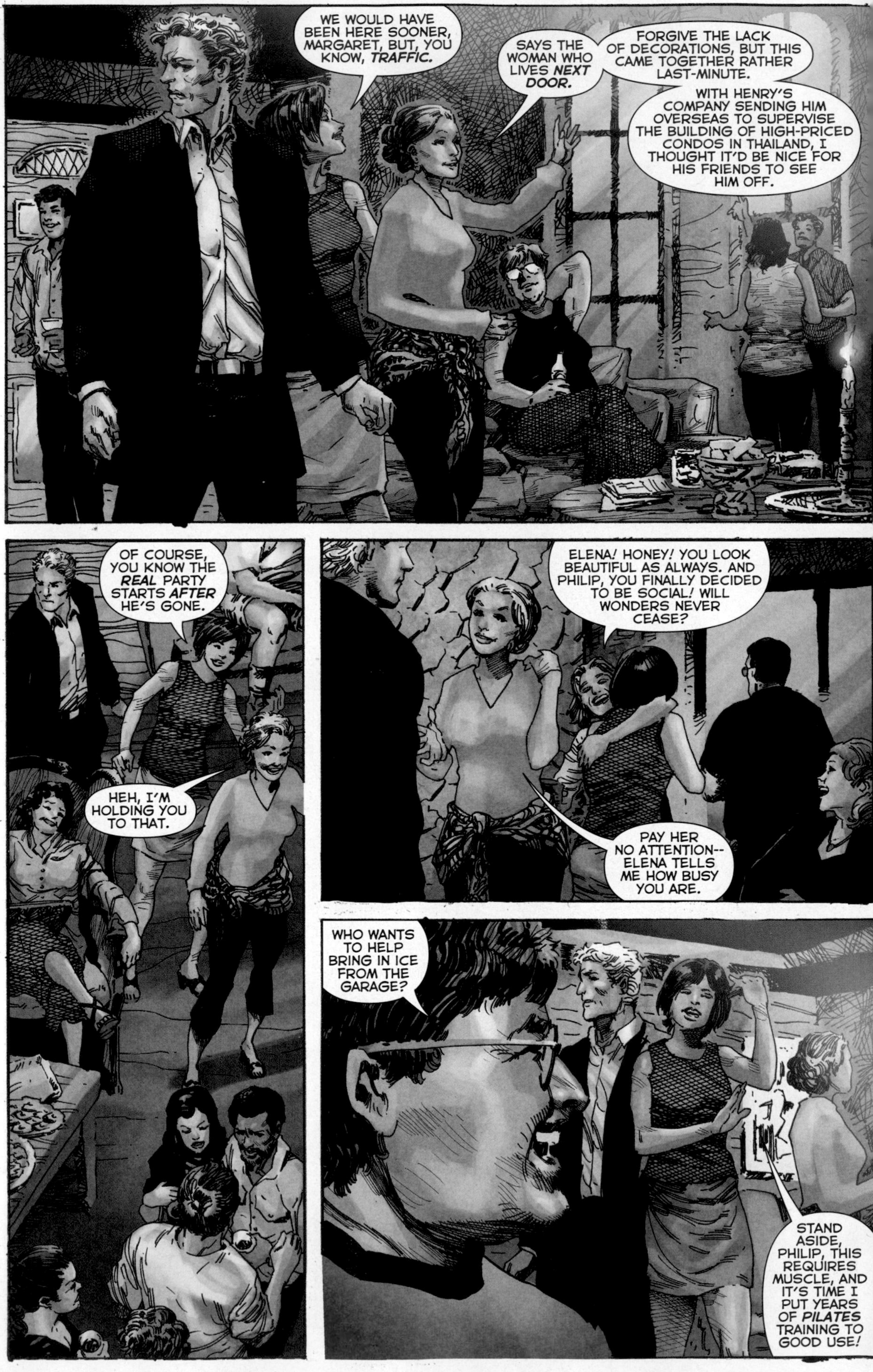
WE WOULD HAVE BEEN HERE SOONER, MARGARET, BUT, YOU KNOW, TRAFFIC.
SAYS THE WOMAN WHO LIVES NEXT DOOR.
FORGIVE THE LACK OF DECORATIONS, BUT THIS CAME TOGETHER RATHER LAST-MINUTE.
WITH HENRY'S COMPANY SENDING HIM OVERSEAS TO SUPERVISE THE BUILDING OF HIGH-PRICED CONDOS IN THAILAND, I THOUGHT IT'D BE NICE FOR HIS FRIENDS TO SEE HIM OFF.
OF COURSE, YOU KNOW THE REAL PARTY STARTS AFTER HE'S GONE.
HEH, I'M HOLDING YOU TO THAT.
ELENA! HONEY! YOU LOOK BEAUTIFUL AS ALWAYS. AND PHILIP, YOU FINALLY DECIDED TO BE SOCIAL! WILL WONDERS NEVER CEASE?
PAY HER NO ATTENTION-- ELENA TELLS ME HOW BUSY YOU ARE.
WHO WANTS TO HELP BRING IN ICE FROM THE GARAGE?
STAND ASIDE, PHILIP, THIS REQUIRES MUSCLE, AND IT'S TIME I PUT YEARS OF PILATES TRAINING TO GOOD USE!

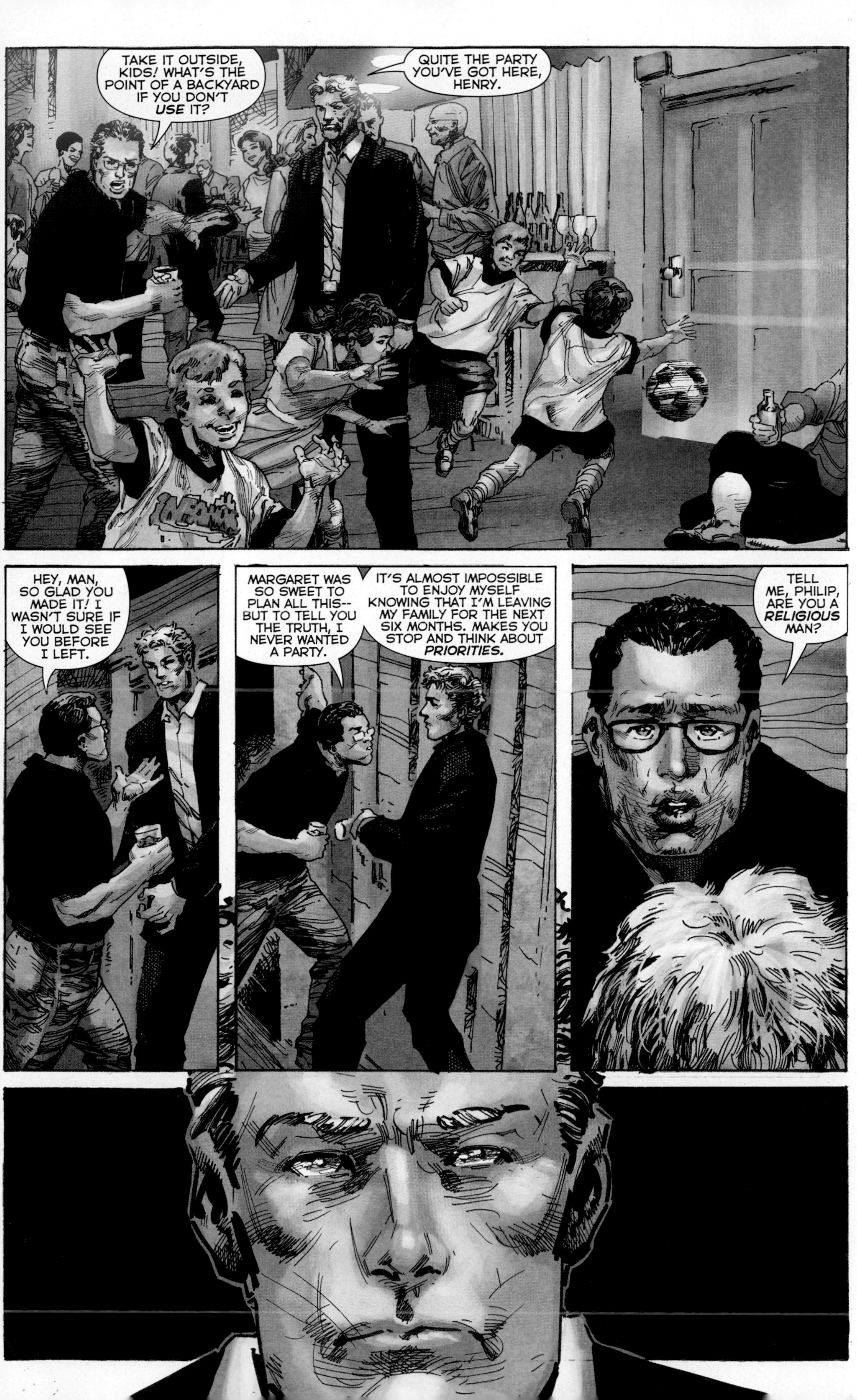
TAKE IT OUTSIDE, KIDS! WHAT'S THE POINT OF A BACKYARD IF YOU DON'T USE IT?
QUITE THE PARTY YOU'VE GOT HERE, HENRY.
HEY, MAN, SO GLAD YOU MADE IT! I WASN'T SURE IF I WOULD SEE YOU BEFORE I LEFT.
MARGARET WAS SO SWEET TO PLAN ALL THIS-- BUT TO TELL YOU THE TRUTH, I NEVER WANTED A PARTY.
IT'S ALMOST IMPOSSIBLE TO ENJOY MYSELF KNOWING THAT I'M LEAVING MY FAMILY FOR THE NEXT SIX MONTHS. MAKES YOU STOP AND THINK ABOUT PRIORITIES.
TELL ME, PHILIP, ARE YOU A RELIGIOUS MAN?

WHY DO YOU ASK?

WELL, WE'RE ALL PUT ON THIS EARTH FOR *SOME* REASON, I JUST DON'T KNOW IF *MY* REASON IS TO BUILD *CONDOS* IN *THAILAND*.

THEN DON'T GO.

EASY FOR YOU TO SAY! YOU'RE SELF-EMPLOYED AND GET TO MAKE YOUR OWN RULES.

FAMILY MATTERS TO ME MORE THAN ANYTHING. I DON'T WANT TO GO, BUT I *HAVE* TO. MY COMPANY DIDN'T GIVE ME MUCH CHOICE--HECK, THEY BASICALLY MADE THE DECISION *FOR* ME.

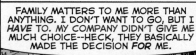

YOU *ALWAYS* HAVE A CHOICE. YOU JUST NEED THE STRENGTH TO MAKE IT.

PHILIP, THEY'RE GOING TO PAY ME A SIX-FIGURE SALARY FOR JUST SIX MONTHS OF WORK. DON'T KNOW IF I'M STRONG ENOUGH TO GIVE *THAT* UP.

BESIDES, I HAVE YOU AND ELENA NEXT DOOR, READY TO HELP WHEN NEEDED, RIGHT?

OF COURSE.

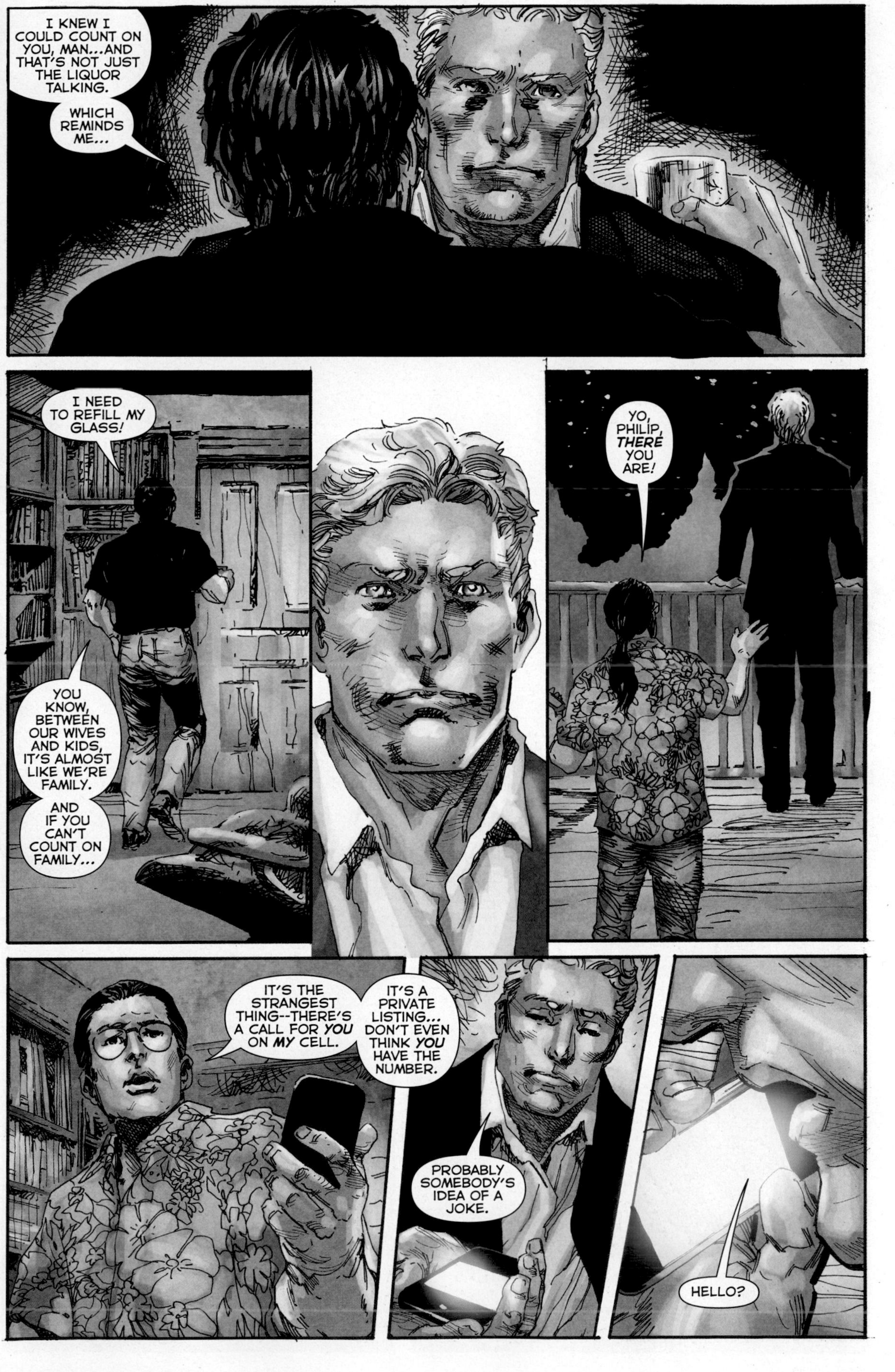
I KNEW I COULD COUNT ON YOU, MAN...AND THAT'S NOT JUST THE LIQUOR TALKING.
WHICH REMINDS ME...
I NEED TO REFILL MY GLASS!
YOU KNOW, BETWEEN OUR WIVES AND KIDS, IT'S ALMOST LIKE WE'RE FAMILY.
AND IF YOU CAN'T COUNT ON FAMILY...
YO, PHILIP, THERE YOU ARE!
IT'S THE STRANGEST THING--THERE'S A CALL FOR YOU ON MY CELL.
IT'S A PRIVATE LISTING... DON'T EVEN THINK YOU HAVE THE NUMBER.
PROBABLY SOMEBODY'S IDEA OF A JOKE.
HELLO?

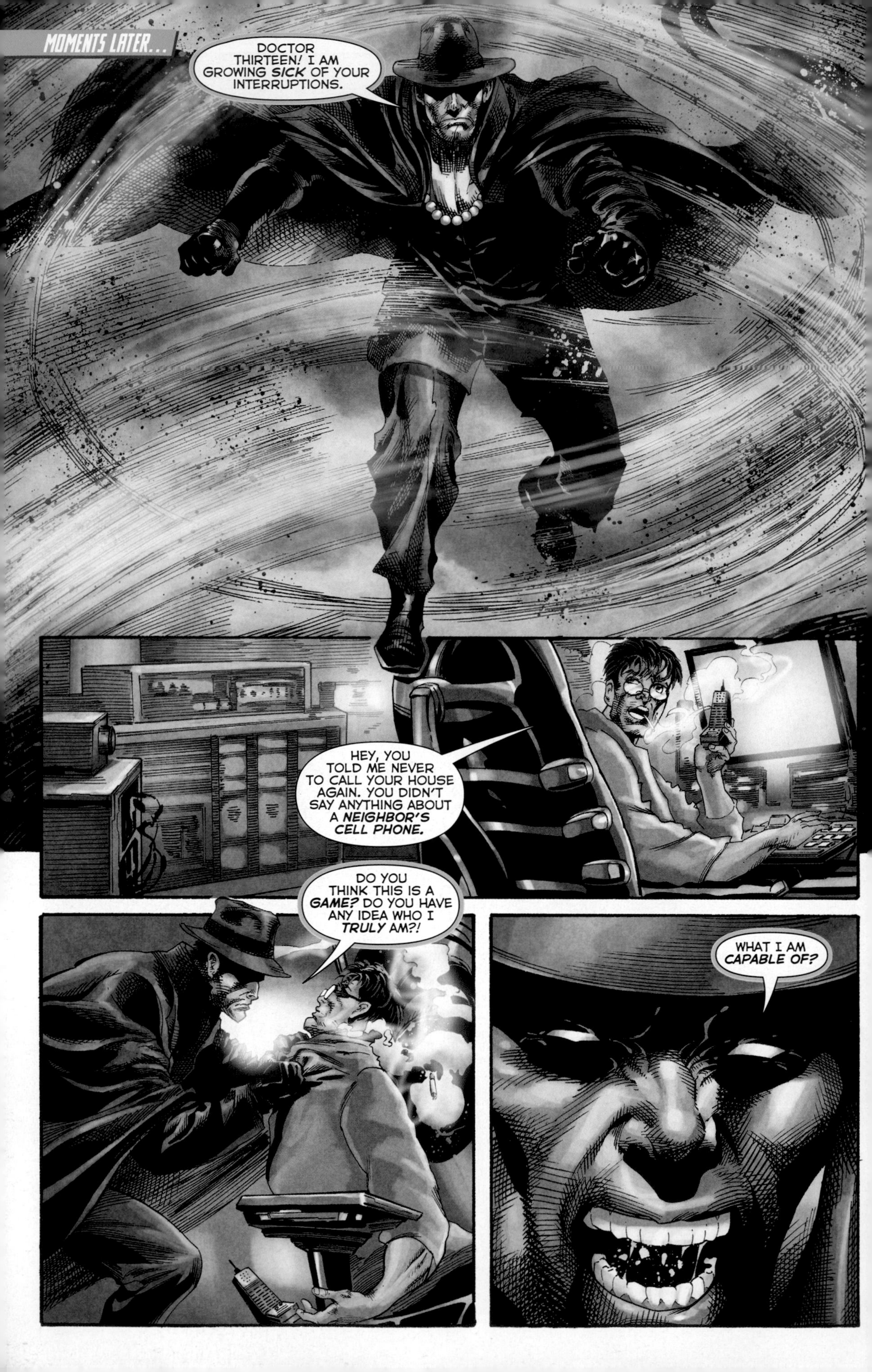
MOMENTS LATER...
DOCTOR THIRTEEN! I AM GROWING SICK OF YOUR INTERRUPTIONS.
HEY, YOU TOLD ME NEVER TO CALL YOUR HOUSE AGAIN. YOU DIDN'T SAY ANYTHING ABOUT A NEIGHBOR'S CELL PHONE.
DO YOU THINK THIS IS A GAME? DO YOU HAVE ANY IDEA WHO I TRULY AM?!
WHAT I AM CAPABLE OF?

I READ THE SCRIPTURES, RESEARCHED *EVERYTHING.* OF COURSE I KNOW WHO YOU ARE, THAT'S WHY I *NEED* YOU.

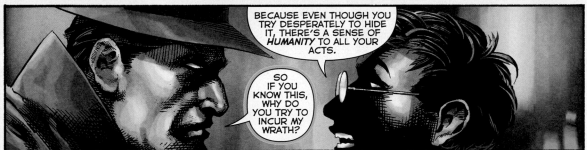

BECAUSE EVEN THOUGH YOU TRY DESPERATELY TO HIDE IT, THERE'S A SENSE OF *HUMANITY* TO ALL YOUR ACTS.

SO IF YOU KNOW THIS, WHY DO YOU TRY TO INCUR MY WRATH?

BECAUSE IF I'M GOING TO DIE TONIGHT, I'D RATHER IT BE AT *YOUR* HANDS...

...THAN HIS.

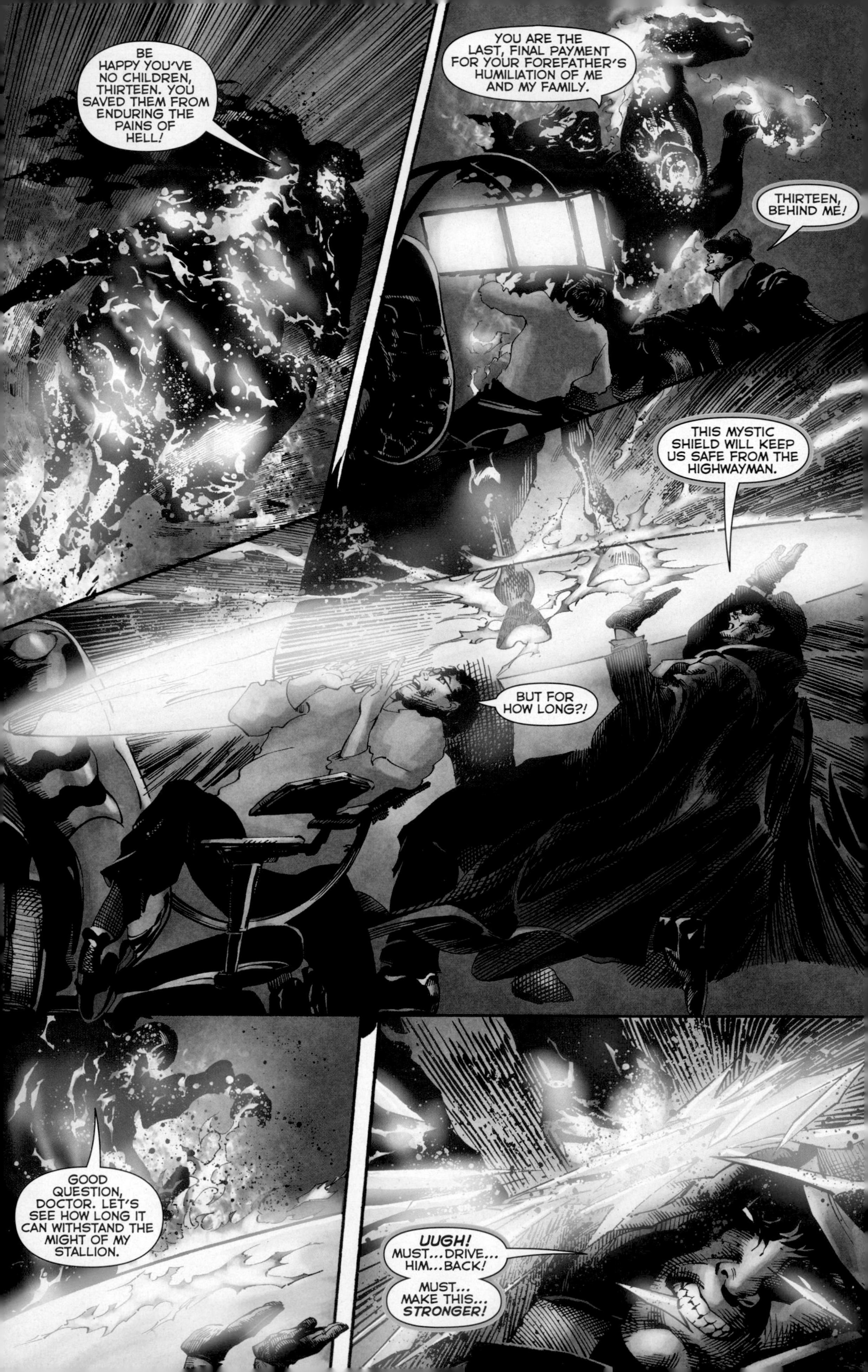
BE HAPPY YOU'VE NO CHILDREN, THIRTEEN. YOU SAVED THEM FROM ENDURING THE PAINS OF HELL!
YOU ARE THE LAST, FINAL PAYMENT FOR YOUR FOREFATHER'S HUMILIATION OF ME AND MY FAMILY.
THIRTEEN, BEHIND ME!
THIS MYSTIC SHIELD WILL KEEP US SAFE FROM THE HIGHWAYMAN.
BUT FOR HOW LONG?!
GOOD QUESTION, DOCTOR. LET'S SEE HOW LONG IT CAN WITHSTAND THE MIGHT OF MY STALLION.
UUGH! MUST...DRIVE... HIM...BACK!
MUST... MAKE THIS... STRONGER!

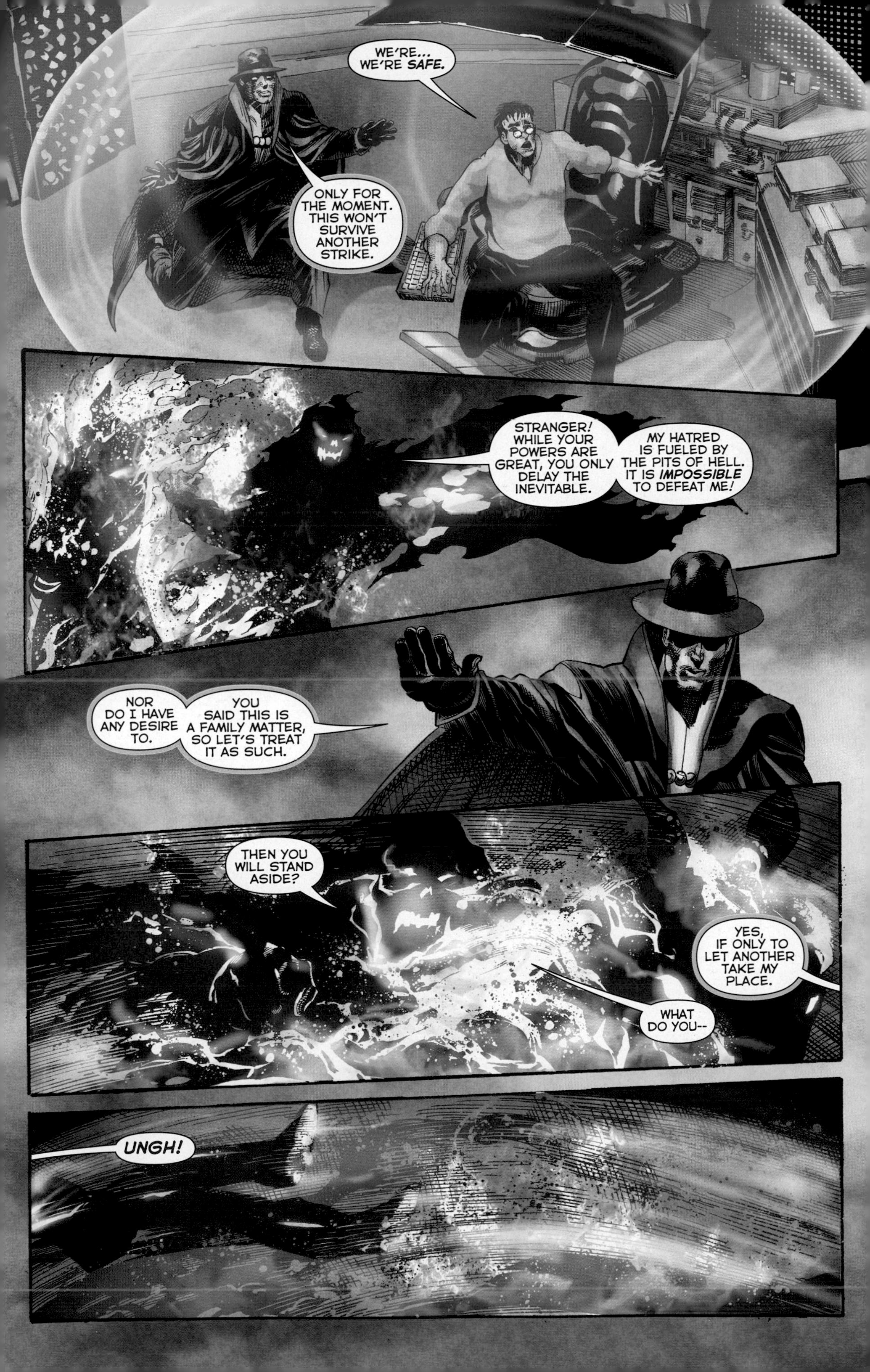
WE'RE... WE'RE SAFE.
ONLY FOR THE MOMENT. THIS WON'T SURVIVE ANOTHER STRIKE.
STRANGER! WHILE YOUR POWERS ARE GREAT, YOU ONLY DELAY THE INEVITABLE.
MY HATRED IS FUELED BY THE PITS OF HELL. IT IS IMPOSSIBLE TO DEFEAT ME!
NOR DO I HAVE ANY DESIRE TO.
YOU SAID THIS IS A FAMILY MATTER, SO LET'S TREAT IT AS SUCH.
THEN YOU WILL STAND ASIDE?
YES, IF ONLY TO LET ANOTHER TAKE MY PLACE.
WHAT DO YOU--
UNGH!

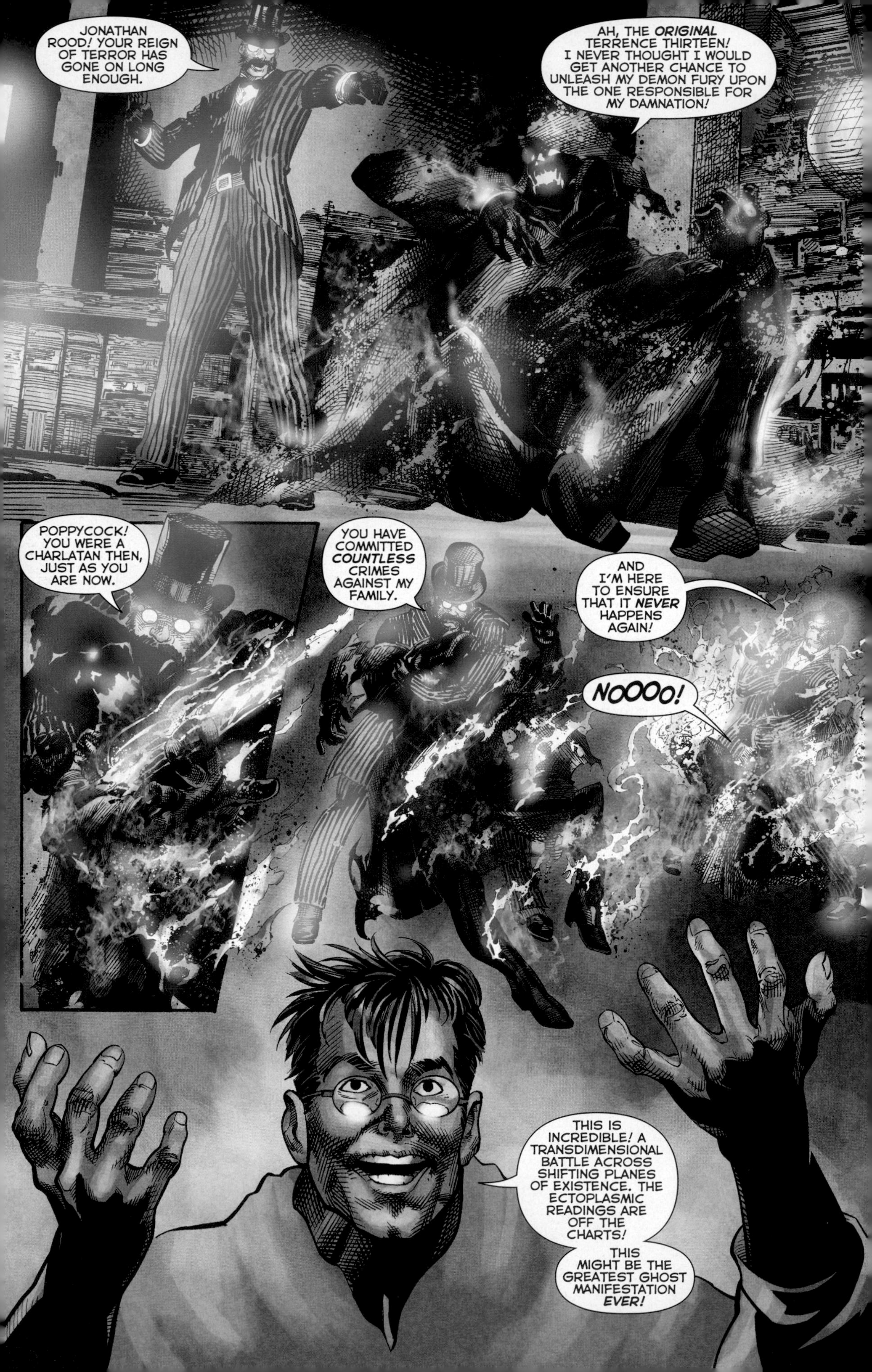
JONATHAN ROOD! YOUR REIGN OF TERROR HAS GONE ON LONG ENOUGH.
AH, THE *ORIGINAL* TERRENCE THIRTEEN! I NEVER THOUGHT I WOULD GET ANOTHER CHANCE TO UNLEASH MY DEMON FURY UPON THE ONE RESPONSIBLE FOR MY DAMNATION!
POPPYCOCK! YOU WERE A CHARLATAN THEN, JUST AS YOU ARE NOW.
YOU HAVE COMMITTED *COUNTLESS* CRIMES AGAINST MY FAMILY.
AND I'M HERE TO ENSURE THAT IT *NEVER* HAPPENS AGAIN!
NOOOO!
THIS IS INCREDIBLE! A TRANSDIMENSIONAL BATTLE ACROSS SHIFTING PLANES OF EXISTENCE. THE ECTOPLASMIC READINGS ARE OFF THE CHARTS!
THIS MIGHT BE THE GREATEST GHOST MANIFESTATION *EVER*!

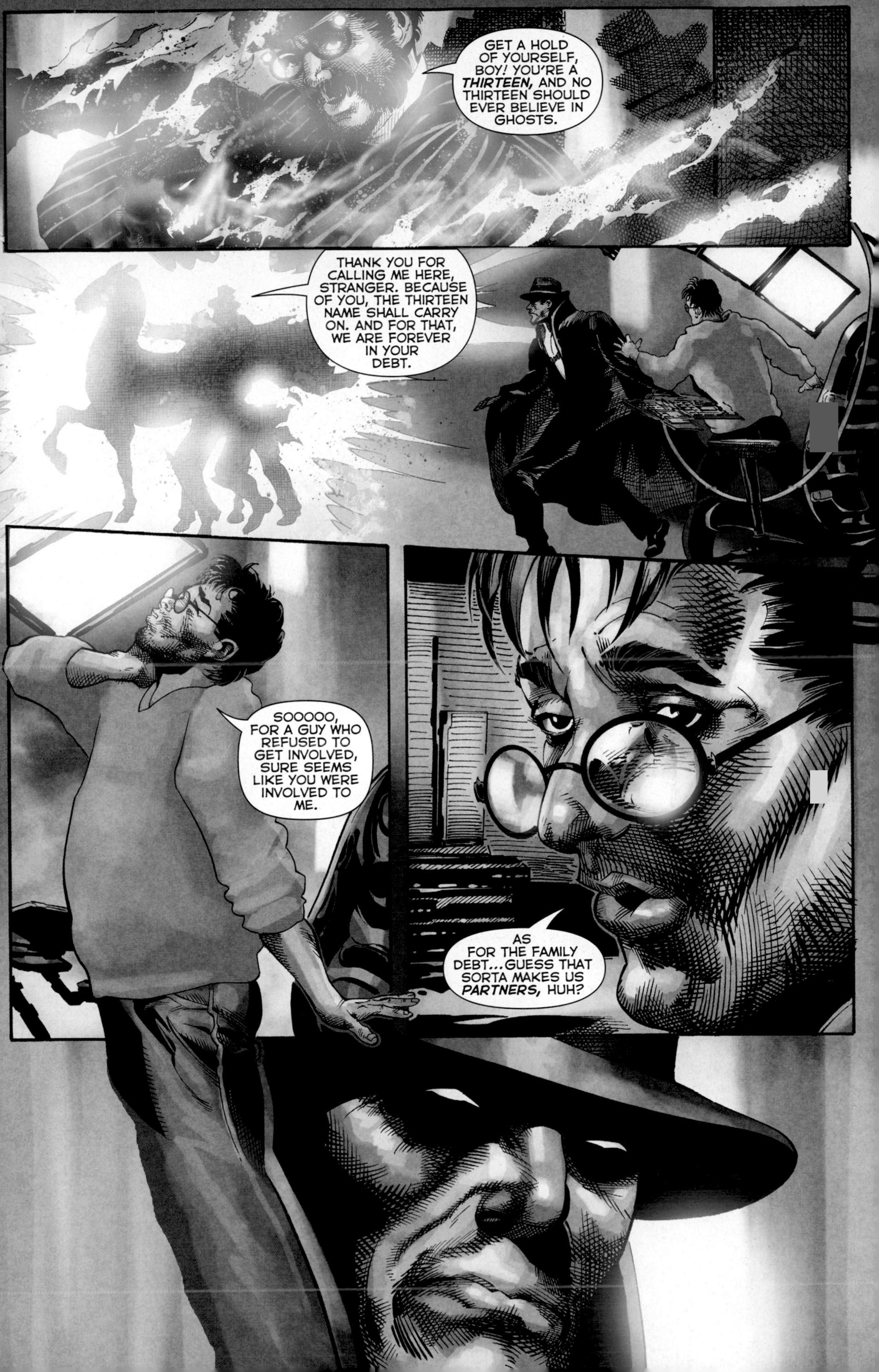
GET A HOLD OF YOURSELF, BOY! YOU'RE A *THIRTEEN,* AND NO THIRTEEN SHOULD EVER BELIEVE IN GHOSTS.
THANK YOU FOR CALLING ME HERE, STRANGER. BECAUSE OF YOU, THE THIRTEEN NAME SHALL CARRY ON. AND FOR THAT, WE ARE FOREVER IN YOUR DEBT.
SOOOOO, FOR A GUY WHO REFUSED TO GET INVOLVED, SURE SEEMS LIKE YOU WERE INVOLVED TO ME.
AS FOR THE FAMILY DEBT...GUESS THAT SORTA MAKES US *PARTNERS,* HUH?

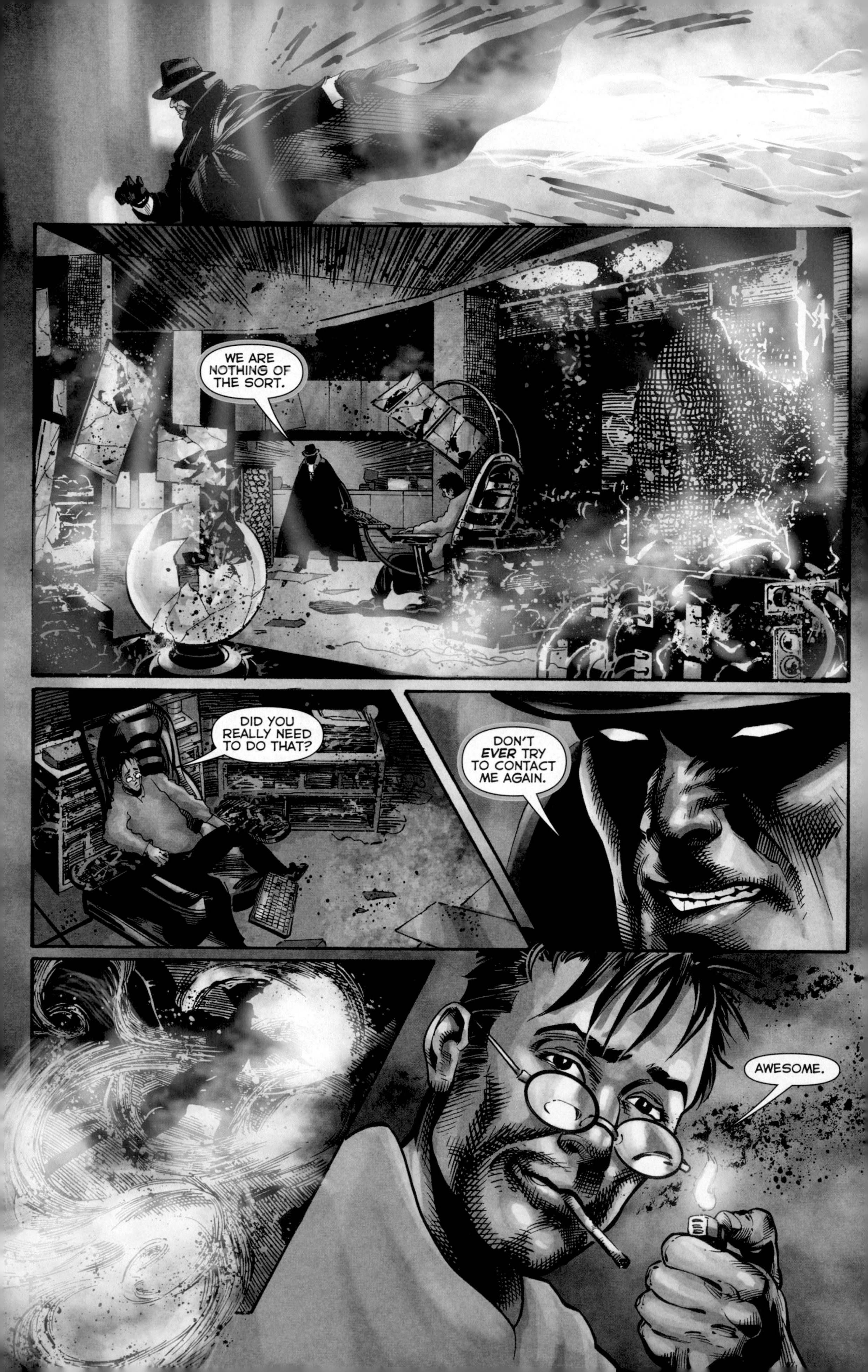
WE ARE NOTHING OF THE SORT.
DID YOU REALLY NEED TO DO THAT?
DON'T *EVER* TRY TO CONTACT ME AGAIN.
AWESOME.

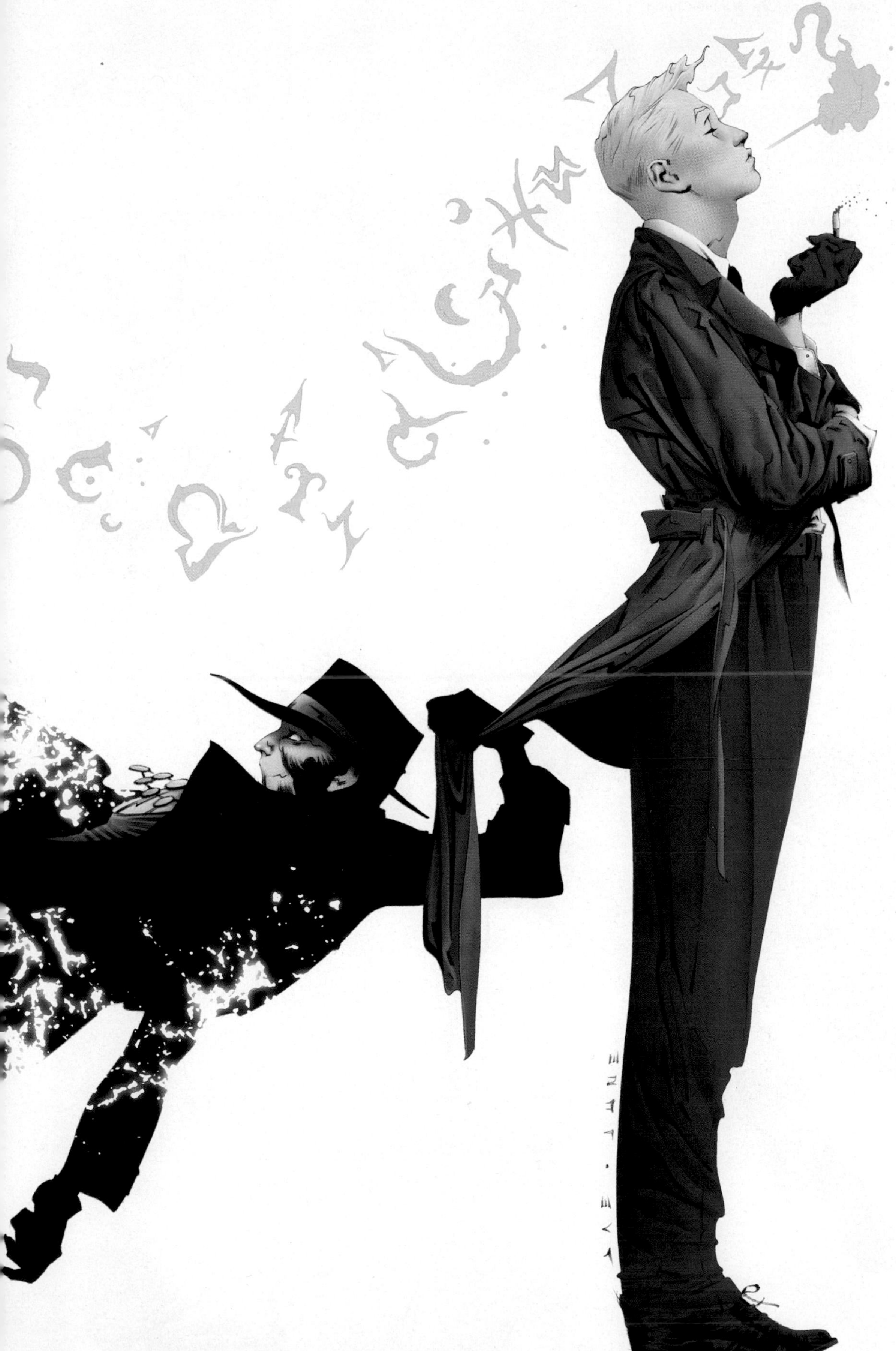

Cover by Jae Lee & June Chung

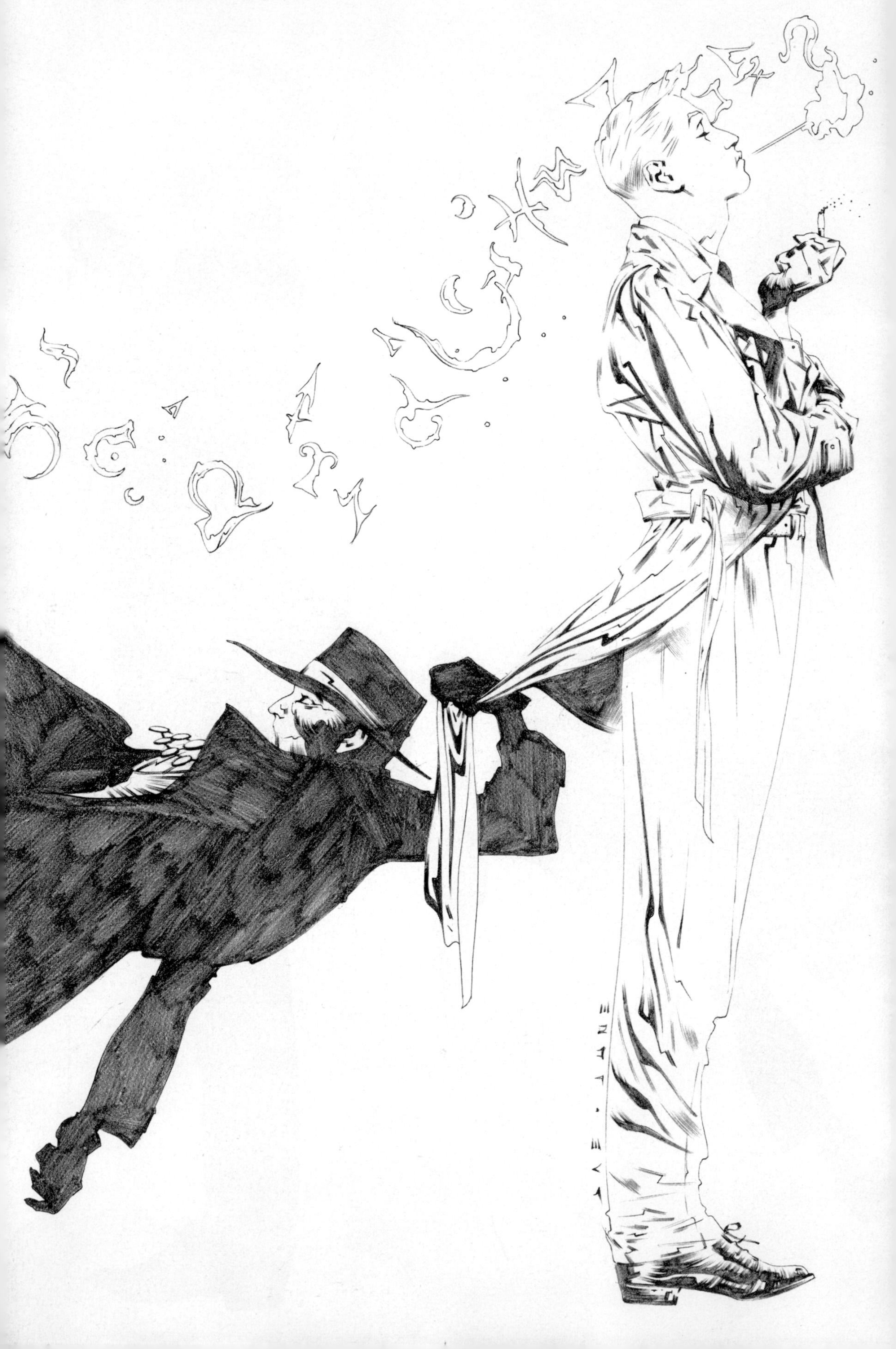

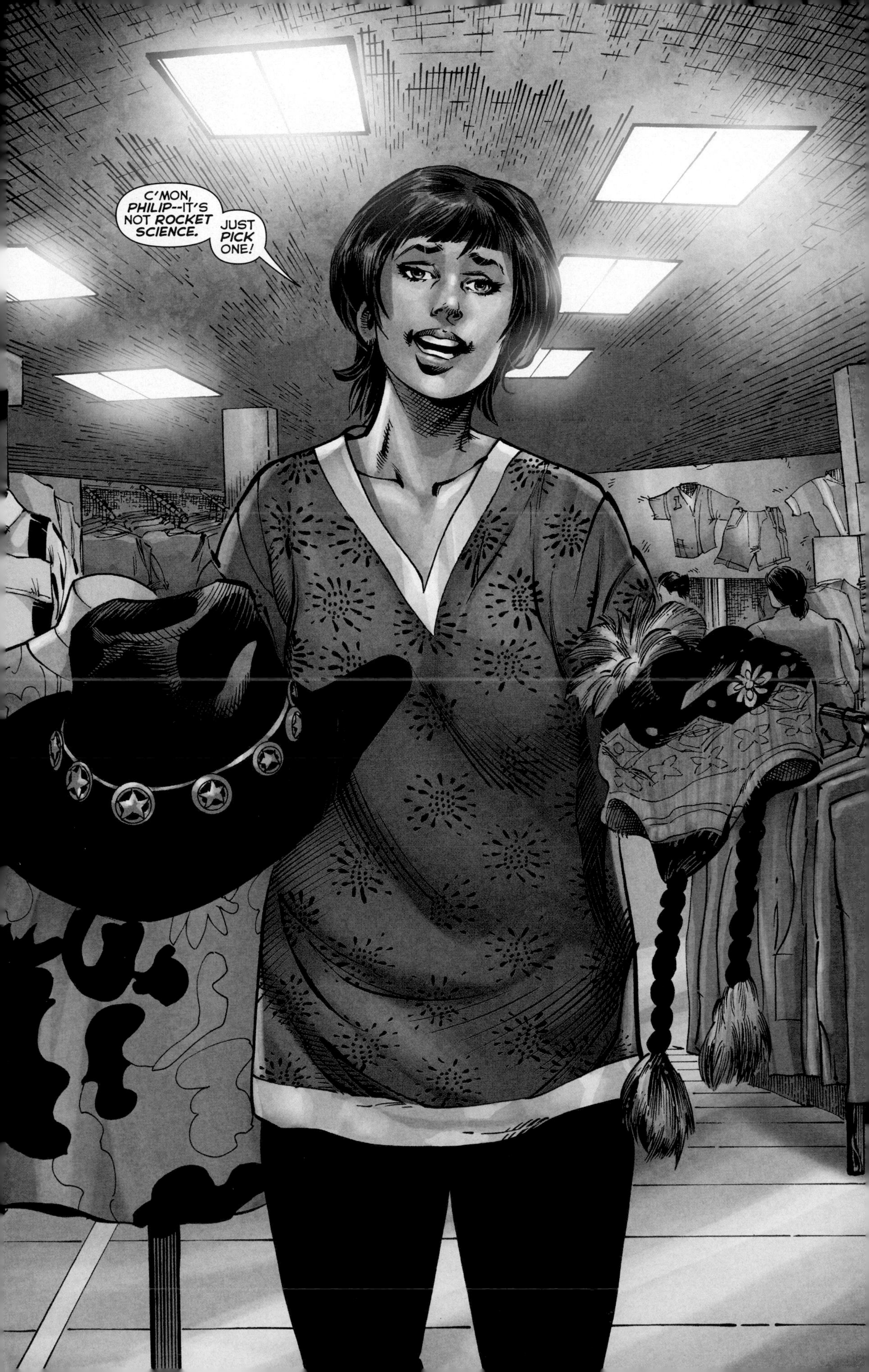
C'MON, PHILIP--IT'S NOT ROCKET SCIENCE.
JUST PICK ONE!

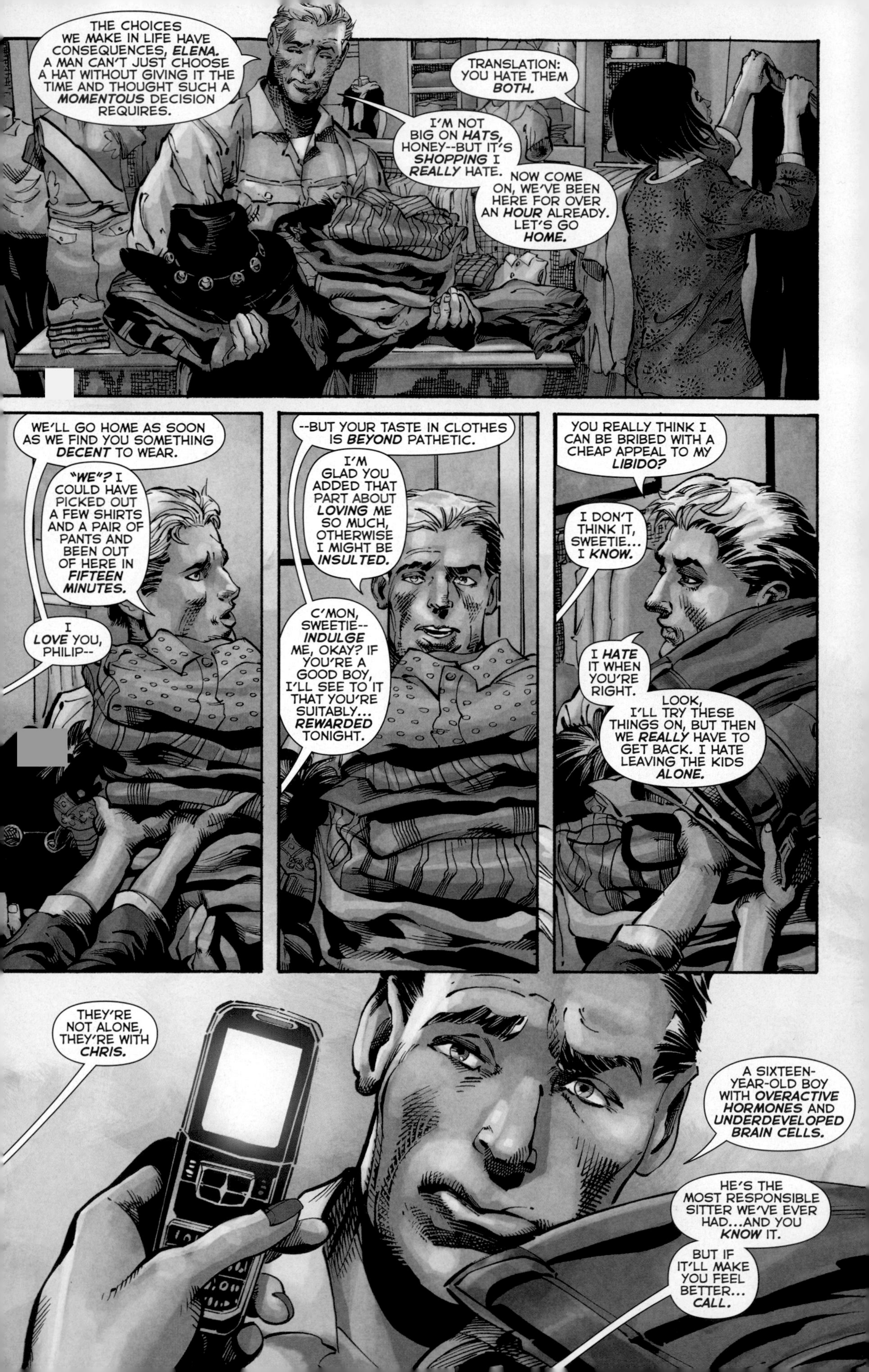
THE CHOICES WE MAKE IN LIFE HAVE CONSEQUENCES, ELENA. A MAN CAN'T JUST CHOOSE A HAT WITHOUT GIVING IT THE TIME AND THOUGHT SUCH A MOMENTOUS DECISION REQUIRES.
TRANSLATION: YOU HATE THEM BOTH.
I'M NOT BIG ON HATS, HONEY--BUT IT'S SHOPPING I REALLY HATE.
NOW COME ON, WE'VE BEEN HERE FOR OVER AN HOUR ALREADY. LET'S GO HOME.
WE'LL GO HOME AS SOON AS WE FIND YOU SOMETHING DECENT TO WEAR.
"WE"? I COULD HAVE PICKED OUT A FEW SHIRTS AND A PAIR OF PANTS AND BEEN OUT OF HERE IN FIFTEEN MINUTES.
I LOVE YOU, PHILIP--
--BUT YOUR TASTE IN CLOTHES IS BEYOND PATHETIC.
I'M GLAD YOU ADDED THAT PART ABOUT LOVING ME SO MUCH, OTHERWISE I MIGHT BE INSULTED.
C'MON, SWEETIE--INDULGE ME, OKAY? IF YOU'RE A GOOD BOY, I'LL SEE TO IT THAT YOU'RE SUITABLY... REWARDED TONIGHT.
YOU REALLY THINK I CAN BE BRIBED WITH A CHEAP APPEAL TO MY LIBIDO?
I DON'T THINK IT, SWEETIE... I KNOW.
I HATE IT WHEN YOU'RE RIGHT.
LOOK, I'LL TRY THESE THINGS ON, BUT THEN WE REALLY HAVE TO GET BACK. I HATE LEAVING THE KIDS ALONE.
THEY'RE NOT ALONE, THEY'RE WITH CHRIS.
A SIXTEEN-YEAR-OLD BOY WITH OVERACTIVE HORMONES AND UNDERDEVELOPED BRAIN CELLS.
HE'S THE MOST RESPONSIBLE SITTER WE'VE EVER HAD...AND YOU KNOW IT.
BUT IF IT'LL MAKE YOU FEEL BETTER... CALL.

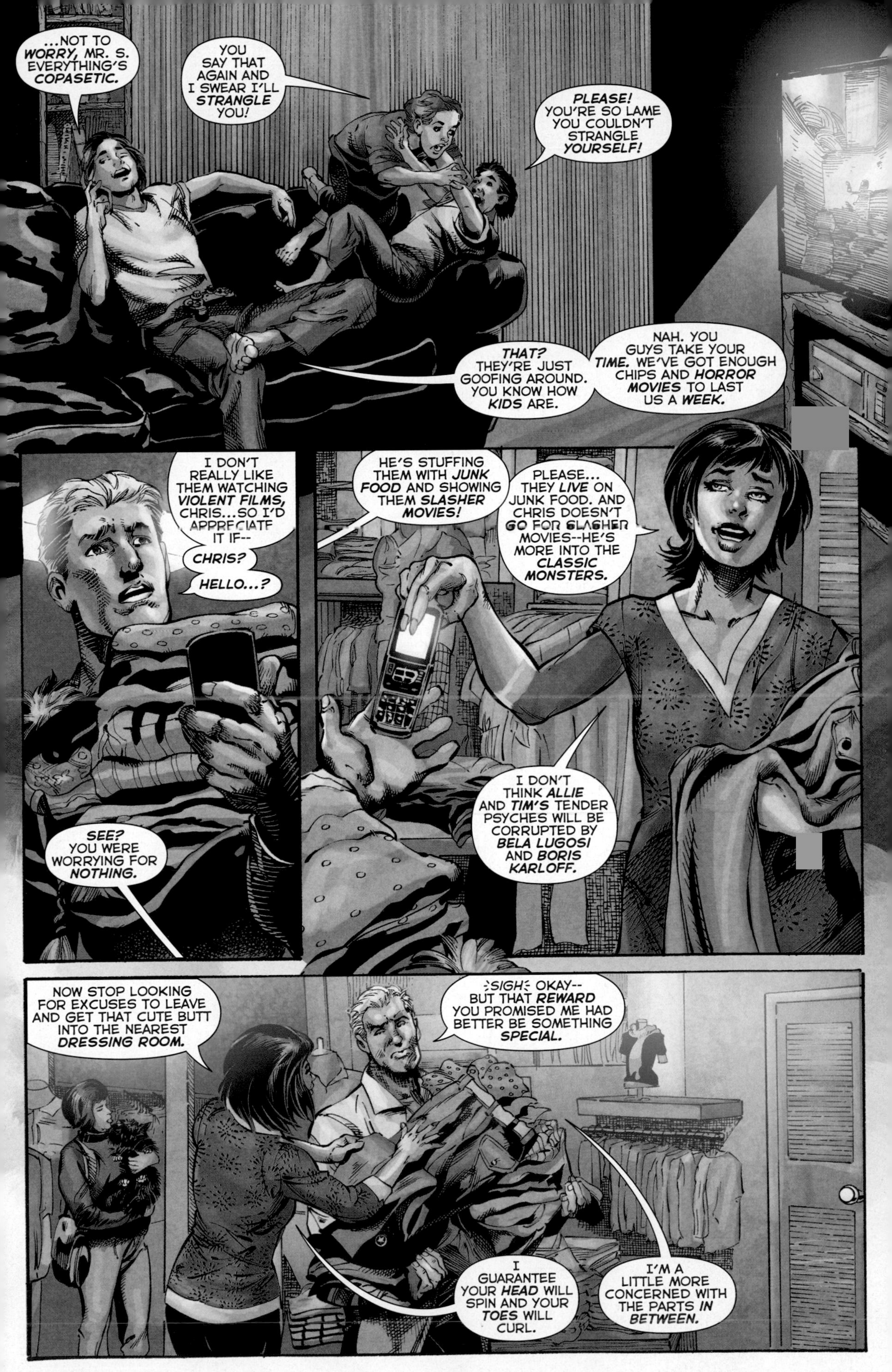

...NOT TO WORRY, MR. S. EVERYTHING'S COPASETIC.
YOU SAY THAT AGAIN AND I SWEAR I'LL STRANGLE YOU!
PLEASE! YOU'RE SO LAME YOU COULDN'T STRANGLE YOURSELF!
THAT? THEY'RE JUST GOOFING AROUND. YOU KNOW HOW KIDS ARE.
NAH. YOU GUYS TAKE YOUR TIME. WE'VE GOT ENOUGH CHIPS AND HORROR MOVIES TO LAST US A WEEK.
I DON'T REALLY LIKE THEM WATCHING VIOLENT FILMS, CHRIS...SO I'D APPRECIATE IT IF--
CHRIS?
HELLO...?
SEE? YOU WERE WORRYING FOR NOTHING.
HE'S STUFFING THEM WITH JUNK FOOD AND SHOWING THEM SLASHER MOVIES!
PLEASE... THEY LIVE ON JUNK FOOD. AND CHRIS DOESN'T GO FOR SLASHER MOVIES--HE'S MORE INTO THE CLASSIC MONSTERS.
I DON'T THINK ALLIE AND TIM'S TENDER PSYCHES WILL BE CORRUPTED BY BELA LUGOSI AND BORIS KARLOFF.
NOW STOP LOOKING FOR EXCUSES TO LEAVE AND GET THAT CUTE BUTT INTO THE NEAREST DRESSING ROOM.
SIGH OKAY-- BUT THAT REWARD YOU PROMISED ME HAD BETTER BE SOMETHING SPECIAL.
I GUARANTEE YOUR HEAD WILL SPIN AND YOUR TOES WILL CURL.
I'M A LITTLE MORE CONCERNED WITH THE PARTS IN BETWEEN.

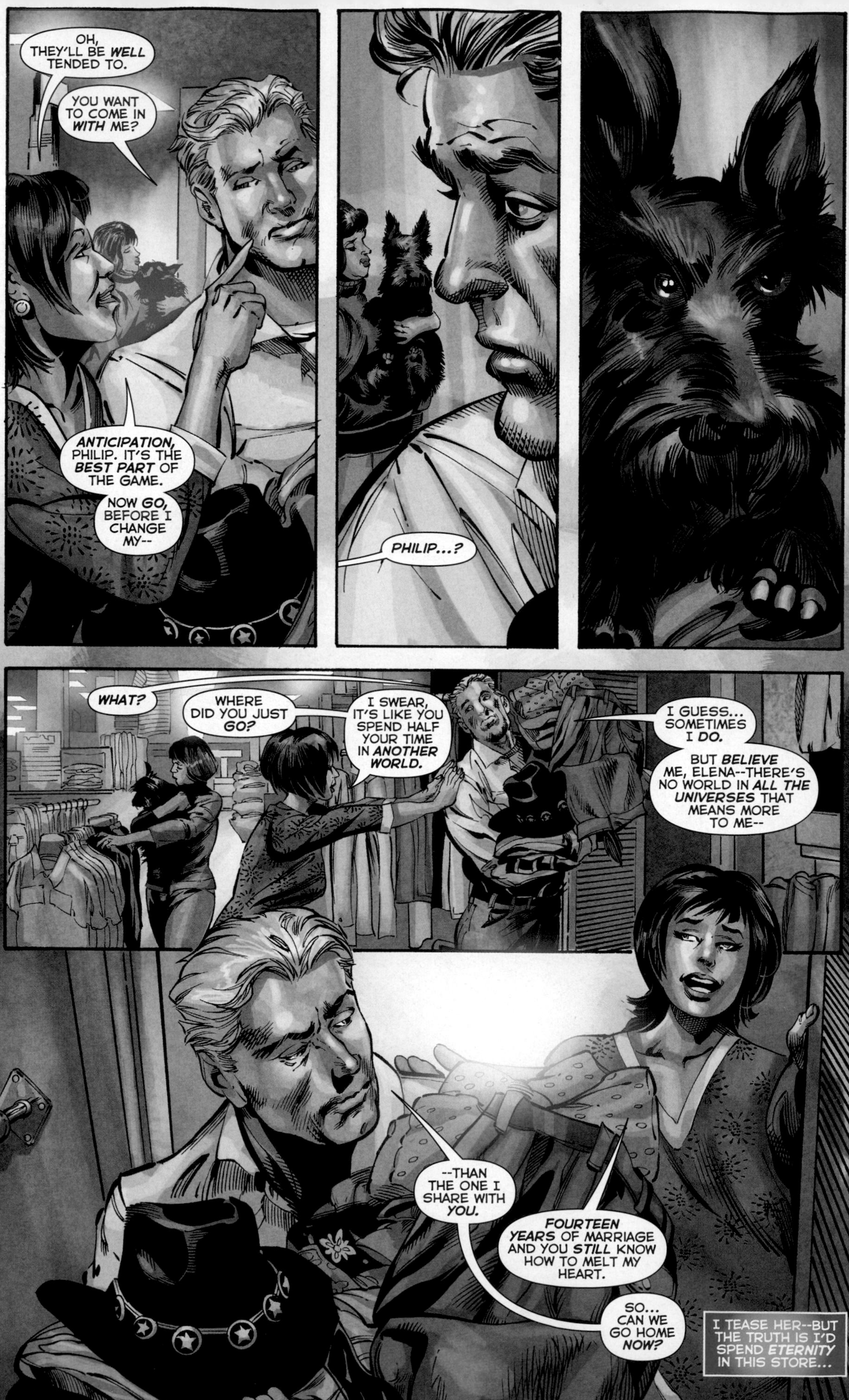
OH, THEY'LL BE WELL TENDED TO.
YOU WANT TO COME IN WITH ME?
ANTICIPATION, PHILIP. IT'S THE BEST PART OF THE GAME.
NOW GO, BEFORE I CHANGE MY--
PHILIP...?
WHAT?
WHERE DID YOU JUST GO?
I SWEAR, IT'S LIKE YOU SPEND HALF YOUR TIME IN ANOTHER WORLD.
I GUESS... SOMETIMES I DO.
BUT BELIEVE ME, ELENA--THERE'S NO WORLD IN ALL THE UNIVERSES THAT MEANS MORE TO ME--
--THAN THE ONE I SHARE WITH YOU.
FOURTEEN YEARS OF MARRIAGE AND YOU STILL KNOW HOW TO MELT MY HEART.
SO... CAN WE GO HOME NOW?
I TEASE HER--BUT THE TRUTH IS I'D SPEND ETERNITY IN THIS STORE...

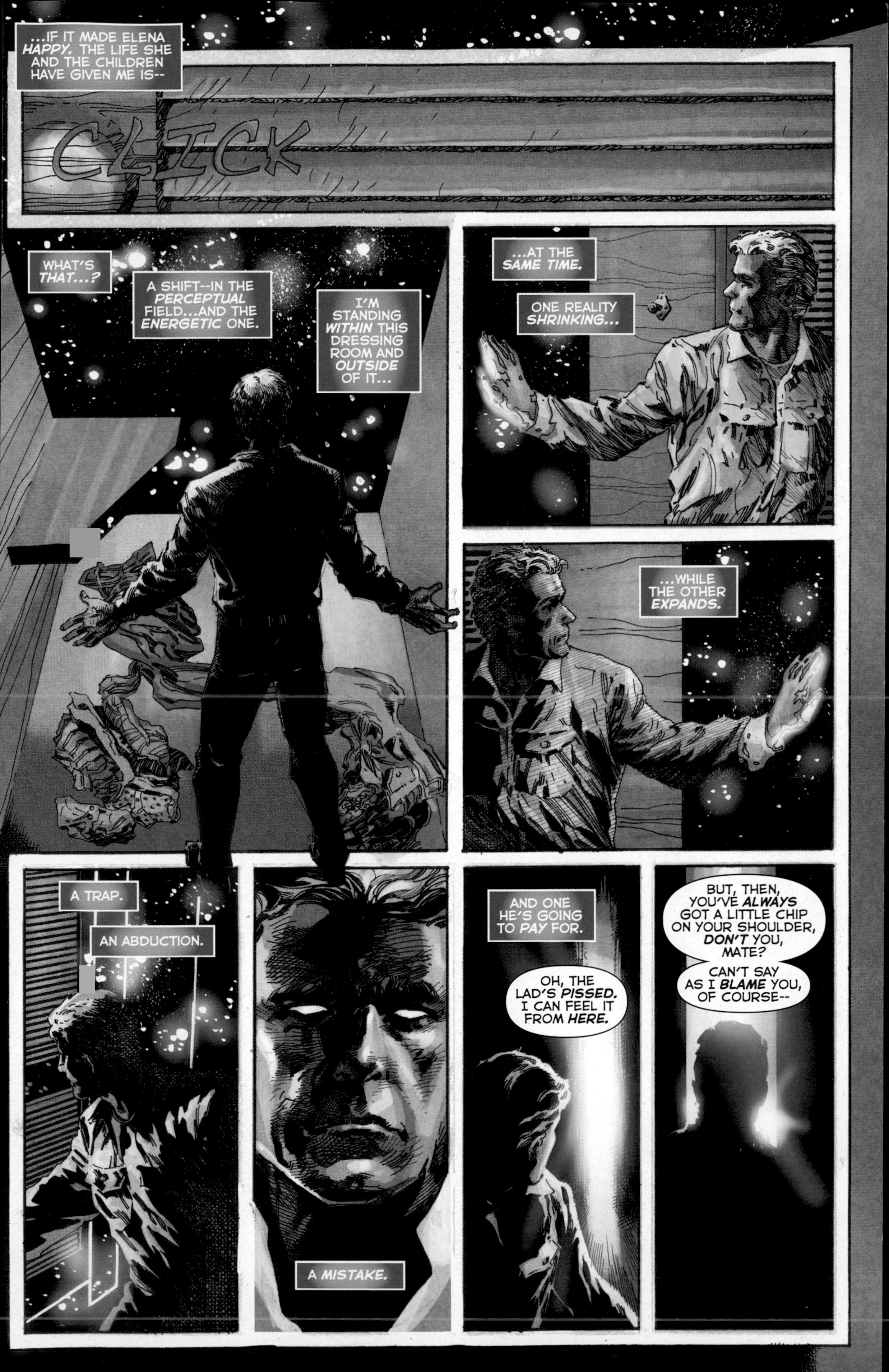
...IF IT MADE ELENA *HAPPY.* THE LIFE SHE AND THE CHILDREN HAVE GIVEN ME IS--
CLICK
WHAT'S *THAT...?*
A SHIFT--IN THE *PERCEPTUAL* FIELD...AND THE *ENERGETIC* ONE.
I'M STANDING *WITHIN* THIS DRESSING ROOM AND *OUTSIDE* OF IT...
...AT THE *SAME TIME.*
ONE REALITY *SHRINKING...*
...WHILE THE OTHER *EXPANDS.*
A TRAP.
AN ABDUCTION.
A *MISTAKE.*
AND ONE HE'S GOING TO *PAY* FOR.
OH, THE LAD'S *PISSED.* I CAN FEEL IT FROM *HERE.*
BUT, THEN, YOU'VE *ALWAYS* GOT A LITTLE CHIP ON YOUR SHOULDER, *DON'T* YOU, MATE?
CAN'T SAY AS I *BLAME* YOU, OF COURSE--

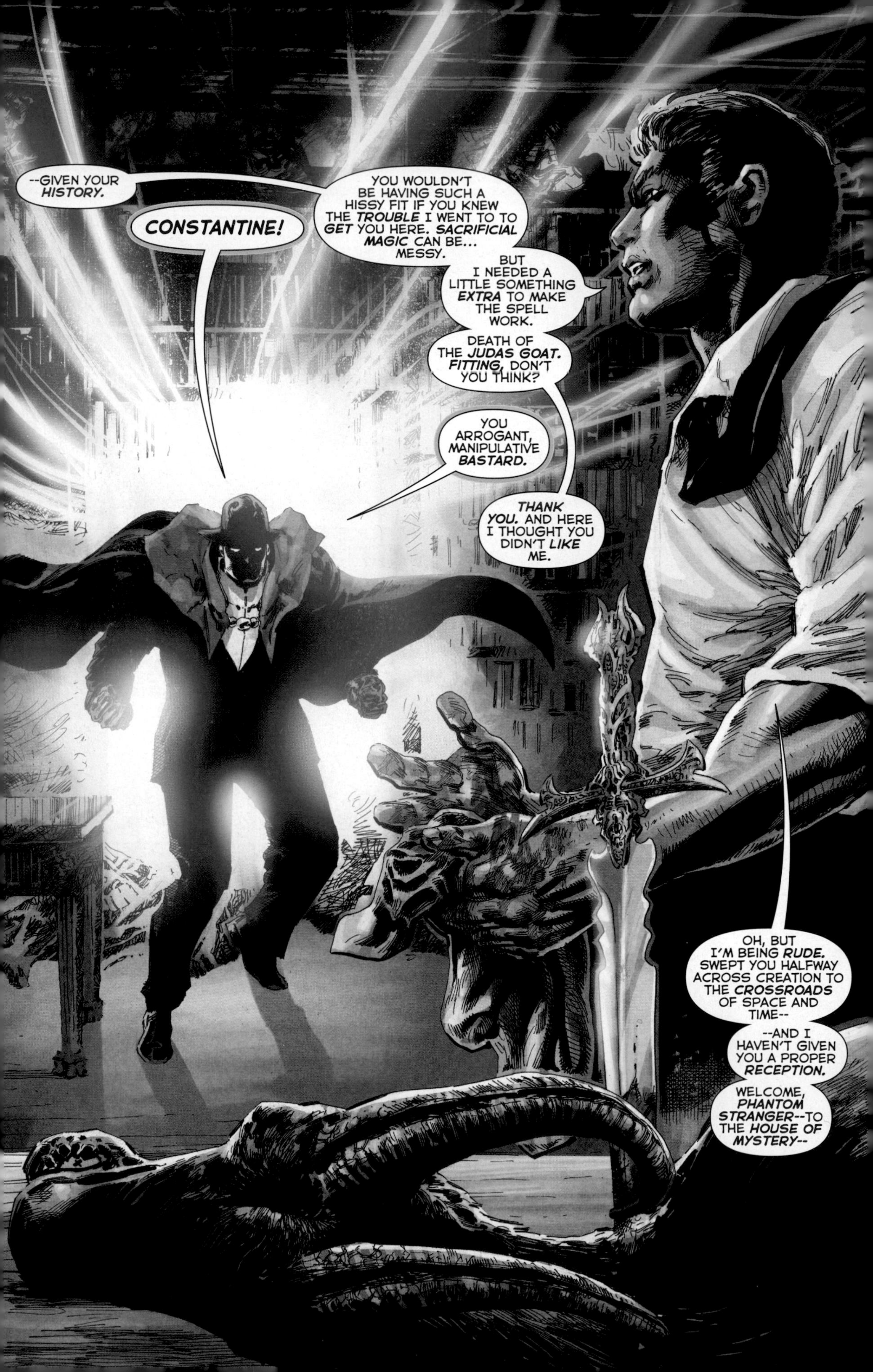
--GIVEN YOUR HISTORY.
CONSTANTINE!
YOU WOULDN'T BE HAVING SUCH A HISSY FIT IF YOU KNEW THE TROUBLE I WENT TO TO GET YOU HERE. SACRIFICIAL MAGIC CAN BE... MESSY.
BUT I NEEDED A LITTLE SOMETHING EXTRA TO MAKE THE SPELL WORK.
DEATH OF THE JUDAS GOAT. FITTING, DON'T YOU THINK?
YOU ARROGANT, MANIPULATIVE BASTARD.
THANK YOU. AND HERE I THOUGHT YOU DIDN'T LIKE ME.
OH, BUT I'M BEING RUDE. SWEPT YOU HALFWAY ACROSS CREATION TO THE CROSSROADS OF SPACE AND TIME--
--AND I HAVEN'T GIVEN YOU A PROPER RECEPTION.
WELCOME, PHANTOM STRANGER--TO THE HOUSE OF MYSTERY--

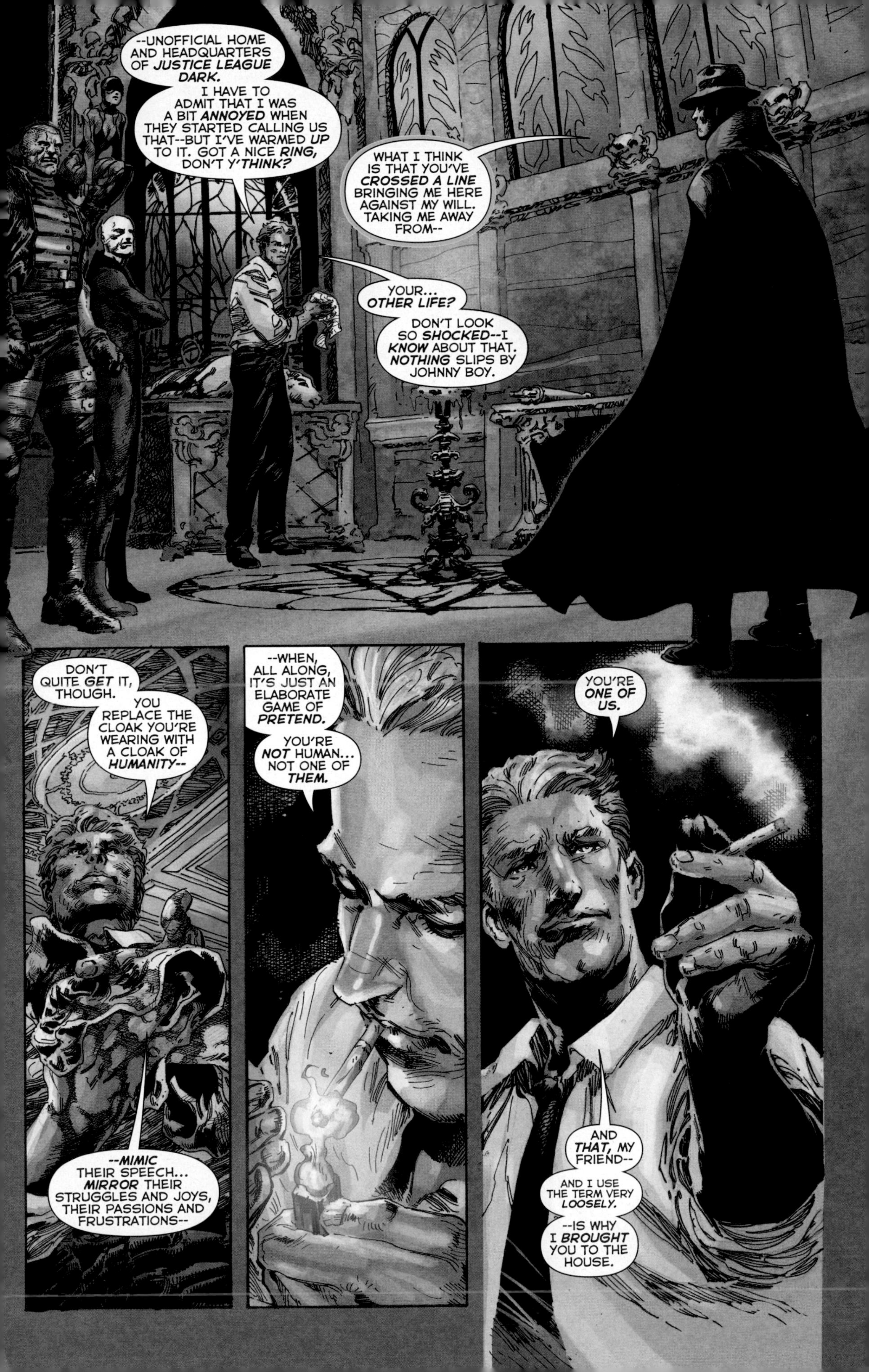
--UNOFFICIAL HOME AND HEADQUARTERS OF JUSTICE LEAGUE DARK.
I HAVE TO ADMIT THAT I WAS A BIT ANNOYED WHEN THEY STARTED CALLING US THAT--BUT I'VE WARMED UP TO IT. GOT A NICE RING, DON'T Y'THINK?
WHAT I THINK IS THAT YOU'VE CROSSED A LINE BRINGING ME HERE AGAINST MY WILL. TAKING ME AWAY FROM--
YOUR... OTHER LIFE?
DON'T LOOK SO SHOCKED--I KNOW ABOUT THAT. NOTHING SLIPS BY JOHNNY BOY.
DON'T QUITE GET IT, THOUGH.
YOU REPLACE THE CLOAK YOU'RE WEARING WITH A CLOAK OF HUMANITY--
--MIMIC THEIR SPEECH... MIRROR THEIR STRUGGLES AND JOYS, THEIR PASSIONS AND FRUSTRATIONS--
--WHEN, ALL ALONG, IT'S JUST AN ELABORATE GAME OF PRETEND.
YOU'RE NOT HUMAN... NOT ONE OF THEM.
YOU'RE ONE OF US.
AND THAT, MY FRIEND--
AND I USE THE TERM VERY LOOSELY.
--IS WHY I BROUGHT YOU TO THE HOUSE.

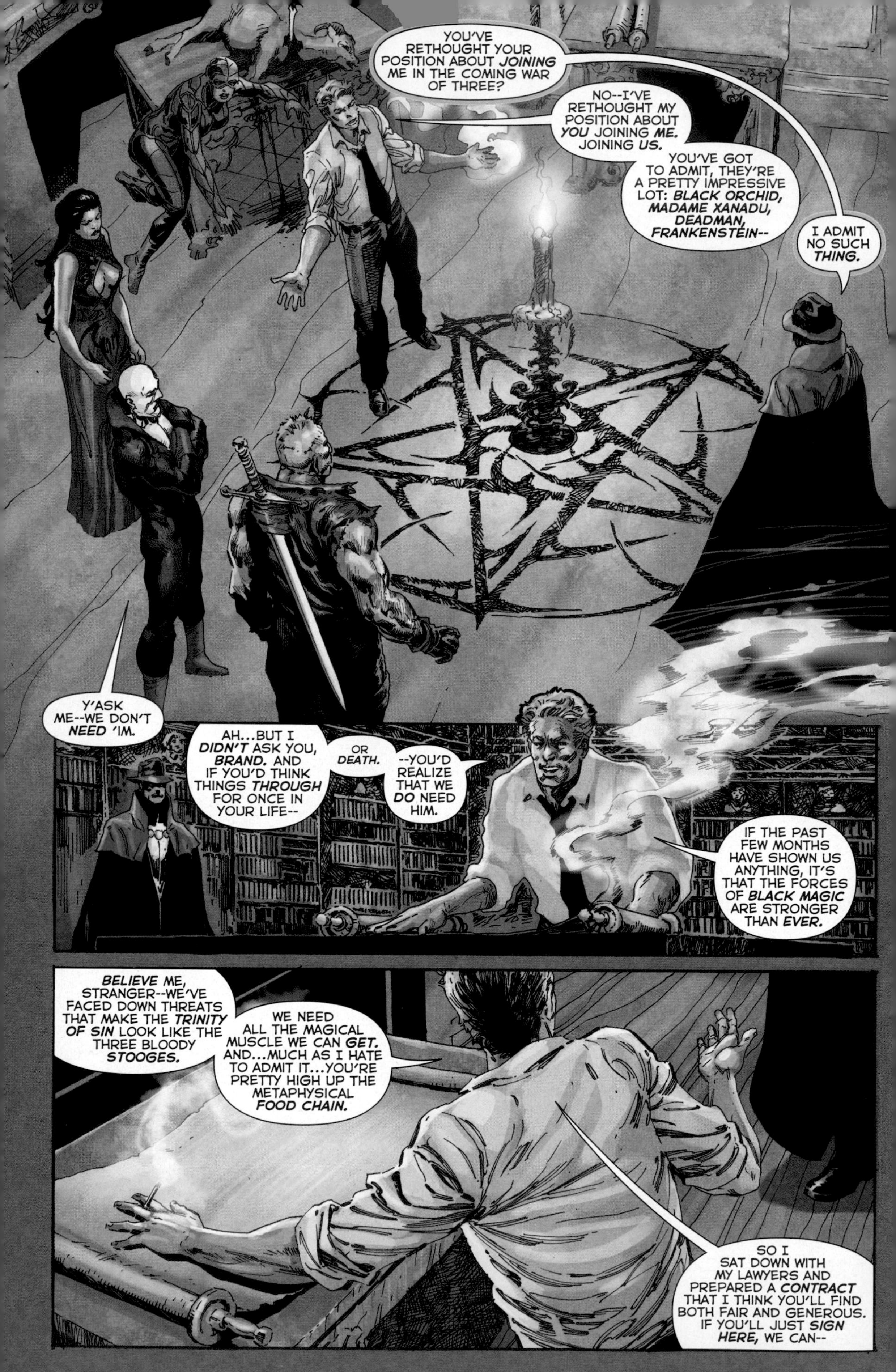
YOU'VE RETHOUGHT YOUR POSITION ABOUT JOINING ME IN THE COMING WAR OF THREE?
NO--I'VE RETHOUGHT MY POSITION ABOUT YOU JOINING ME. JOINING US.
YOU'VE GOT TO ADMIT, THEY'RE A PRETTY IMPRESSIVE LOT: BLACK ORCHID, MADAME XANADU, DEADMAN, FRANKENSTEIN--
I ADMIT NO SUCH THING.
Y'ASK ME--WE DON'T NEED 'IM.
AH...BUT I DIDN'T ASK YOU, BRAND. AND IF YOU'D THINK THINGS THROUGH FOR ONCE IN YOUR LIFE--
OR DEATH.
--YOU'D REALIZE THAT WE DO NEED HIM.
IF THE PAST FEW MONTHS HAVE SHOWN US ANYTHING, IT'S THAT THE FORCES OF BLACK MAGIC ARE STRONGER THAN EVER.
BELIEVE ME, STRANGER--WE'VE FACED DOWN THREATS THAT MAKE THE TRINITY OF SIN LOOK LIKE THE THREE BLOODY STOOGES.
WE NEED ALL THE MAGICAL MUSCLE WE CAN GET. AND...MUCH AS I HATE TO ADMIT IT...YOU'RE PRETTY HIGH UP THE METAPHYSICAL FOOD CHAIN.
SO I SAT DOWN WITH MY LAWYERS AND PREPARED A CONTRACT THAT I THINK YOU'LL FIND BOTH FAIR AND GENEROUS. IF YOU'LL JUST SIGN HERE, WE CAN--

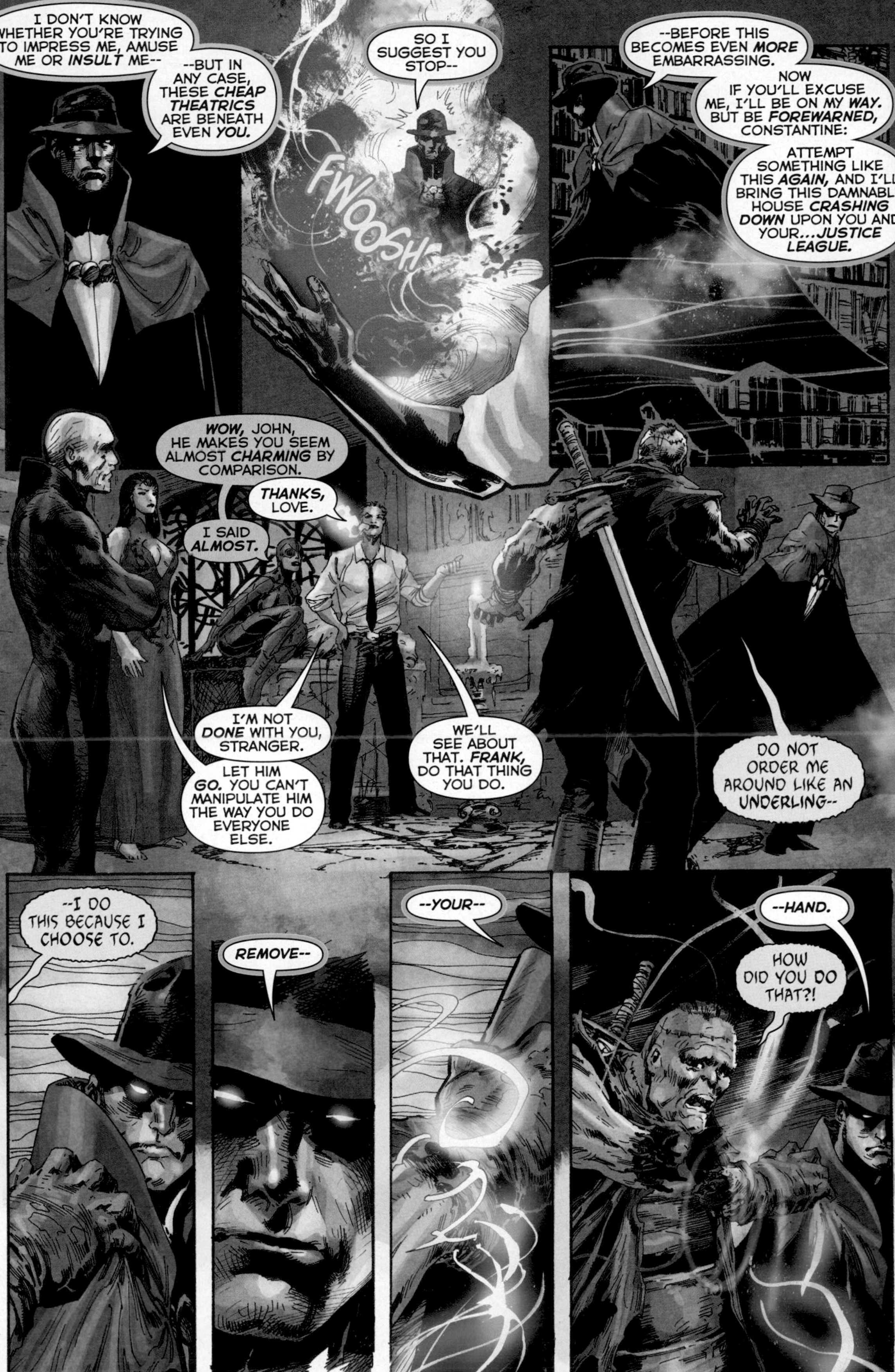
I DON'T KNOW WHETHER YOU'RE TRYING TO IMPRESS ME, AMUSE ME OR INSULT ME--
--BUT IN ANY CASE, THESE CHEAP THEATRICS ARE BENEATH EVEN YOU.
SO I SUGGEST YOU STOP--
FWOOSH
--BEFORE THIS BECOMES EVEN MORE EMBARRASSING.
NOW IF YOU'LL EXCUSE ME, I'LL BE ON MY WAY. BUT BE FOREWARNED, CONSTANTINE:
ATTEMPT SOMETHING LIKE THIS AGAIN, AND I'LL BRING THIS DAMNABLE HOUSE CRASHING DOWN UPON YOU AND YOUR...JUSTICE LEAGUE.
WOW, JOHN, HE MAKES YOU SEEM ALMOST CHARMING BY COMPARISON.
THANKS, LOVE.
I SAID ALMOST.
I'M NOT DONE WITH YOU, STRANGER.
LET HIM GO. YOU CAN'T MANIPULATE HIM THE WAY YOU DO EVERYONE ELSE.
WE'LL SEE ABOUT THAT. FRANK, DO THAT THING YOU DO.
DO NOT ORDER ME AROUND LIKE AN UNDERLING--
--I DO THIS BECAUSE I CHOOSE TO.
REMOVE--
--YOUR--
--HAND.
HOW DID YOU DO THAT?!

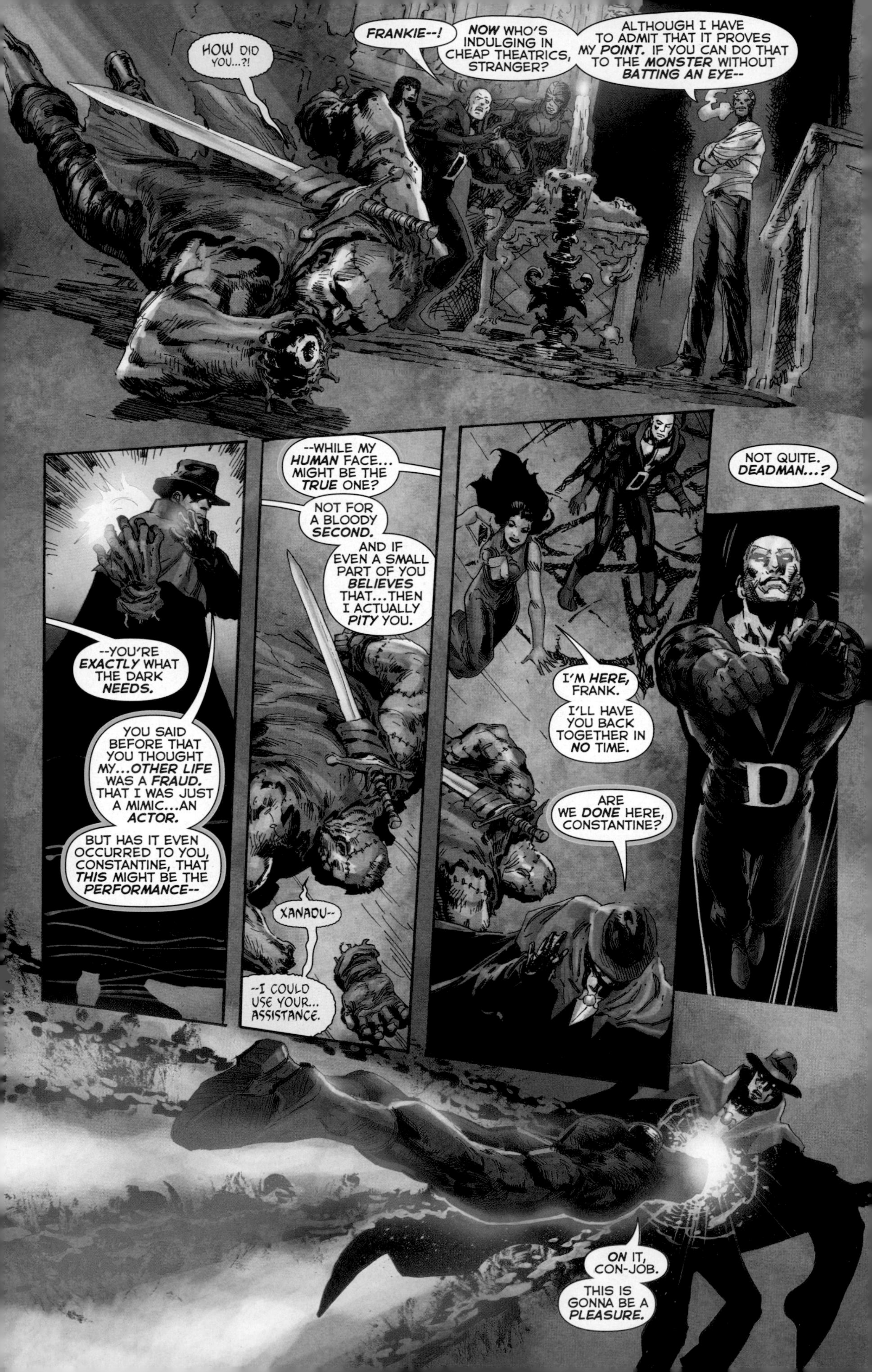
HOW DID YOU...?!
FRANKIE--!
NOW WHO'S INDULGING IN CHEAP THEATRICS, STRANGER?
ALTHOUGH I HAVE TO ADMIT THAT IT PROVES MY POINT. IF YOU CAN DO THAT TO THE MONSTER WITHOUT BATTING AN EYE--
--YOU'RE EXACTLY WHAT THE DARK NEEDS.
YOU SAID BEFORE THAT YOU THOUGHT MY...OTHER LIFE WAS A FRAUD. THAT I WAS JUST A MIMIC...AN ACTOR.
BUT HAS IT EVEN OCCURRED TO YOU, CONSTANTINE, THAT THIS MIGHT BE THE PERFORMANCE--
--WHILE MY HUMAN FACE... MIGHT BE THE TRUE ONE?
NOT FOR A BLOODY SECOND.
AND IF EVEN A SMALL PART OF YOU BELIEVES THAT...THEN I ACTUALLY PITY YOU.
XANADU--
--I COULD USE YOUR... ASSISTANCE.
I'M HERE, FRANK.
I'LL HAVE YOU BACK TOGETHER IN NO TIME.
ARE WE DONE HERE, CONSTANTINE?
NOT QUITE. DEADMAN...?
ON IT, CON-JOB.
THIS IS GONNA BE A PLEASURE.

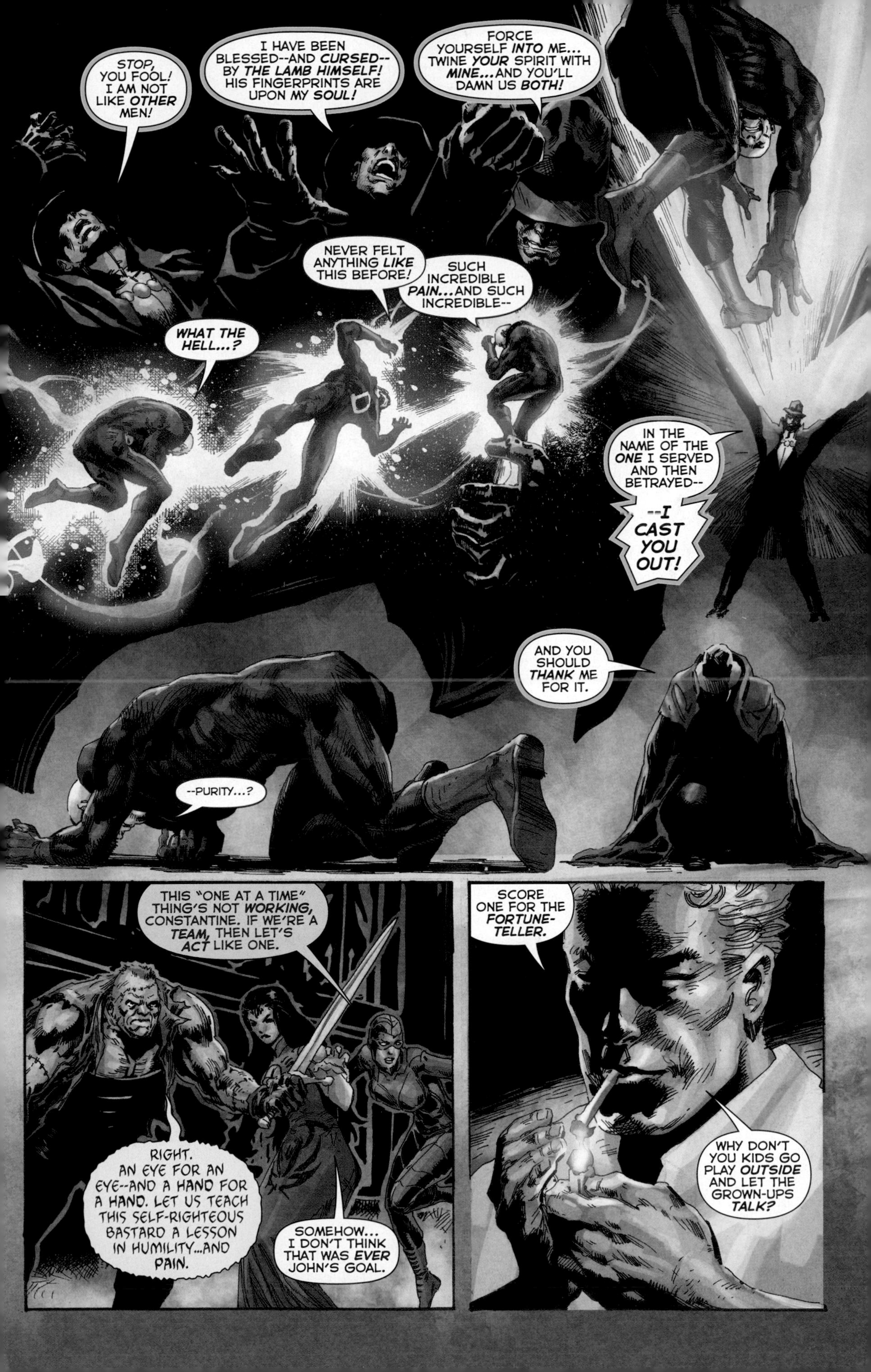
STOP, YOU FOOL! I AM NOT LIKE OTHER MEN!
I HAVE BEEN BLESSED--AND CURSED--BY THE LAMB HIMSELF! HIS FINGERPRINTS ARE UPON MY SOUL!
FORCE YOURSELF INTO ME... TWINE YOUR SPIRIT WITH MINE...AND YOU'LL DAMN US BOTH!
NEVER FELT ANYTHING LIKE THIS BEFORE!
SUCH INCREDIBLE PAIN...AND SUCH INCREDIBLE--
WHAT THE HELL...?
IN THE NAME OF THE ONE I SERVED AND THEN BETRAYED--
--I CAST YOU OUT!
AND YOU SHOULD THANK ME FOR IT.
--PURITY...?
THIS "ONE AT A TIME" THING'S NOT WORKING, CONSTANTINE. IF WE'RE A TEAM, THEN LET'S ACT LIKE ONE.
RIGHT. AN EYE FOR AN EYE--AND A HAND FOR A HAND. LET US TEACH THIS SELF-RIGHTEOUS BASTARD A LESSON IN HUMILITY...AND PAIN.
SOMEHOW... I DON'T THINK THAT WAS EVER JOHN'S GOAL.
SCORE ONE FOR THE FORTUNE-TELLER.
WHY DON'T YOU KIDS GO PLAY OUTSIDE AND LET THE GROWN-UPS TALK?

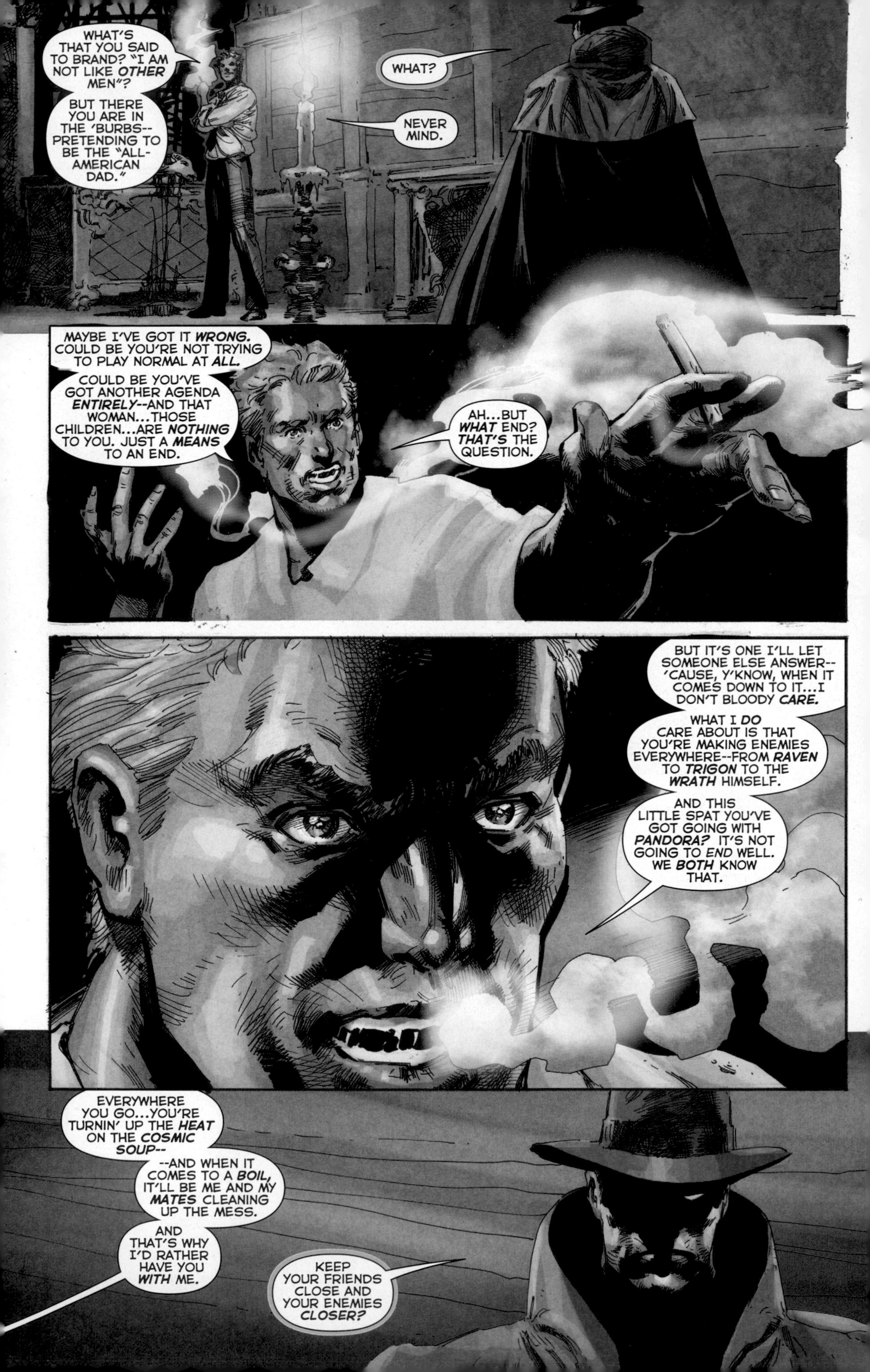
WHAT'S THAT YOU SAID TO BRAND? "I AM NOT LIKE OTHER MEN"?
BUT THERE YOU ARE IN THE 'BURBS--PRETENDING TO BE THE "ALL-AMERICAN DAD."
WHAT?
NEVER MIND.
MAYBE I'VE GOT IT WRONG. COULD BE YOU'RE NOT TRYING TO PLAY NORMAL AT ALL.
COULD BE YOU'VE GOT ANOTHER AGENDA ENTIRELY--AND THAT WOMAN...THOSE CHILDREN...ARE NOTHING TO YOU. JUST A MEANS TO AN END.
AH...BUT WHAT END? THAT'S THE QUESTION.
BUT IT'S ONE I'LL LET SOMEONE ELSE ANSWER--'CAUSE, Y'KNOW, WHEN IT COMES DOWN TO IT...I DON'T BLOODY CARE.
WHAT I DO CARE ABOUT IS THAT YOU'RE MAKING ENEMIES EVERYWHERE--FROM RAVEN TO TRIGON TO THE WRATH HIMSELF.
AND THIS LITTLE SPAT YOU'VE GOT GOING WITH PANDORA? IT'S NOT GOING TO END WELL. WE BOTH KNOW THAT.
EVERYWHERE YOU GO...YOU'RE TURNIN' UP THE HEAT ON THE COSMIC SOUP--
--AND WHEN IT COMES TO A BOIL, IT'LL BE ME AND MY MATES CLEANING UP THE MESS.
AND THAT'S WHY I'D RATHER HAVE YOU WITH ME.
KEEP YOUR FRIENDS CLOSE AND YOUR ENEMIES CLOSER?

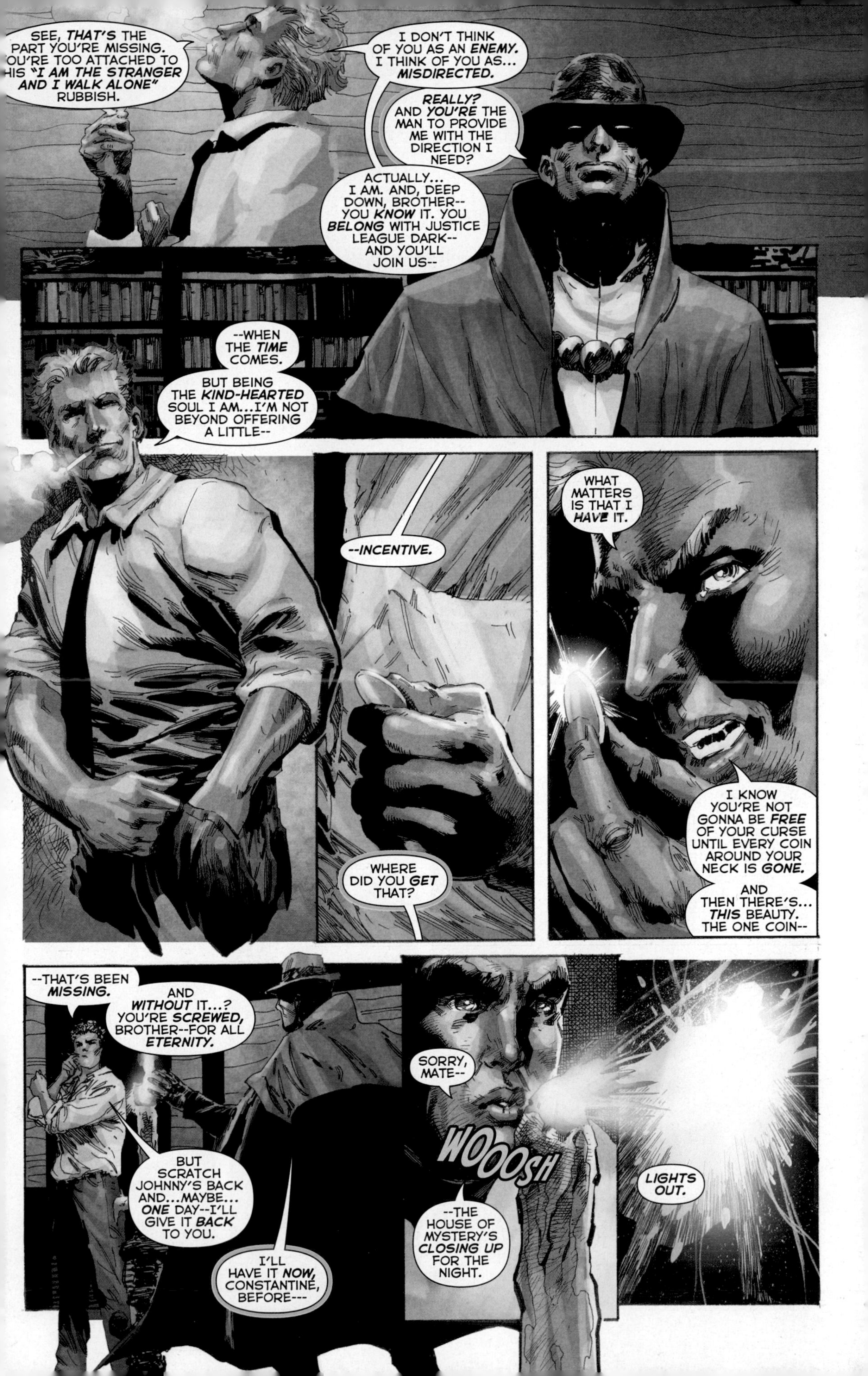
SEE, THAT'S THE PART YOU'RE MISSING. YOU'RE TOO ATTACHED TO THIS "I AM THE STRANGER AND I WALK ALONE" RUBBISH.
I DON'T THINK OF YOU AS AN ENEMY. I THINK OF YOU AS... MISDIRECTED.
REALLY? AND YOU'RE THE MAN TO PROVIDE ME WITH THE DIRECTION I NEED?
ACTUALLY... I AM. AND, DEEP DOWN, BROTHER-- YOU KNOW IT. YOU BELONG WITH JUSTICE LEAGUE DARK-- AND YOU'LL JOIN US--
--WHEN THE TIME COMES.
BUT BEING THE KIND-HEARTED SOUL I AM...I'M NOT BEYOND OFFERING A LITTLE--
--INCENTIVE.
WHERE DID YOU GET THAT?
WHAT MATTERS IS THAT I HAVE IT.
I KNOW YOU'RE NOT GONNA BE FREE OF YOUR CURSE UNTIL EVERY COIN AROUND YOUR NECK IS GONE.
AND THEN THERE'S... THIS BEAUTY. THE ONE COIN--
--THAT'S BEEN MISSING.
AND WITHOUT IT...? YOU'RE SCREWED, BROTHER--FOR ALL ETERNITY.
BUT SCRATCH JOHNNY'S BACK AND...MAYBE... ONE DAY--I'LL GIVE IT BACK TO YOU.
I'LL HAVE IT NOW, CONSTANTINE, BEFORE---
SORRY, MATE--
WOOOSH
--THE HOUSE OF MYSTERY'S CLOSING UP FOR THE NIGHT.
LIGHTS OUT.

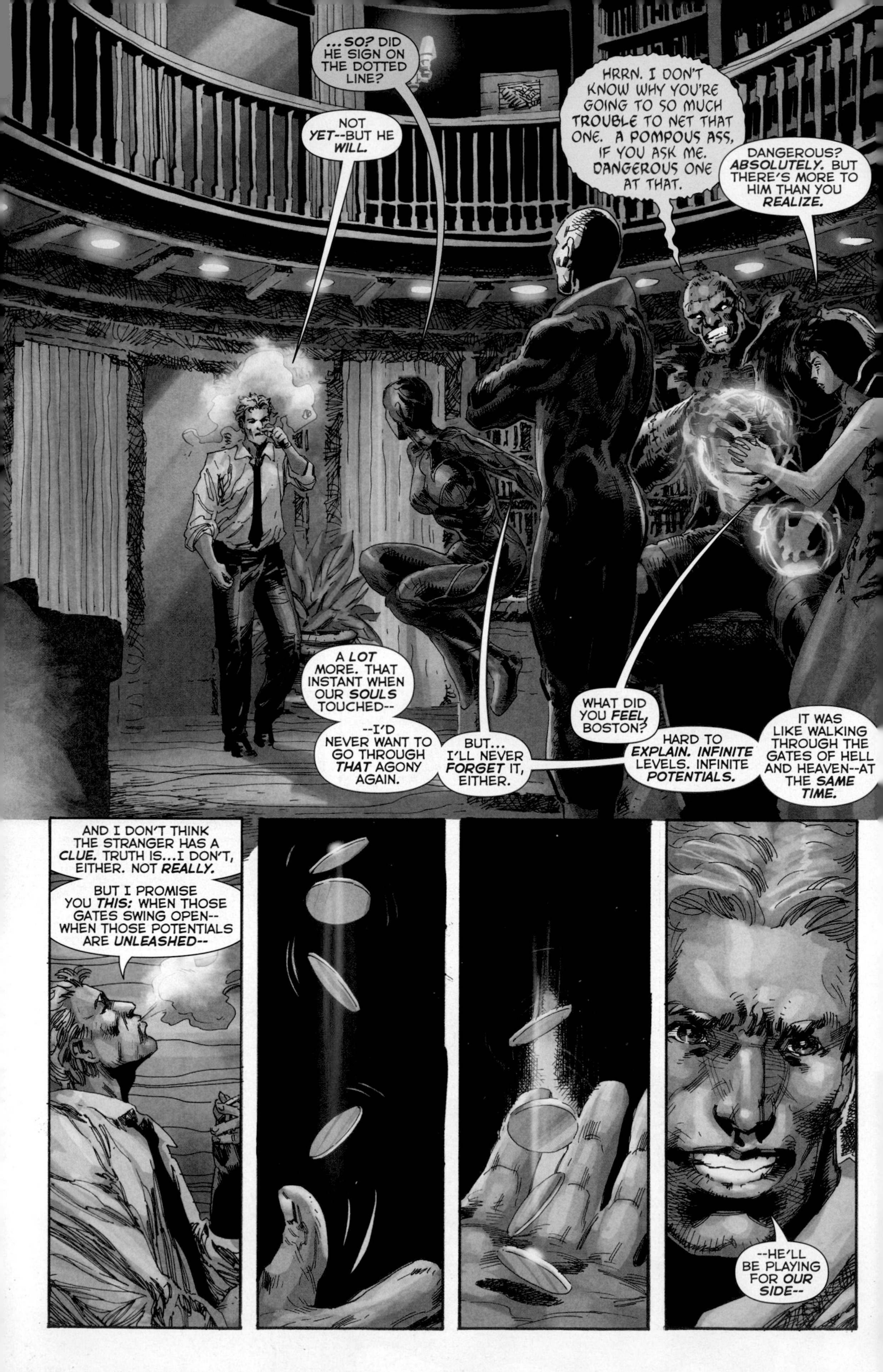
...SO? DID HE SIGN ON THE DOTTED LINE?
NOT YET--BUT HE WILL.
HRRN. I DON'T KNOW WHY YOU'RE GOING TO SO MUCH TROUBLE TO NET THAT ONE. A POMPOUS ASS, IF YOU ASK ME. DANGEROUS ONE AT THAT.
DANGEROUS? ABSOLUTELY. BUT THERE'S MORE TO HIM THAN YOU REALIZE.
A LOT MORE. THAT INSTANT WHEN OUR SOULS TOUCHED--
--I'D NEVER WANT TO GO THROUGH THAT AGONY AGAIN.
BUT... I'LL NEVER FORGET IT, EITHER.
WHAT DID YOU FEEL, BOSTON?
HARD TO EXPLAIN. INFINITE LEVELS. INFINITE POTENTIALS.
IT WAS LIKE WALKING THROUGH THE GATES OF HELL AND HEAVEN--AT THE SAME TIME.
AND I DON'T THINK THE STRANGER HAS A CLUE. TRUTH IS...I DON'T, EITHER. NOT REALLY.
BUT I PROMISE YOU THIS: WHEN THOSE GATES SWING OPEN-- WHEN THOSE POTENTIALS ARE UNLEASHED--
--HE'LL BE PLAYING FOR OUR SIDE--

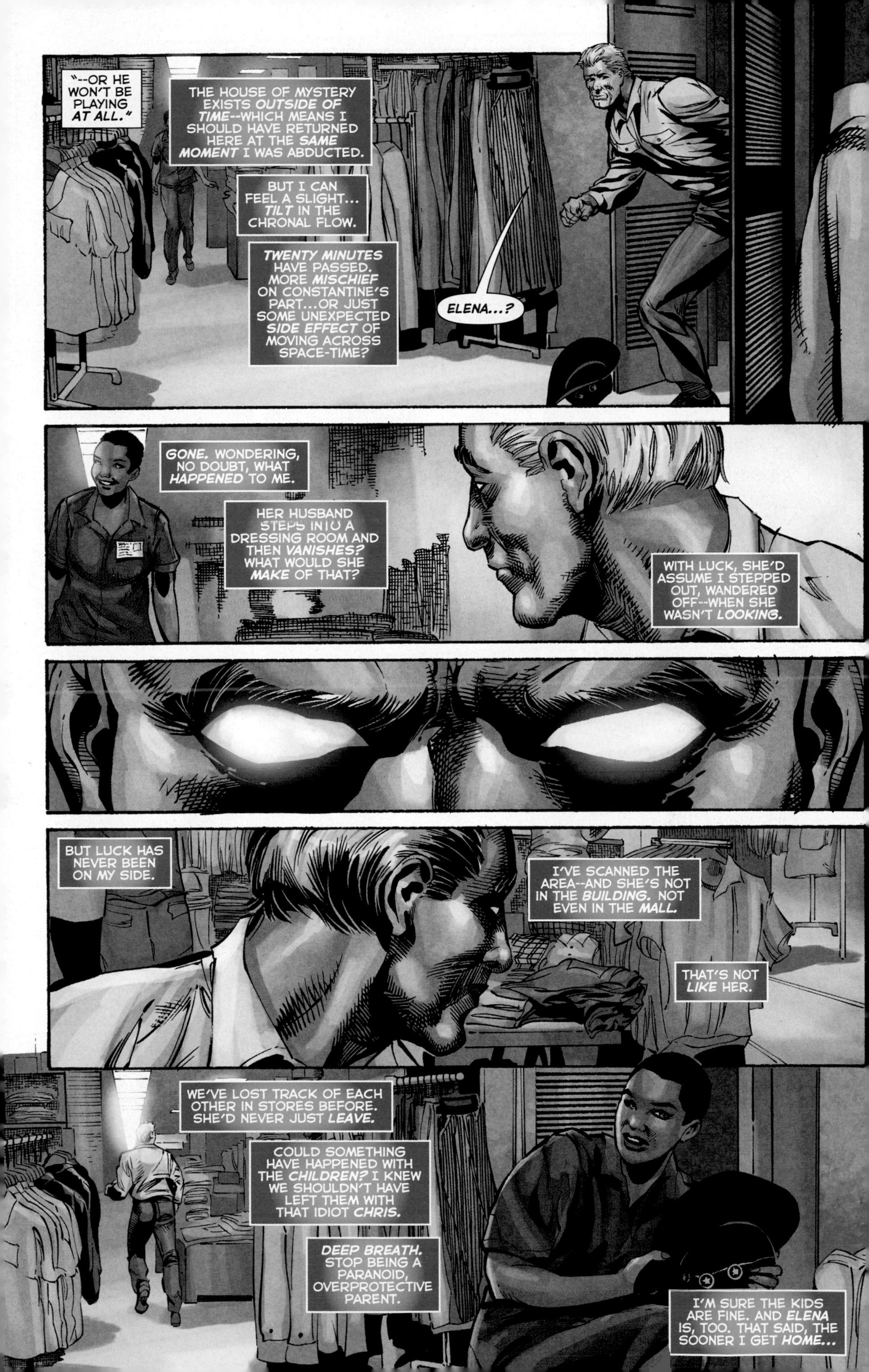
"--OR HE WON'T BE PLAYING AT ALL."
THE HOUSE OF MYSTERY EXISTS OUTSIDE OF TIME--WHICH MEANS I SHOULD HAVE RETURNED HERE AT THE SAME MOMENT I WAS ABDUCTED.
BUT I CAN FEEL A SLIGHT... TILT IN THE CHRONAL FLOW.
TWENTY MINUTES HAVE PASSED. MORE MISCHIEF ON CONSTANTINE'S PART...OR JUST SOME UNEXPECTED SIDE EFFECT OF MOVING ACROSS SPACE-TIME?
ELENA...?
GONE. WONDERING, NO DOUBT, WHAT HAPPENED TO ME.
HER HUSBAND STEPS INTO A DRESSING ROOM AND THEN VANISHES? WHAT WOULD SHE MAKE OF THAT?
WITH LUCK, SHE'D ASSUME I STEPPED OUT, WANDERED OFF--WHEN SHE WASN'T LOOKING.
BUT LUCK HAS NEVER BEEN ON MY SIDE.
I'VE SCANNED THE AREA--AND SHE'S NOT IN THE BUILDING. NOT EVEN IN THE MALL.
THAT'S NOT LIKE HER.
WE'VE LOST TRACK OF EACH OTHER IN STORES BEFORE. SHE'D NEVER JUST LEAVE.
COULD SOMETHING HAVE HAPPENED WITH THE CHILDREN? I KNEW WE SHOULDN'T HAVE LEFT THEM WITH THAT IDIOT CHRIS.
DEEP BREATH. STOP BEING A PARANOID, OVERPROTECTIVE PARENT.
I'M SURE THE KIDS ARE FINE. AND ELENA IS, TOO. THAT SAID, THE SOONER I GET HOME...

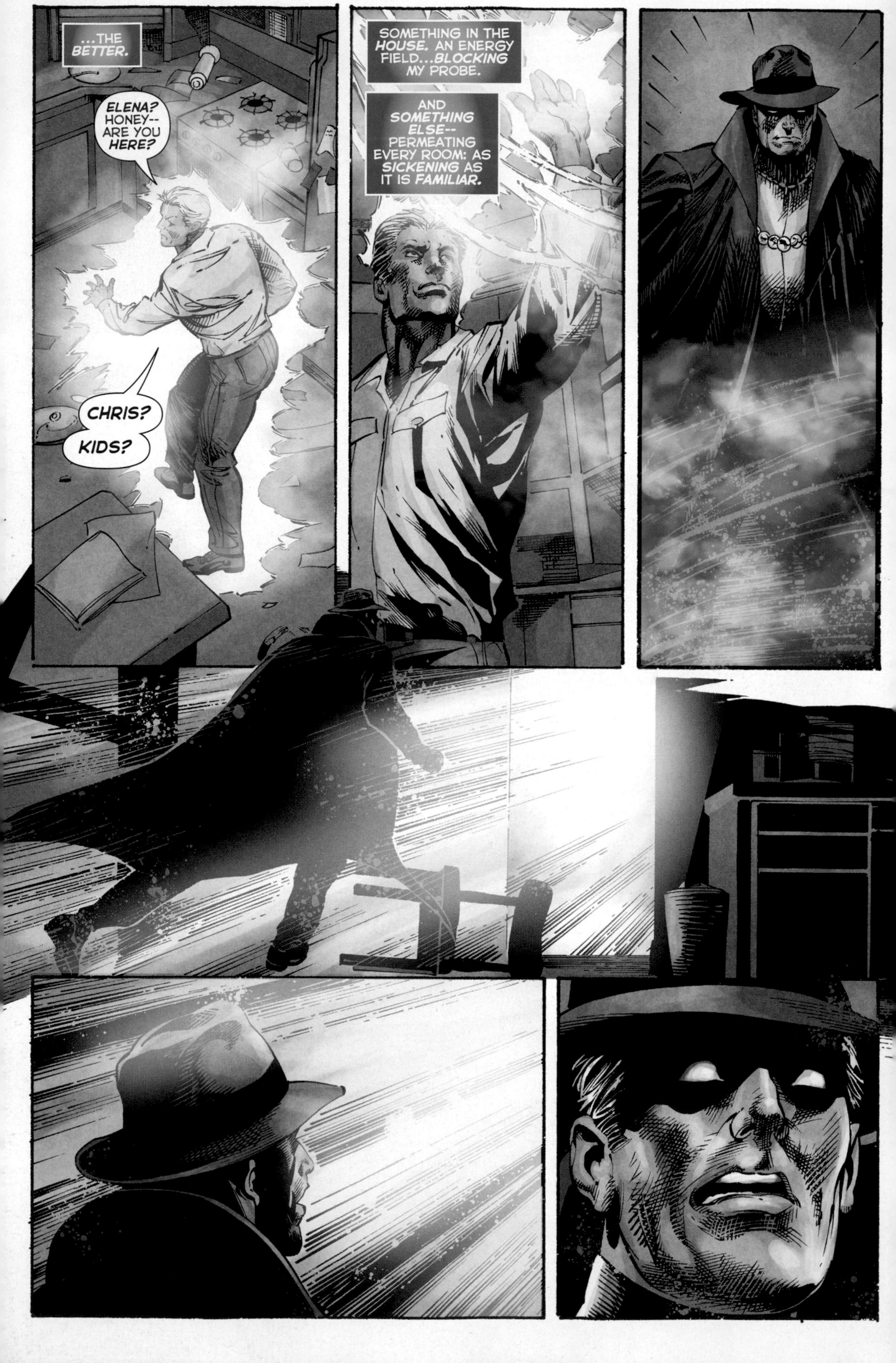

...THE BETTER.
ELENA? HONEY-- ARE YOU HERE?
CHRIS?
KIDS?
SOMETHING IN THE HOUSE. AN ENERGY FIELD...BLOCKING MY PROBE.
AND SOMETHING ELSE-- PERMEATING EVERY ROOM: AS SICKENING AS IT IS FAMILIAR.

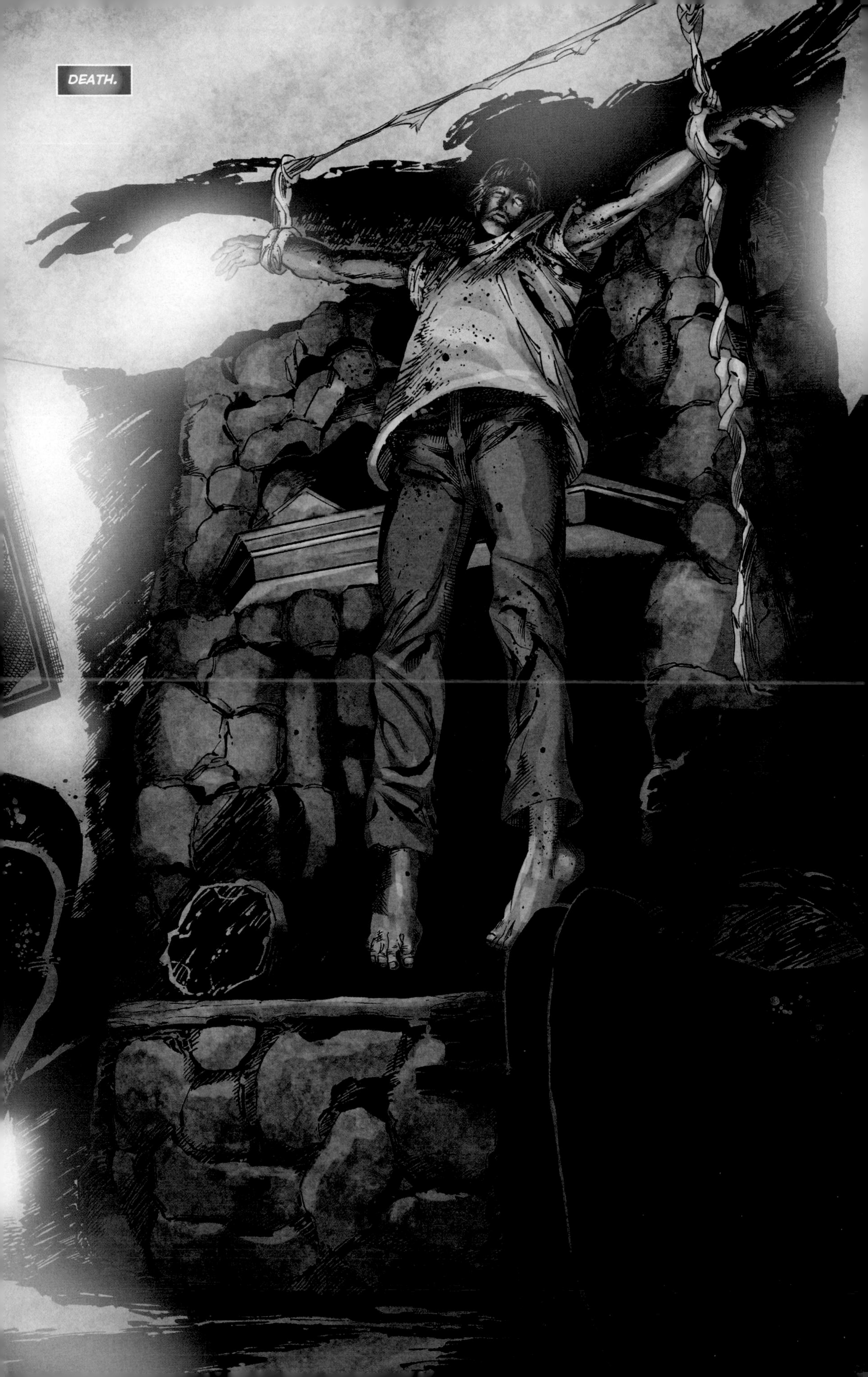
DEATH.

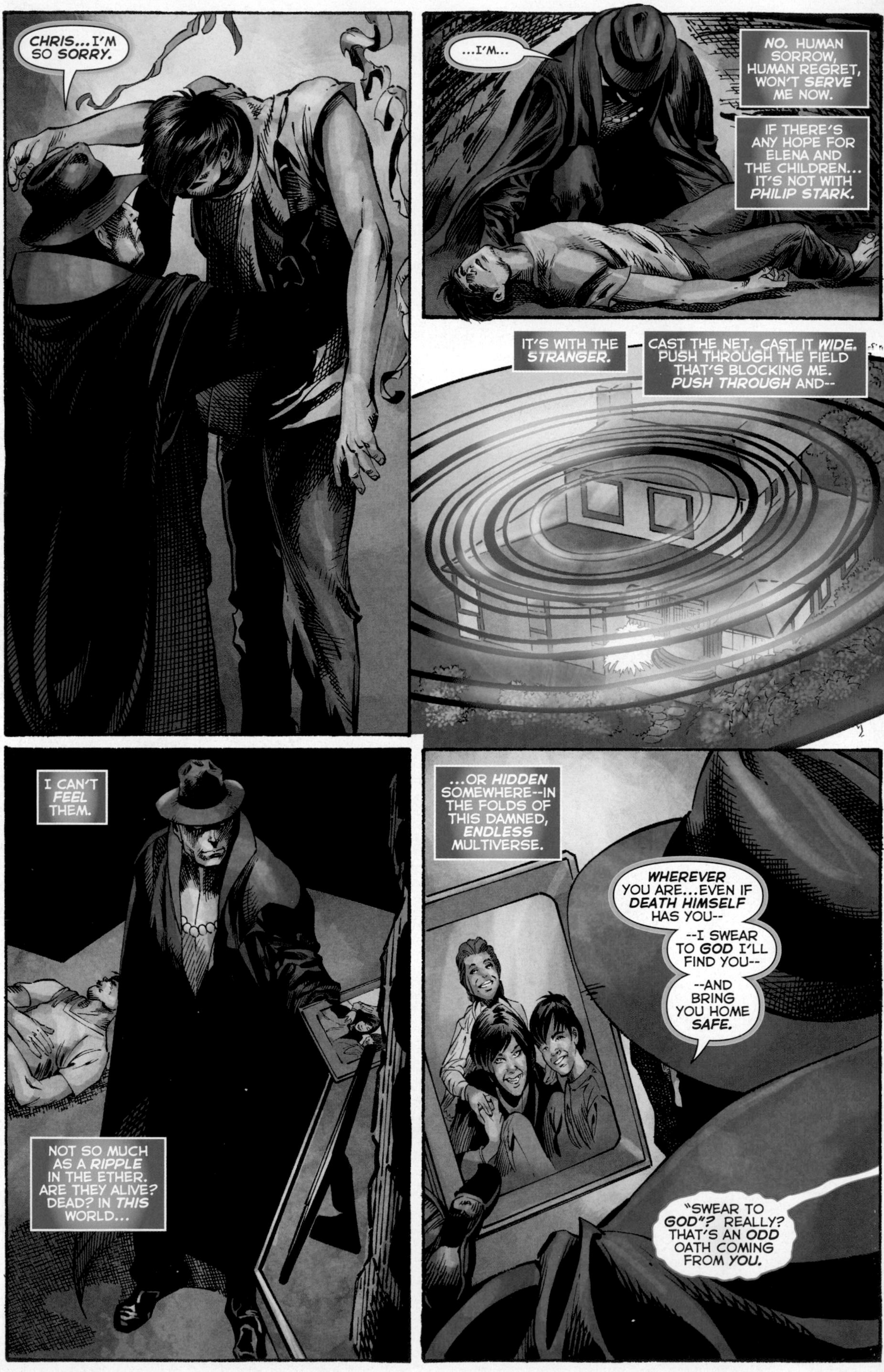
CHRIS... I'M SO SORRY.
...I'M...
NO. HUMAN SORROW, HUMAN REGRET, WON'T SERVE ME NOW.
IF THERE'S ANY HOPE FOR ELENA AND THE CHILDREN... IT'S NOT WITH PHILIP STARK.
IT'S WITH THE STRANGER.
CAST THE NET. CAST IT WIDE. PUSH THROUGH THE FIELD THAT'S BLOCKING ME. PUSH THROUGH AND--
I CAN'T FEEL THEM.
NOT SO MUCH AS A RIPPLE IN THE ETHER. ARE THEY ALIVE? DEAD? IN THIS WORLD...
...OR HIDDEN SOMEWHERE--IN THE FOLDS OF THIS DAMNED, ENDLESS MULTIVERSE.
WHEREVER YOU ARE...EVEN IF DEATH HIMSELF HAS YOU--
--I SWEAR TO GOD I'LL FIND YOU--
--AND BRING YOU HOME SAFE.
"SWEAR TO GOD"? REALLY? THAT'S AN ODD OATH COMING FROM YOU.

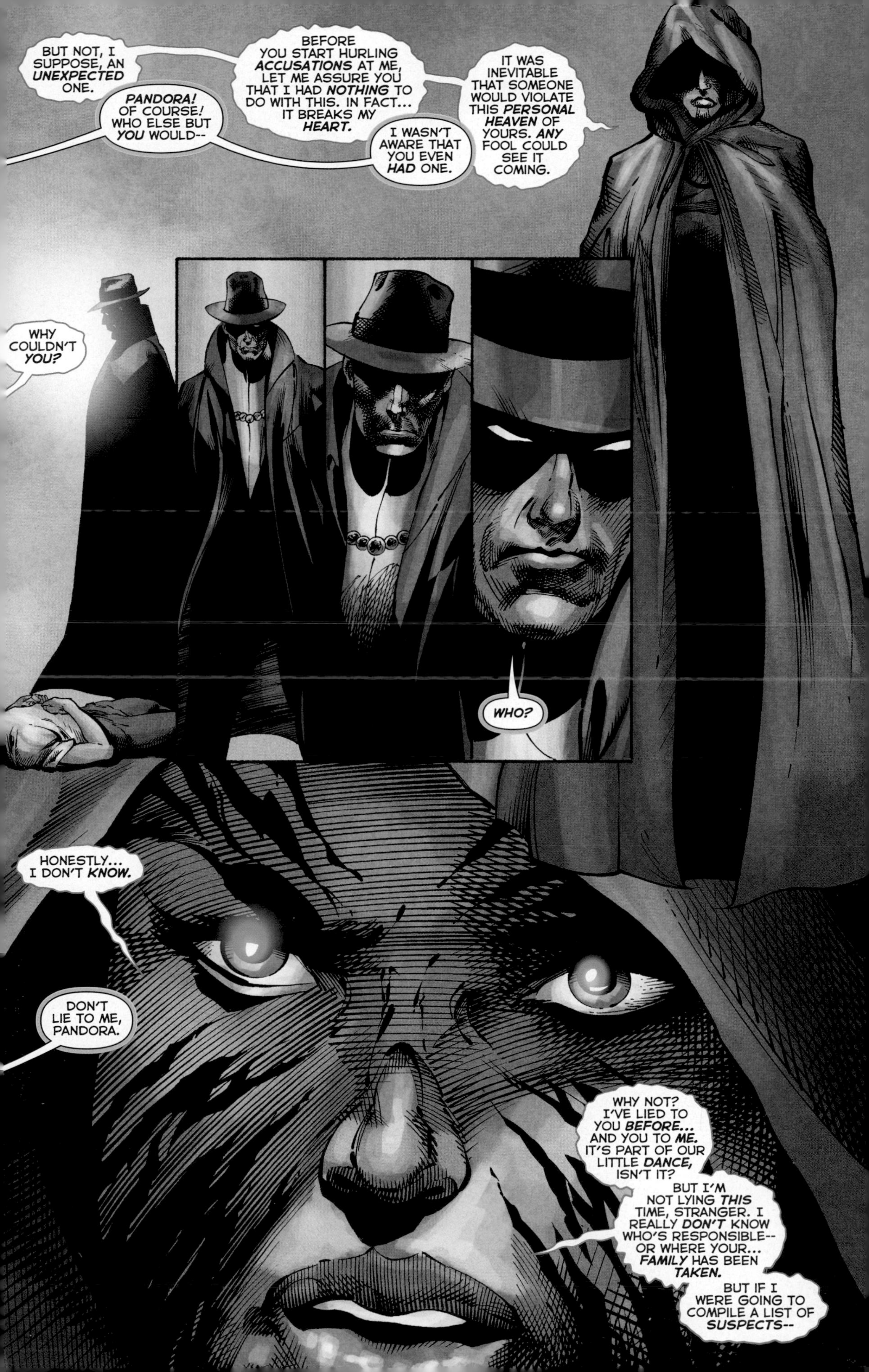
BUT NOT, I SUPPOSE, AN *UNEXPECTED* ONE.
PANDORA! OF COURSE! WHO ELSE BUT *YOU* WOULD--
BEFORE YOU START HURLING *ACCUSATIONS* AT ME, LET ME ASSURE YOU THAT I HAD *NOTHING* TO DO WITH THIS. IN FACT... IT BREAKS MY *HEART.*
I WASN'T AWARE THAT YOU EVEN *HAD* ONE.
IT WAS INEVITABLE THAT SOMEONE WOULD VIOLATE THIS *PERSONAL HEAVEN* OF YOURS. *ANY* FOOL COULD SEE IT COMING.
WHY COULDN'T *YOU?*
WHO?
HONESTLY... I DON'T *KNOW.*
DON'T LIE TO ME, PANDORA.
WHY NOT? I'VE LIED TO YOU *BEFORE...* AND YOU TO *ME.* IT'S PART OF OUR LITTLE *DANCE,* ISN'T IT?
BUT I'M NOT LYING *THIS* TIME, STRANGER. I REALLY *DON'T* KNOW WHO'S RESPONSIBLE-- OR WHERE YOUR... *FAMILY* HAS BEEN *TAKEN.*
BUT IF I WERE GOING TO COMPILE A LIST OF *SUSPECTS--*

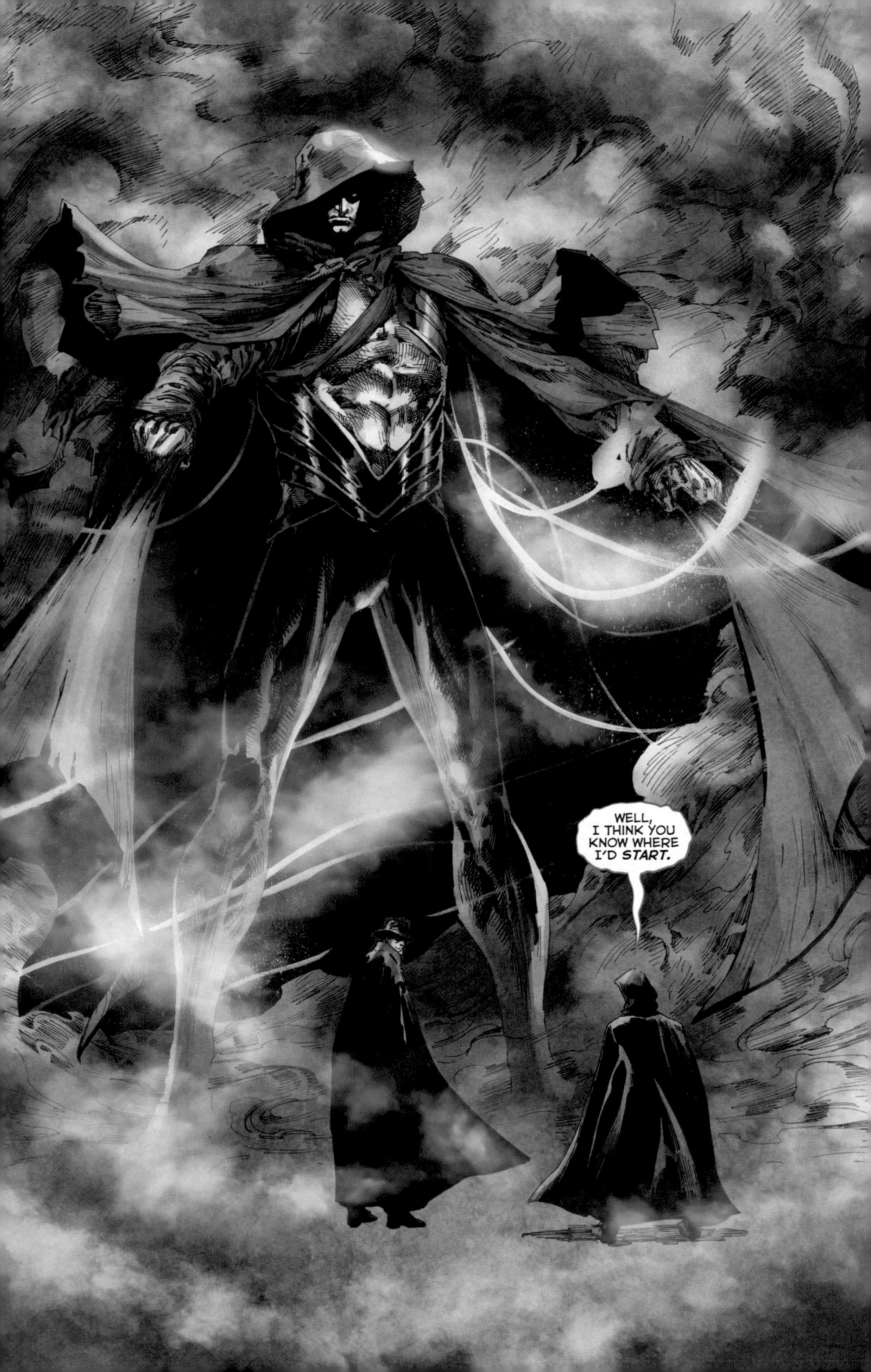
WELL, I THINK YOU KNOW WHERE I'D START.

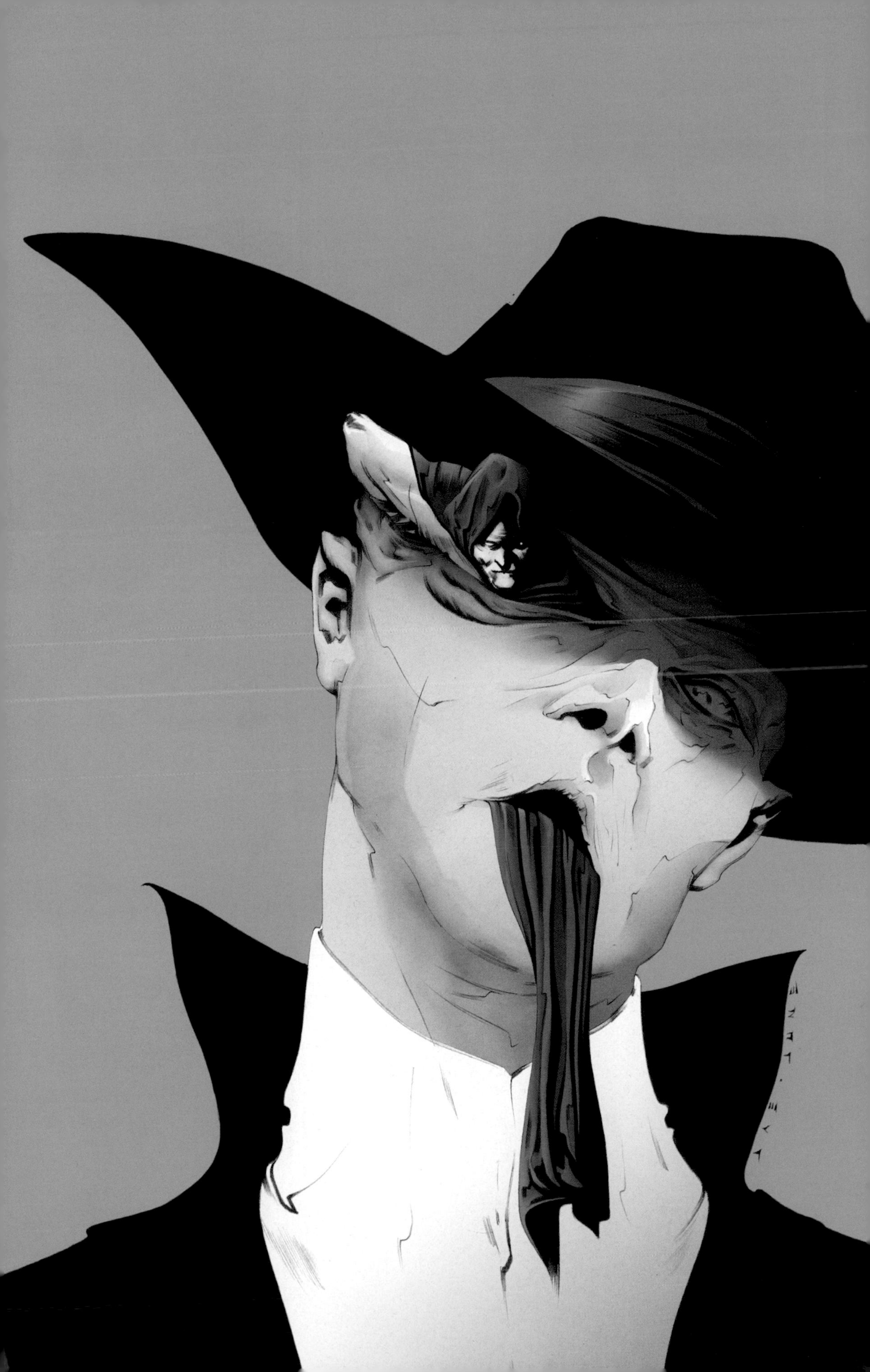

Cover by Jae Lee & June Chung

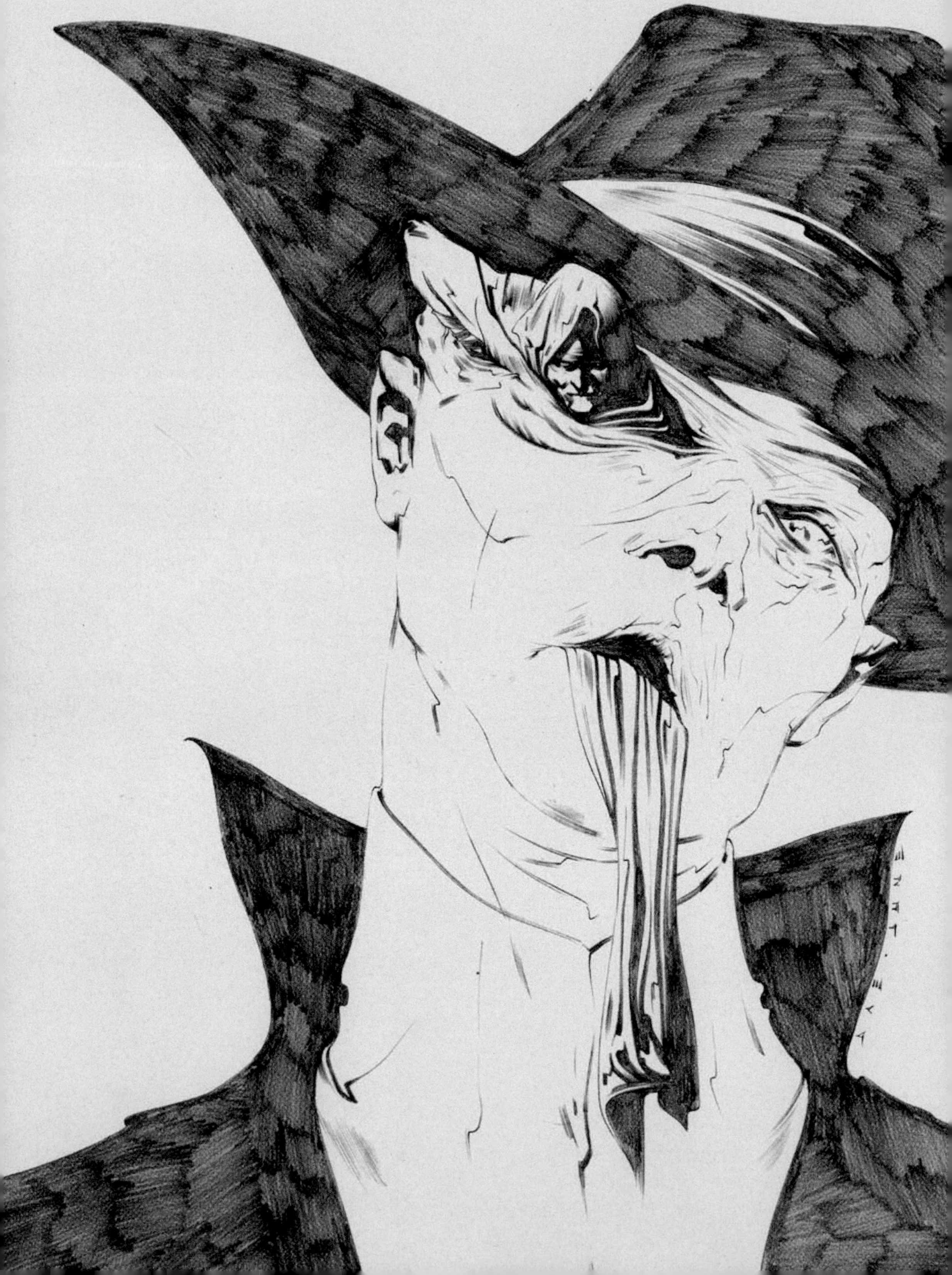

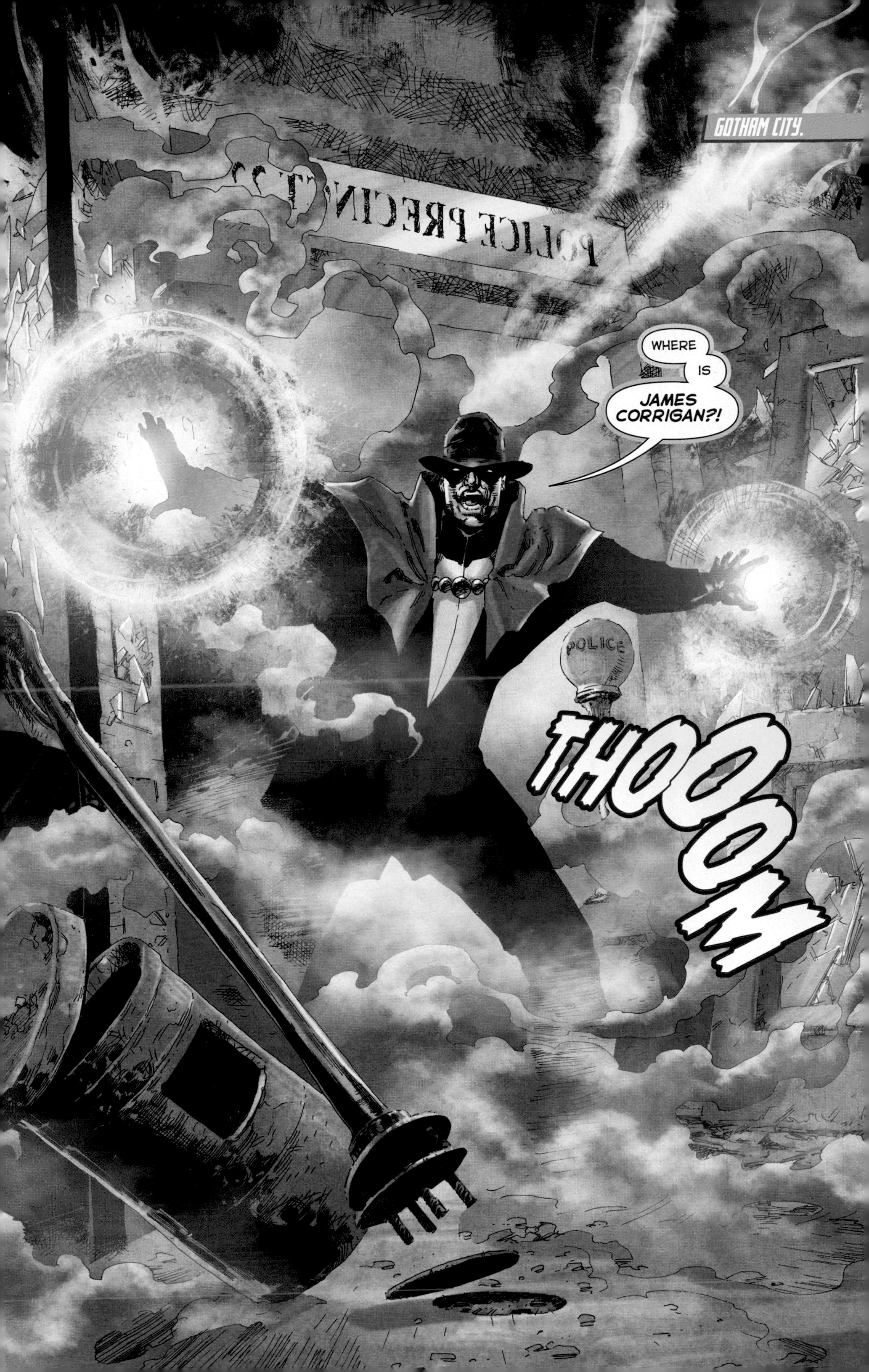
GOTHAM CITY.
POLICE PRECINCT
WHERE IS JAMES CORRIGAN?!
POLICE
THOOOOM

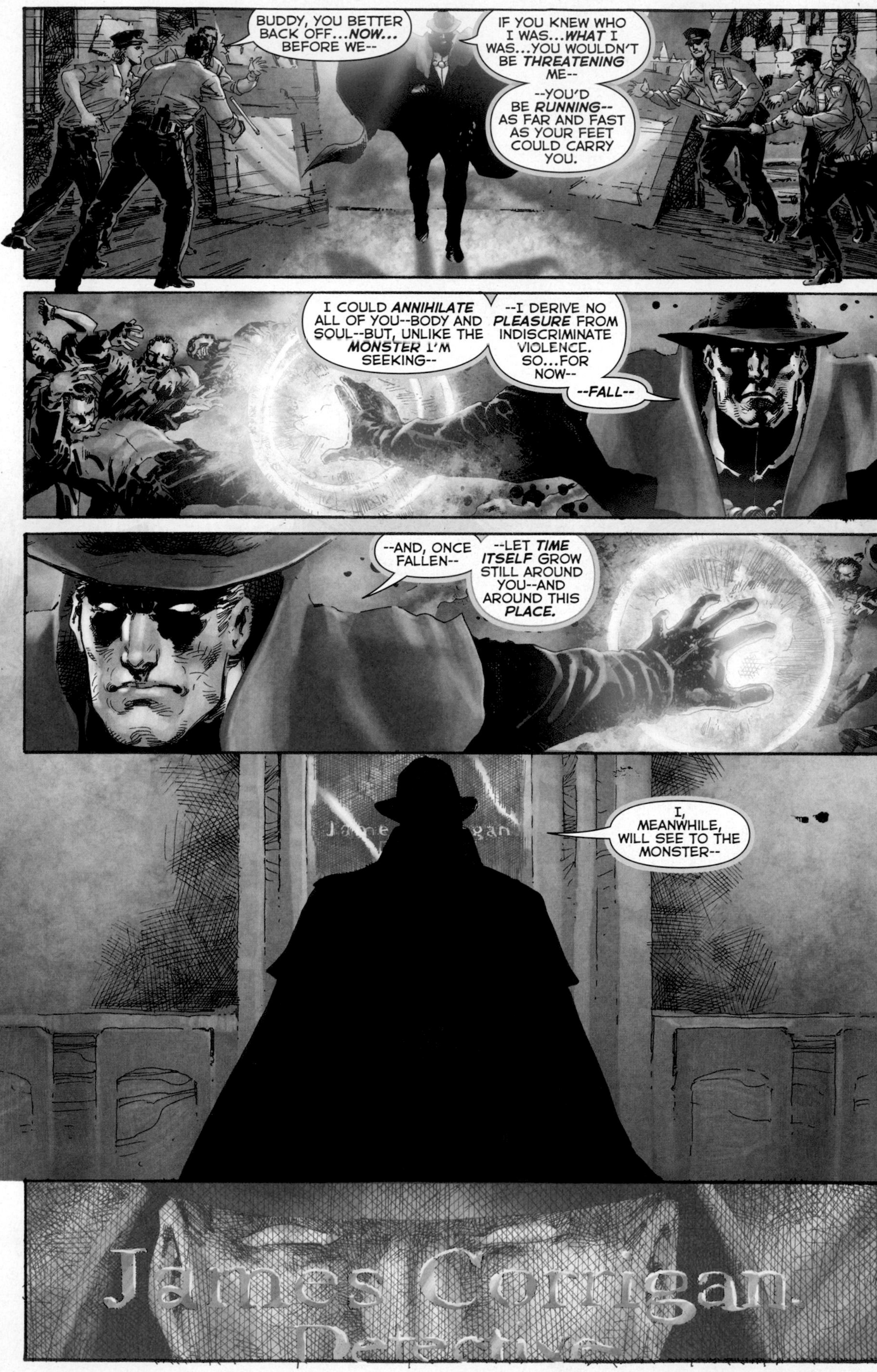
BUDDY, YOU BETTER BACK OFF...NOW... BEFORE WE--
IF YOU KNEW WHO I WAS...WHAT I WAS...YOU WOULDN'T BE THREATENING ME--
--YOU'D BE RUNNING-- AS FAR AND FAST AS YOUR FEET COULD CARRY YOU.
I COULD ANNIHILATE ALL OF YOU--BODY AND SOUL--BUT, UNLIKE THE MONSTER I'M SEEKING--
--I DERIVE NO PLEASURE FROM INDISCRIMINATE VIOLENCE. SO...FOR NOW--
--FALL--
--AND, ONCE FALLEN--
--LET TIME ITSELF GROW STILL AROUND YOU--AND AROUND THIS PLACE.
I, MEANWHILE, WILL SEE TO THE MONSTER--
James Corrigan. Detective

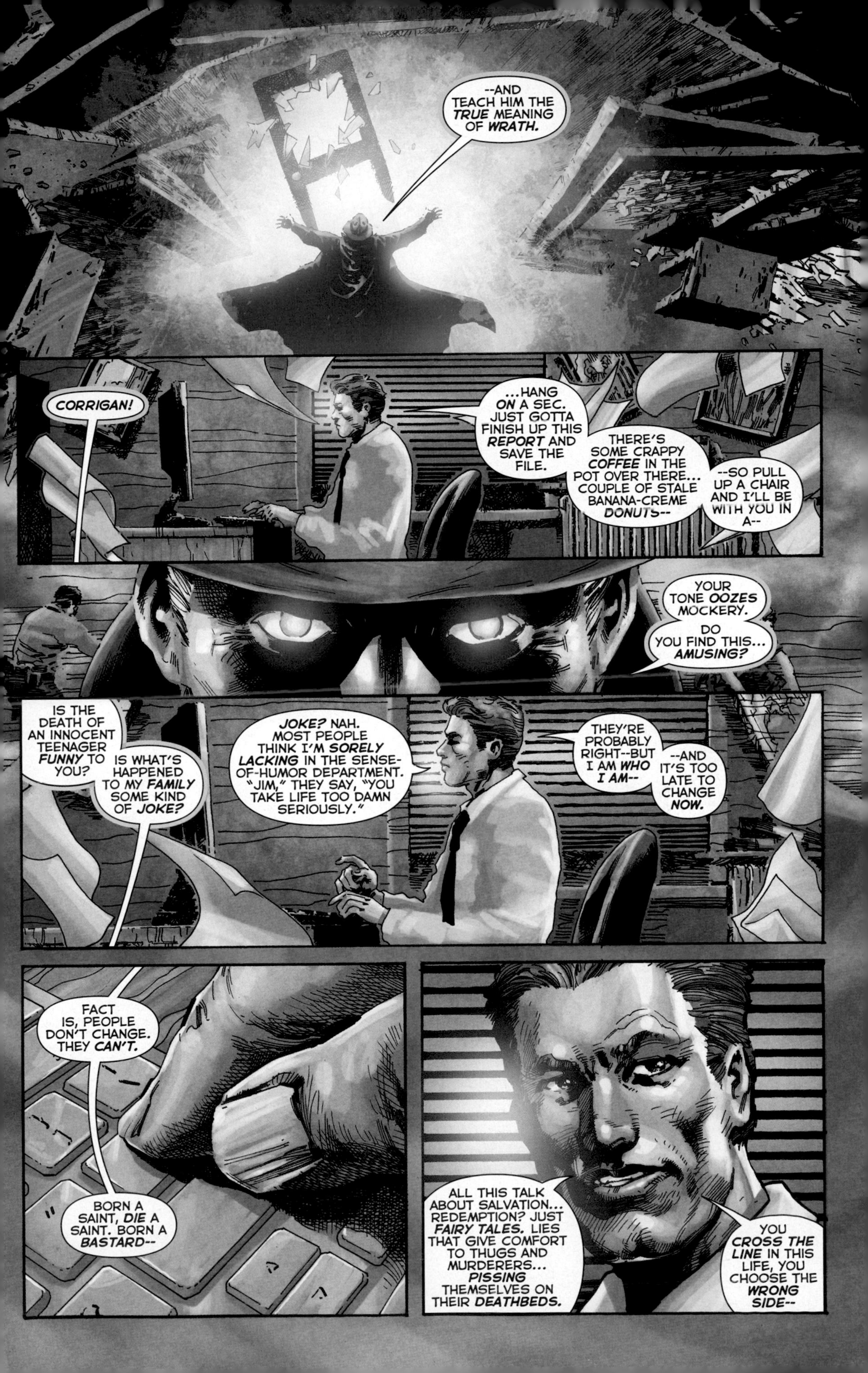
--AND TEACH HIM THE TRUE MEANING OF WRATH.
CORRIGAN!
...HANG ON A SEC. JUST GOTTA FINISH UP THIS REPORT AND SAVE THE FILE.
THERE'S SOME CRAPPY COFFEE IN THE POT OVER THERE... COUPLE OF STALE BANANA-CREME DONUTS--
--SO PULL UP A CHAIR AND I'LL BE WITH YOU IN A--
YOUR TONE OOZES MOCKERY.
DO YOU FIND THIS... AMUSING?
IS THE DEATH OF AN INNOCENT TEENAGER FUNNY TO YOU?
IS WHAT'S HAPPENED TO MY FAMILY SOME KIND OF JOKE?
JOKE? NAH. MOST PEOPLE THINK I'M SORELY LACKING IN THE SENSE-OF-HUMOR DEPARTMENT. "JIM," THEY SAY, "YOU TAKE LIFE TOO DAMN SERIOUSLY."
THEY'RE PROBABLY RIGHT--BUT I AM WHO I AM--
--AND IT'S TOO LATE TO CHANGE NOW.
FACT IS, PEOPLE DON'T CHANGE. THEY CAN'T.
BORN A SAINT, DIE A SAINT. BORN A BASTARD--
ALL THIS TALK ABOUT SALVATION... REDEMPTION? JUST FAIRY TALES. LIES THAT GIVE COMFORT TO THUGS AND MURDERERS... PISSING THEMSELVES ON THEIR DEATHBEDS.
YOU CROSS THE LINE IN THIS LIFE, YOU CHOOSE THE WRONG SIDE--

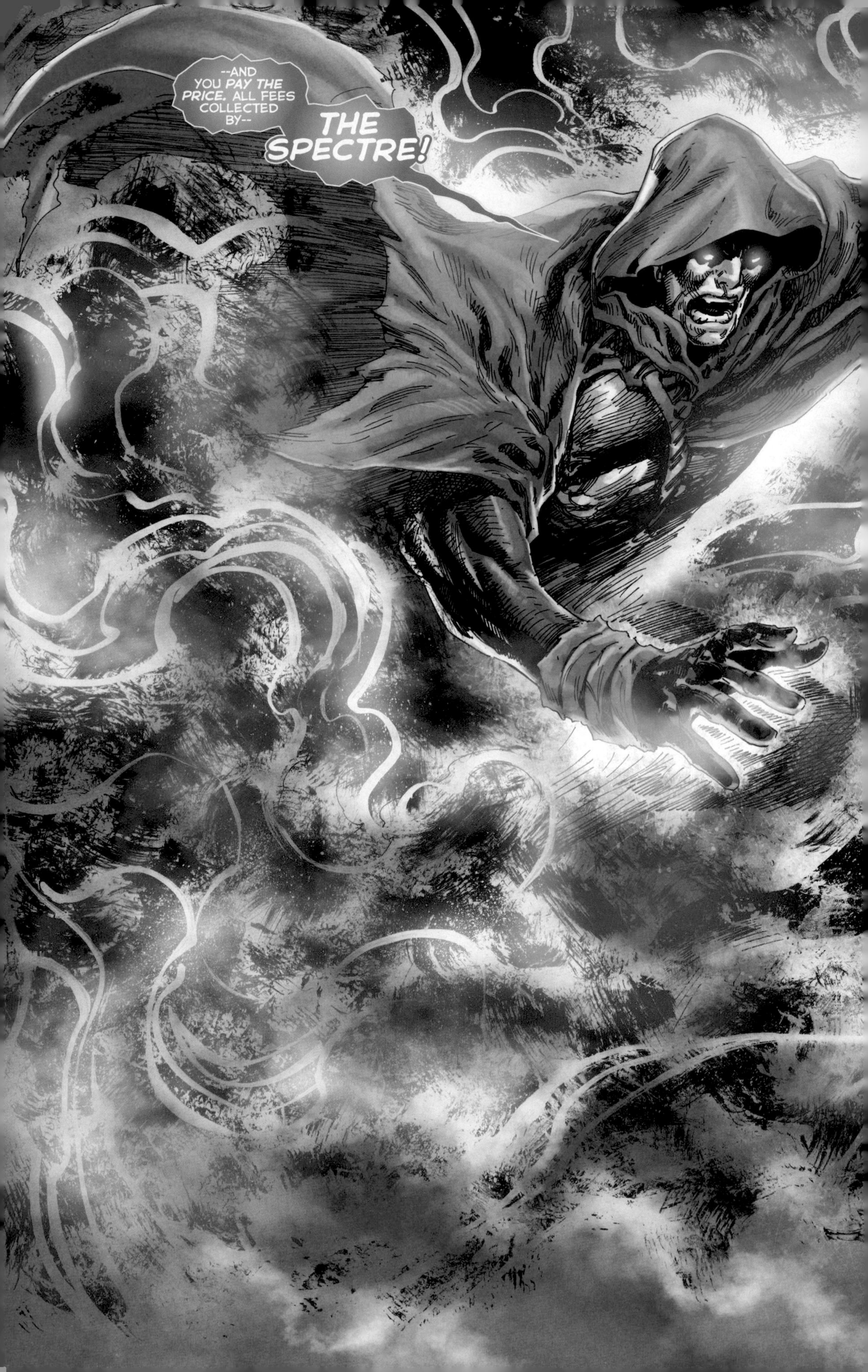
--AND YOU PAY THE PRICE. ALL FEES COLLECTED BY--
THE SPECTRE!

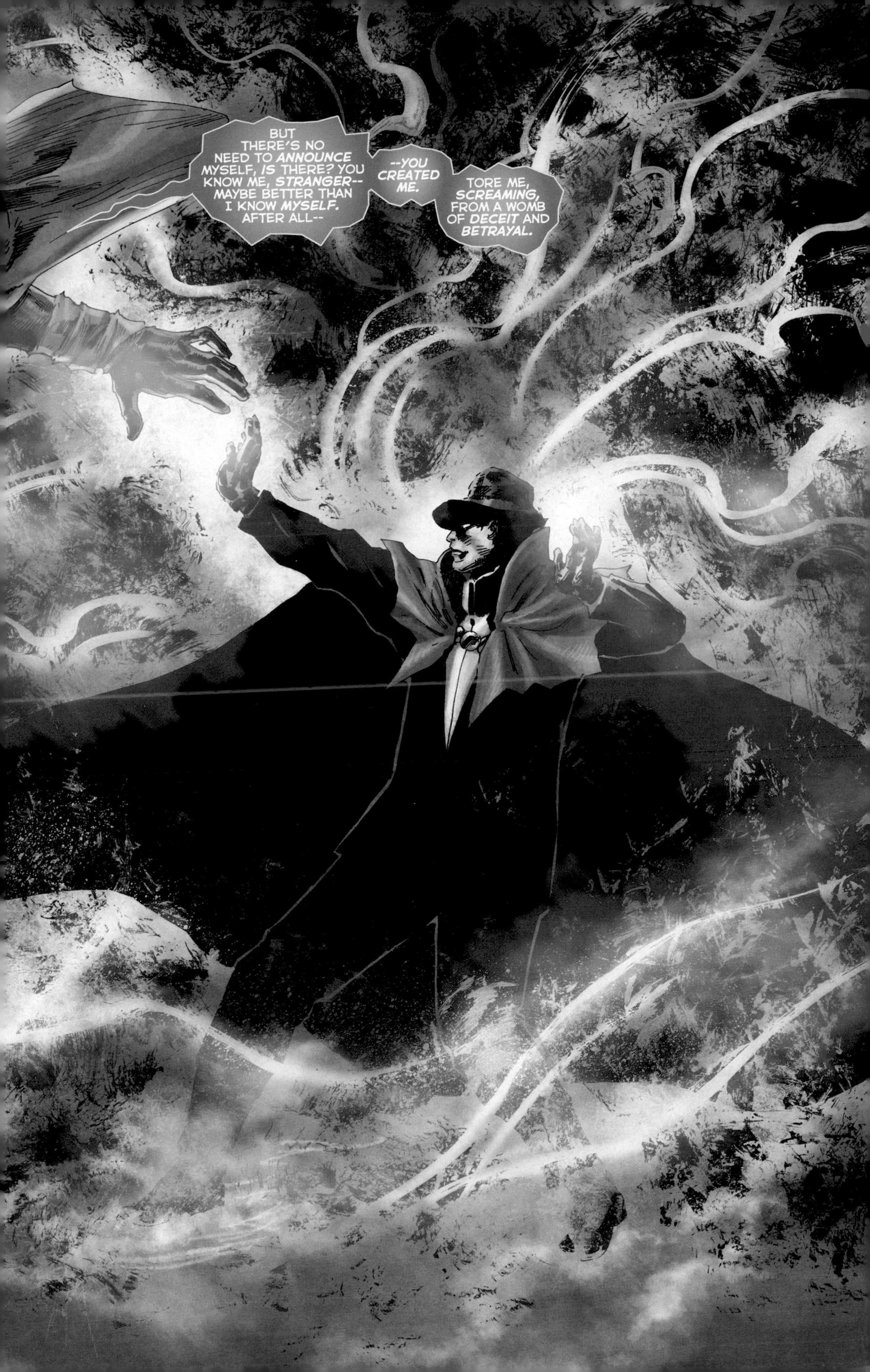
BUT THERE'S NO NEED TO ANNOUNCE MYSELF, IS THERE? YOU KNOW ME, STRANGER--MAYBE BETTER THAN I KNOW MYSELF. AFTER ALL--
--YOU CREATED ME.
TORE ME, SCREAMING, FROM A WOMB OF DECEIT AND BETRAYAL.

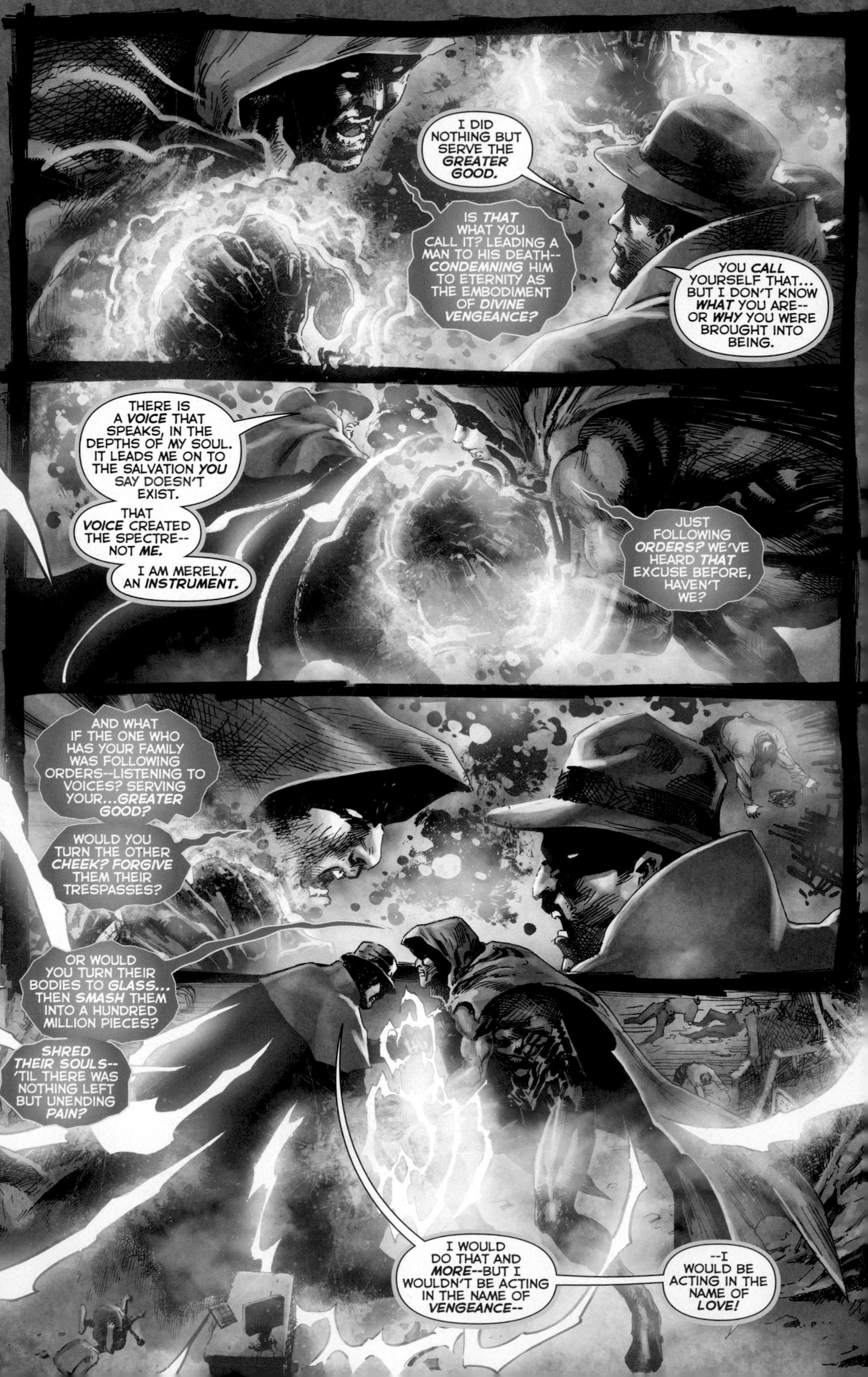
I DID NOTHING BUT SERVE THE GREATER GOOD.
IS THAT WHAT YOU CALL IT? LEADING A MAN TO HIS DEATH--CONDEMNING HIM TO ETERNITY AS THE EMBODIMENT OF DIVINE VENGEANCE?
YOU CALL YOURSELF THAT... BUT I DON'T KNOW WHAT YOU ARE--OR WHY YOU WERE BROUGHT INTO BEING.
THERE IS A VOICE THAT SPEAKS, IN THE DEPTHS OF MY SOUL. IT LEADS ME ON TO THE SALVATION YOU SAY DOESN'T EXIST.
THAT VOICE CREATED THE SPECTRE--NOT ME.
I AM MERELY AN INSTRUMENT.
JUST FOLLOWING ORDERS? WE'VE HEARD THAT EXCUSE BEFORE, HAVEN'T WE?
AND WHAT IF THE ONE WHO HAS YOUR FAMILY WAS FOLLOWING ORDERS--LISTENING TO VOICES? SERVING YOUR...GREATER GOOD?
WOULD YOU TURN THE OTHER CHEEK? FORGIVE THEM THEIR TRESPASSES?
OR WOULD YOU TURN THEIR BODIES TO GLASS... THEN SMASH THEM INTO A HUNDRED MILLION PIECES?
SHRED THEIR SOULS--'TIL THERE WAS NOTHING LEFT BUT UNENDING PAIN?
I WOULD DO THAT AND MORE--BUT I WOULDN'T BE ACTING IN THE NAME OF VENGEANCE--
--I WOULD BE ACTING IN THE NAME OF LOVE!

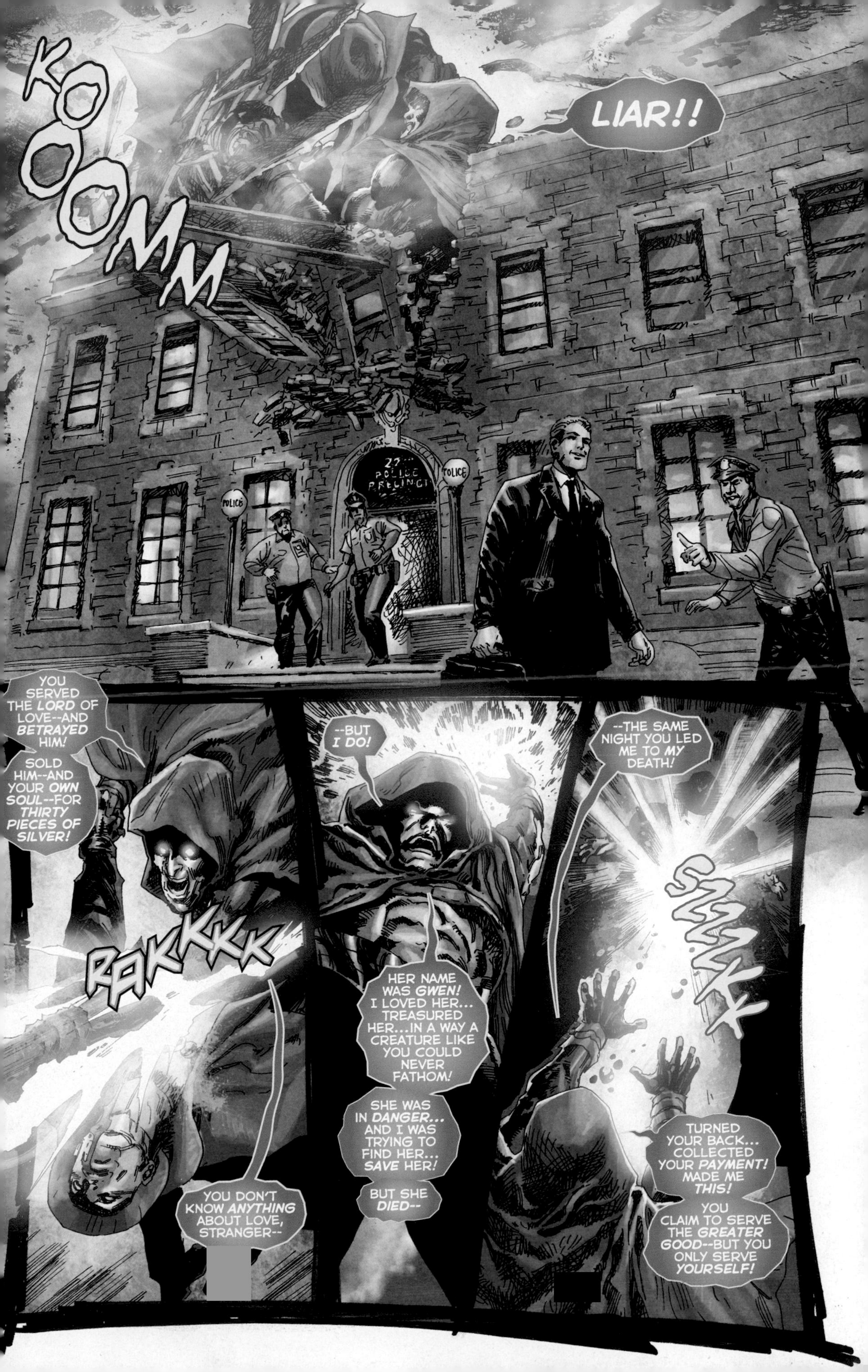
KOOOMM
LIAR!!
POLICE
POLICE
YOU SERVED THE LORD OF LOVE--AND BETRAYED HIM!
SOLD HIM--AND YOUR OWN SOUL--FOR THIRTY PIECES OF SILVER!
RAKKKK
YOU DON'T KNOW ANYTHING ABOUT LOVE, STRANGER--
--BUT I DO!
HER NAME WAS GWEN! I LOVED HER... TREASURED HER...IN A WAY A CREATURE LIKE YOU COULD NEVER FATHOM!
SHE WAS IN DANGER... AND I WAS TRYING TO FIND HER... SAVE HER!
BUT SHE DIED--
--THE SAME NIGHT YOU LED ME TO MY DEATH!
SZZZKK
TURNED YOUR BACK... COLLECTED YOUR PAYMENT! MADE ME THIS!
YOU CLAIM TO SERVE THE GREATER GOOD--BUT YOU ONLY SERVE YOURSELF!

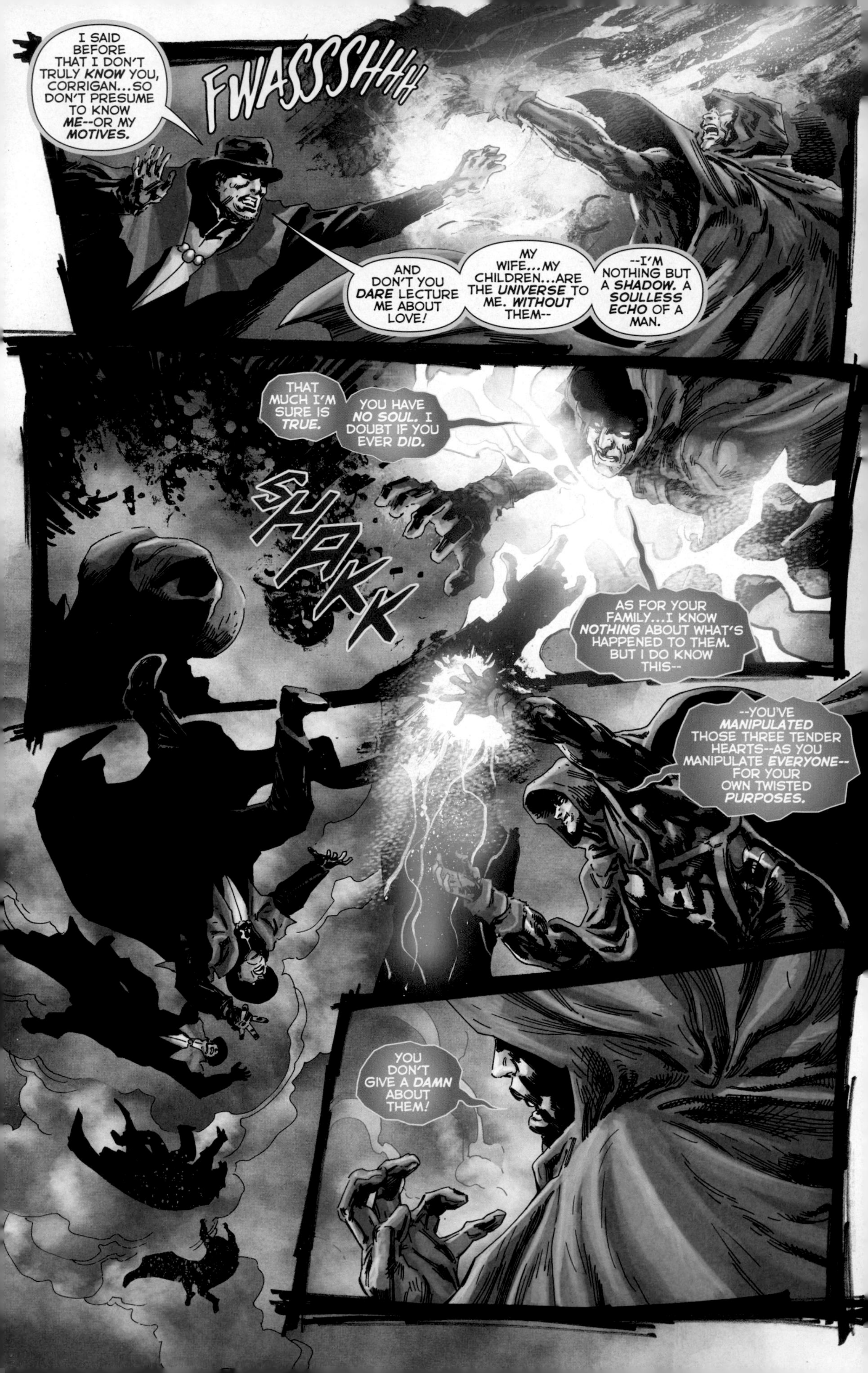
I SAID BEFORE THAT I DON'T TRULY KNOW YOU, CORRIGAN...SO DON'T PRESUME TO KNOW ME--OR MY MOTIVES.
FWASSSHHH
AND DON'T YOU DARE LECTURE ME ABOUT LOVE!
MY WIFE...MY CHILDREN...ARE THE UNIVERSE TO ME. WITHOUT THEM--
--I'M NOTHING BUT A SHADOW. A SOULLESS ECHO OF A MAN.
THAT MUCH I'M SURE IS TRUE.
YOU HAVE NO SOUL. I DOUBT IF YOU EVER DID.
SHAKK
AS FOR YOUR FAMILY...I KNOW NOTHING ABOUT WHAT'S HAPPENED TO THEM. BUT I DO KNOW THIS--
--YOU'VE MANIPULATED THOSE THREE TENDER HEARTS--AS YOU MANIPULATE EVERYONE--FOR YOUR OWN TWISTED PURPOSES.
YOU DON'T GIVE A DAMN ABOUT THEM!

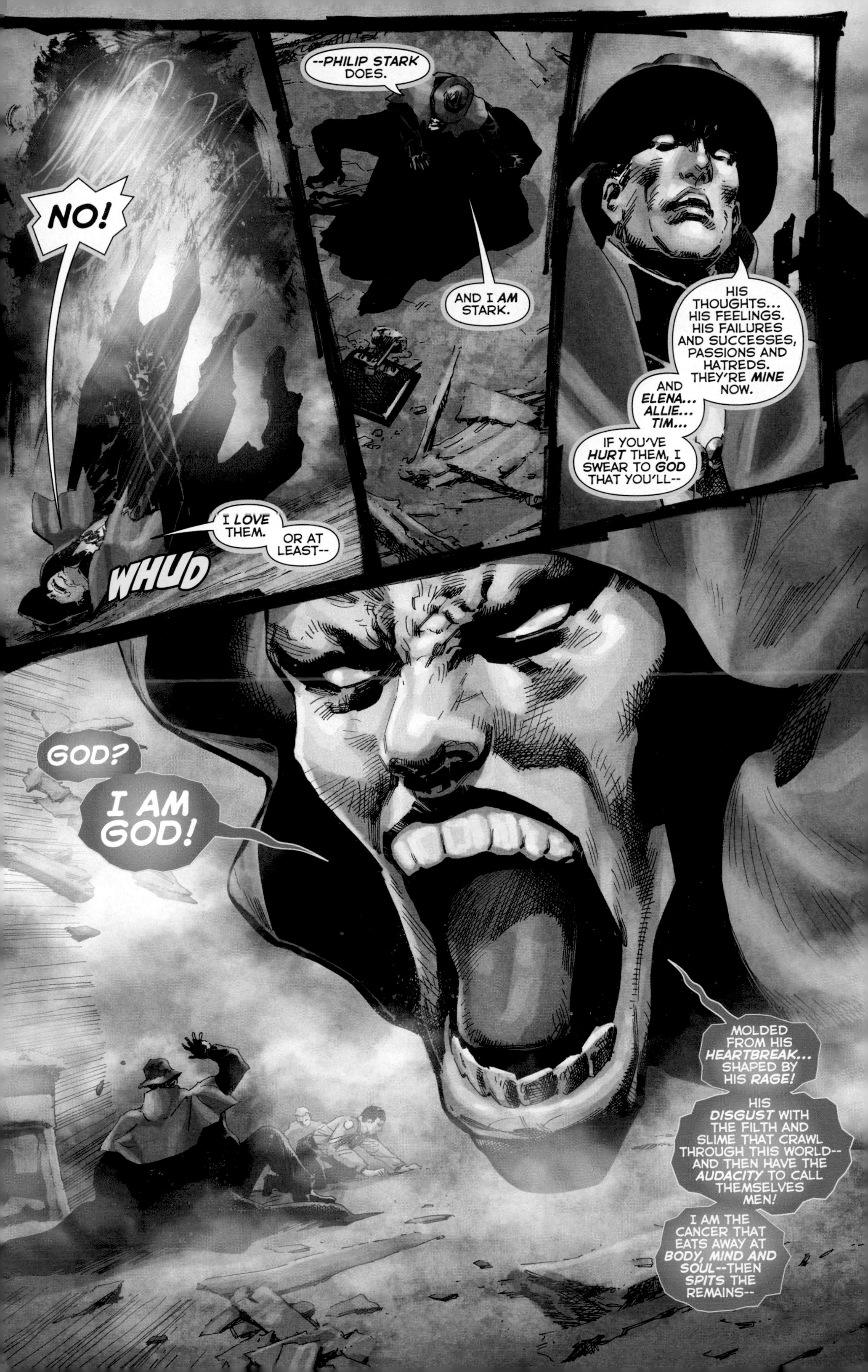
NO!
I LOVE THEM.
OR AT LEAST--
WHUD
--PHILIP STARK DOES.
AND I AM STARK.
HIS THOUGHTS... HIS FEELINGS. HIS FAILURES AND SUCCESSES, PASSIONS AND HATREDS. THEY'RE MINE NOW.
AND ELENA... ALLIE... TIM...
IF YOU'VE HURT THEM, I SWEAR TO GOD THAT YOU'LL--
GOD?
I AM GOD!
MOLDED FROM HIS HEARTBREAK... SHAPED BY HIS RAGE!
HIS DISGUST WITH THE FILTH AND SLIME THAT CRAWL THROUGH THIS WORLD--AND THEN HAVE THE AUDACITY TO CALL THEMSELVES MEN!
I AM THE CANCER THAT EATS AWAY AT BODY, MIND AND SOUL--THEN SPITS THE REMAINS--

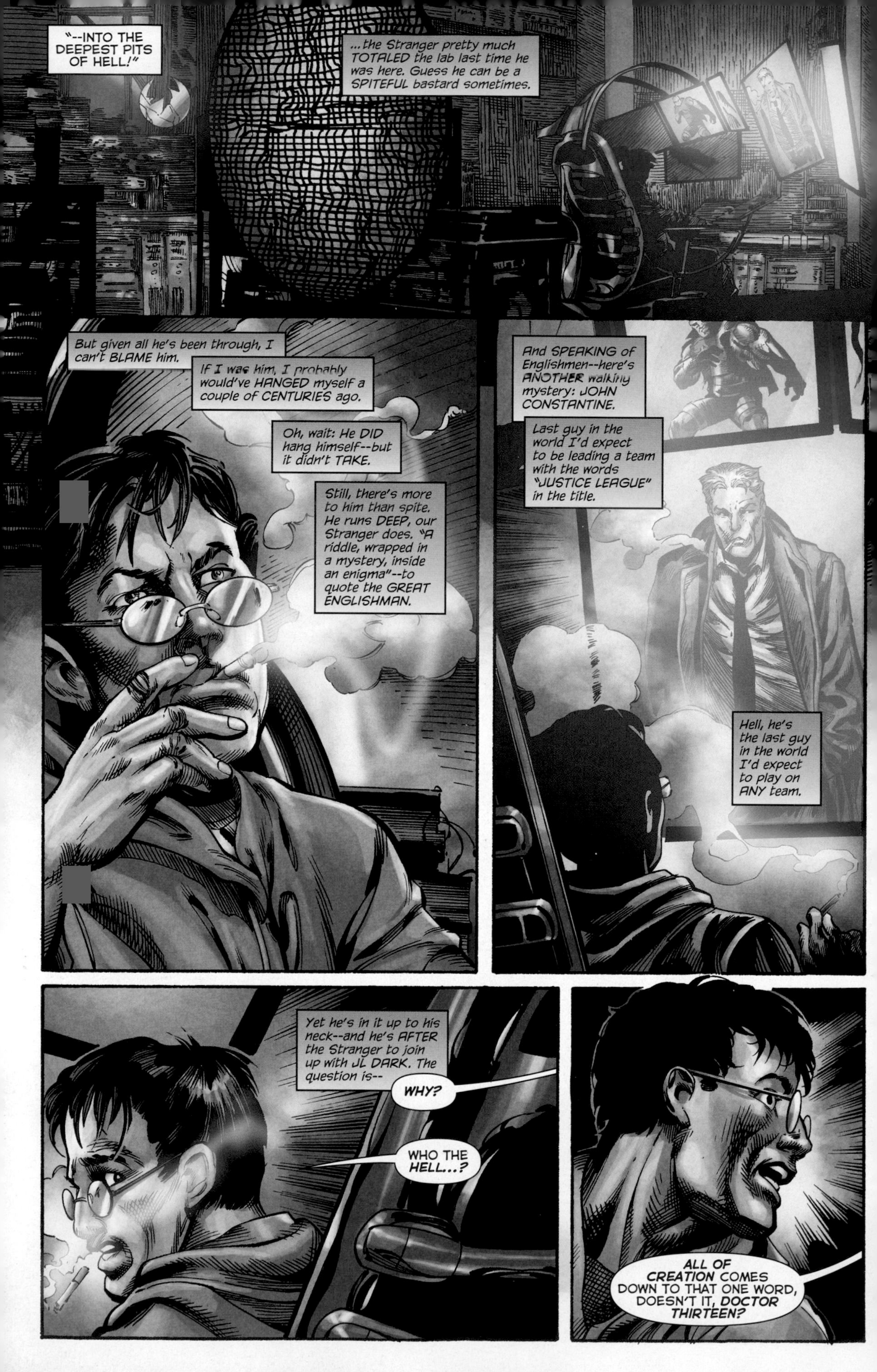
"--INTO THE DEEPEST PITS OF HELL!"
...the Stranger pretty much TOTALED the lab last time he was here. Guess he can be a SPITEFUL bastard sometimes.
But given all he's been through, I can't BLAME him.
If I was him, I probably would've HANGED myself a couple of CENTURIES ago.
Oh, wait: He DID hang himself--but it didn't TAKE.
Still, there's more to him than spite. He runs DEEP, our Stranger does. "A riddle, wrapped in a mystery, inside an enigma"--to quote the GREAT ENGLISHMAN.
And SPEAKING of Englishmen--here's ANOTHER walking mystery: JOHN CONSTANTINE.
Last guy in the world I'd expect to be leading a team with the words "JUSTICE LEAGUE" in the title.
Hell, he's the last guy in the world I'd expect to play on ANY team.
Yet he's in it up to his neck--and he's AFTER the Stranger to join up with JL DARK. The question is--
WHY?
WHO THE HELL...?
ALL OF CREATION COMES DOWN TO THAT ONE WORD, DOESN'T IT, DOCTOR THIRTEEN?

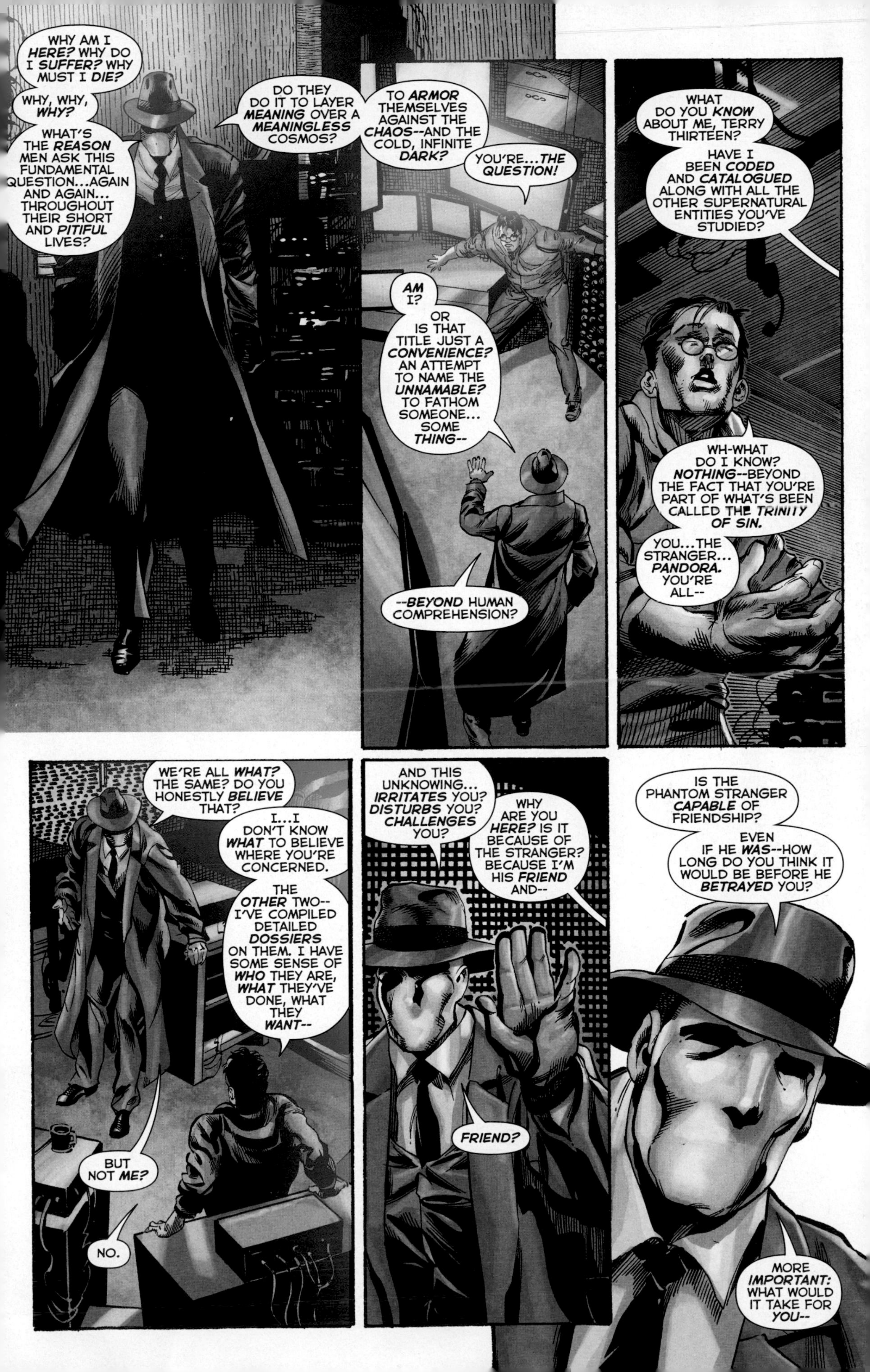
WHY AM I HERE? WHY DO I SUFFER? WHY MUST I DIE?
WHY, WHY, WHY?
WHAT'S THE REASON MEN ASK THIS FUNDAMENTAL QUESTION...AGAIN AND AGAIN... THROUGHOUT THEIR SHORT AND PITIFUL LIVES?
DO THEY DO IT TO LAYER MEANING OVER A MEANINGLESS COSMOS?
TO ARMOR THEMSELVES AGAINST THE CHAOS--AND THE COLD, INFINITE DARK?
YOU'RE...THE QUESTION!
AM I?
OR IS THAT TITLE JUST A CONVENIENCE? AN ATTEMPT TO NAME THE UNNAMABLE? TO FATHOM SOMEONE... SOME THING--
--BEYOND HUMAN COMPREHENSION?
WHAT DO YOU KNOW ABOUT ME, TERRY THIRTEEN?
HAVE I BEEN CODED AND CATALOGUED ALONG WITH ALL THE OTHER SUPERNATURAL ENTITIES YOU'VE STUDIED?
WH-WHAT DO I KNOW? NOTHING--BEYOND THE FACT THAT YOU'RE PART OF WHAT'S BEEN CALLED THE TRINITY OF SIN.
YOU...THE STRANGER... PANDORA. YOU'RE ALL--
WE'RE ALL WHAT? THE SAME? DO YOU HONESTLY BELIEVE THAT?
I...I DON'T KNOW WHAT TO BELIEVE WHERE YOU'RE CONCERNED.
THE OTHER TWO-- I'VE COMPILED DETAILED DOSSIERS ON THEM. I HAVE SOME SENSE OF WHO THEY ARE, WHAT THEY'VE DONE, WHAT THEY WANT--
BUT NOT ME?
NO.
AND THIS UNKNOWING... IRRITATES YOU? DISTURBS YOU? CHALLENGES YOU?
WHY ARE YOU HERE? IS IT BECAUSE OF THE STRANGER? BECAUSE I'M HIS FRIEND AND--
FRIEND?
IS THE PHANTOM STRANGER CAPABLE OF FRIENDSHIP?
EVEN IF HE WAS--HOW LONG DO YOU THINK IT WOULD BE BEFORE HE BETRAYED YOU?
MORE IMPORTANT: WHAT WOULD IT TAKE FOR YOU--

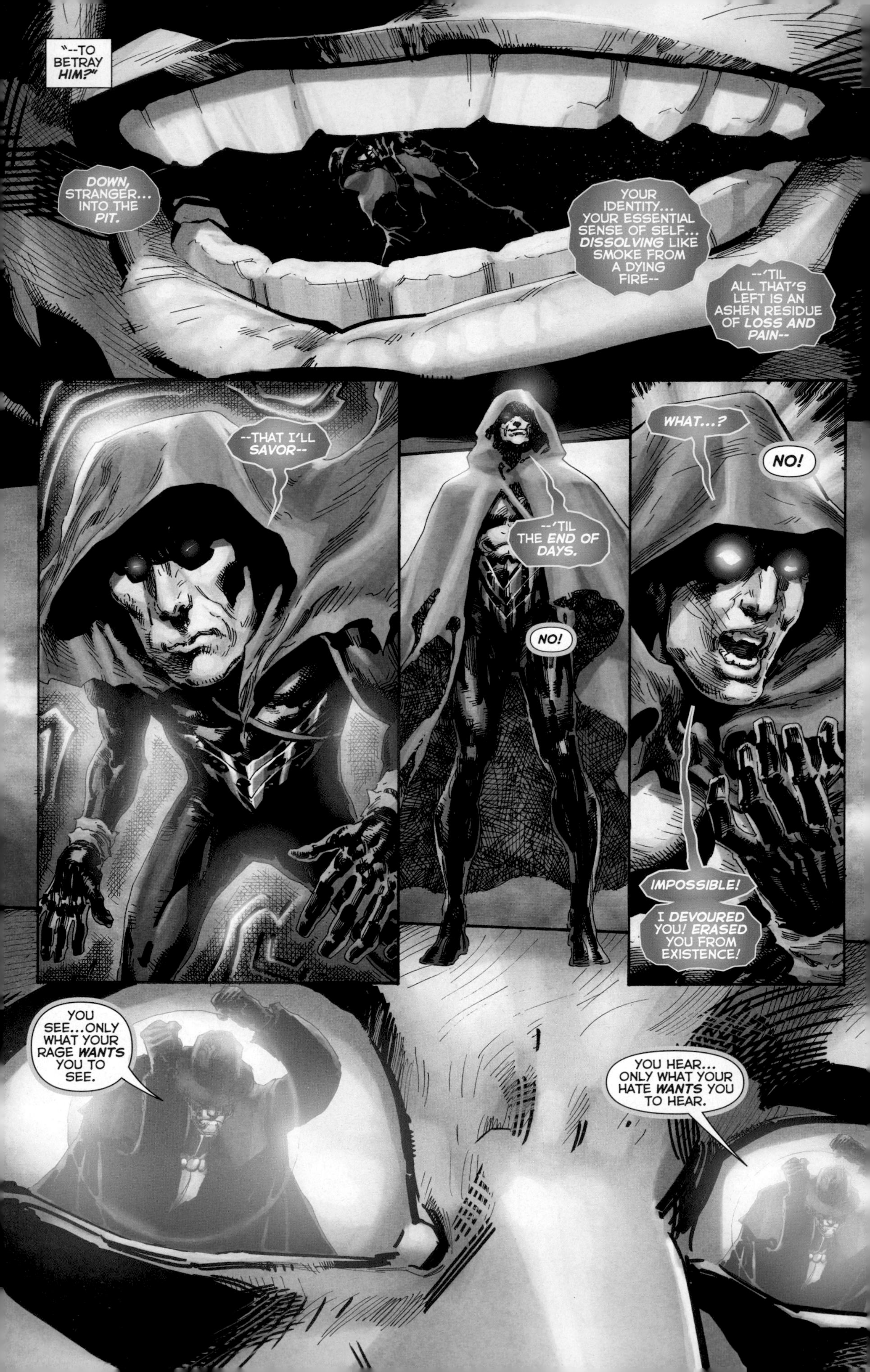
"--TO BETRAY HIM?"
DOWN, STRANGER... INTO THE PIT.
YOUR IDENTITY... YOUR ESSENTIAL SENSE OF SELF... DISSOLVING LIKE SMOKE FROM A DYING FIRE--
--'TIL ALL THAT'S LEFT IS AN ASHEN RESIDUE OF LOSS AND PAIN--
--THAT I'LL SAVOR--
--'TIL THE END OF DAYS.
NO!
WHAT...?
NO!
IMPOSSIBLE!
I DEVOURED YOU! ERASED YOU FROM EXISTENCE!
YOU SEE...ONLY WHAT YOUR RAGE WANTS YOU TO SEE.
YOU HEAR... ONLY WHAT YOUR HATE WANTS YOU TO HEAR.

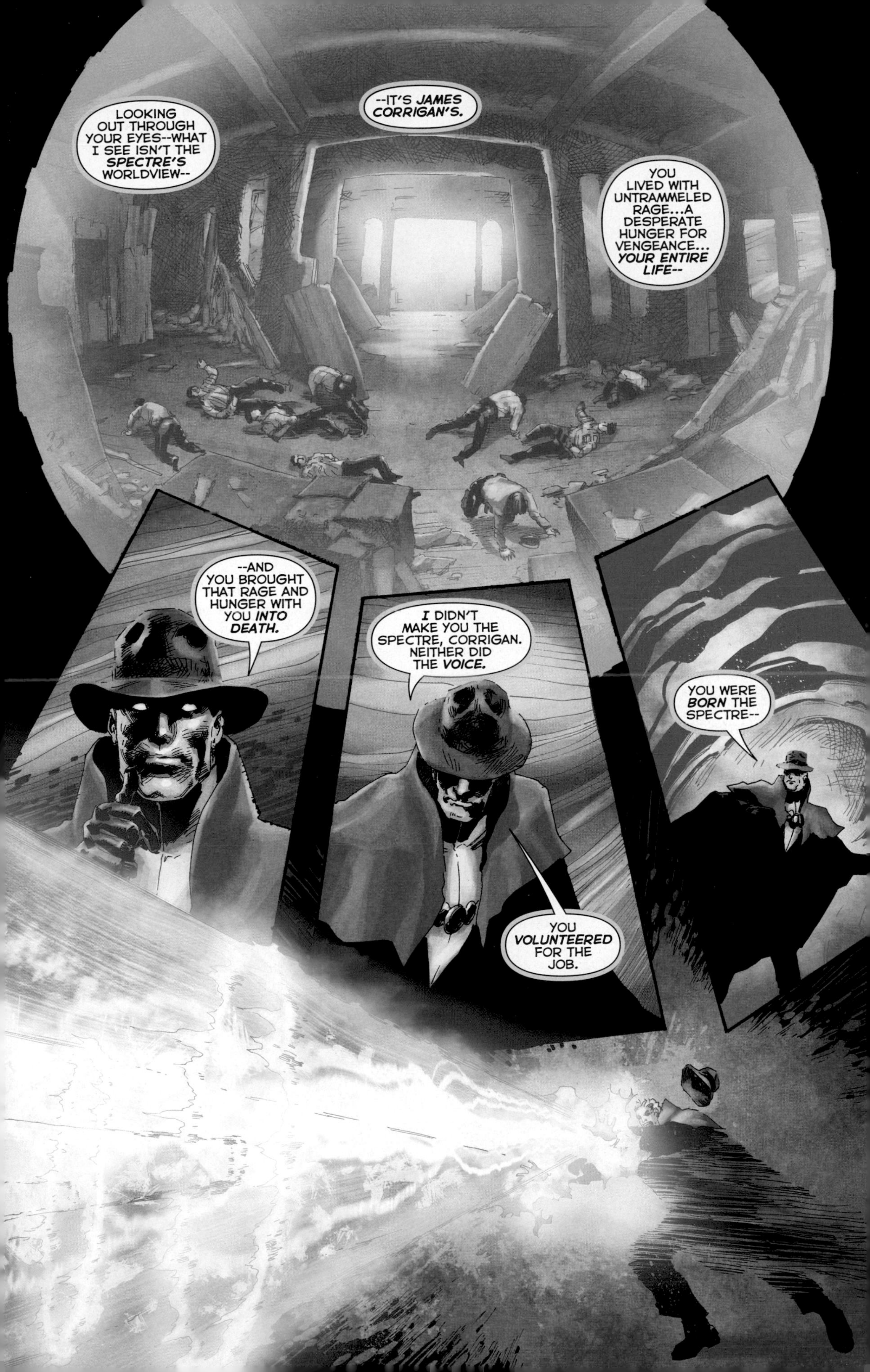
LOOKING OUT THROUGH YOUR EYES--WHAT I SEE ISN'T THE SPECTRE'S WORLDVIEW--
--IT'S JAMES CORRIGAN'S.
YOU LIVED WITH UNTRAMMELED RAGE...A DESPERATE HUNGER FOR VENGEANCE... YOUR ENTIRE LIFE--
--AND YOU BROUGHT THAT RAGE AND HUNGER WITH YOU INTO DEATH.
I DIDN'T MAKE YOU THE SPECTRE, CORRIGAN. NEITHER DID THE VOICE.
YOU VOLUNTEERED FOR THE JOB.
YOU WERE BORN THE SPECTRE--

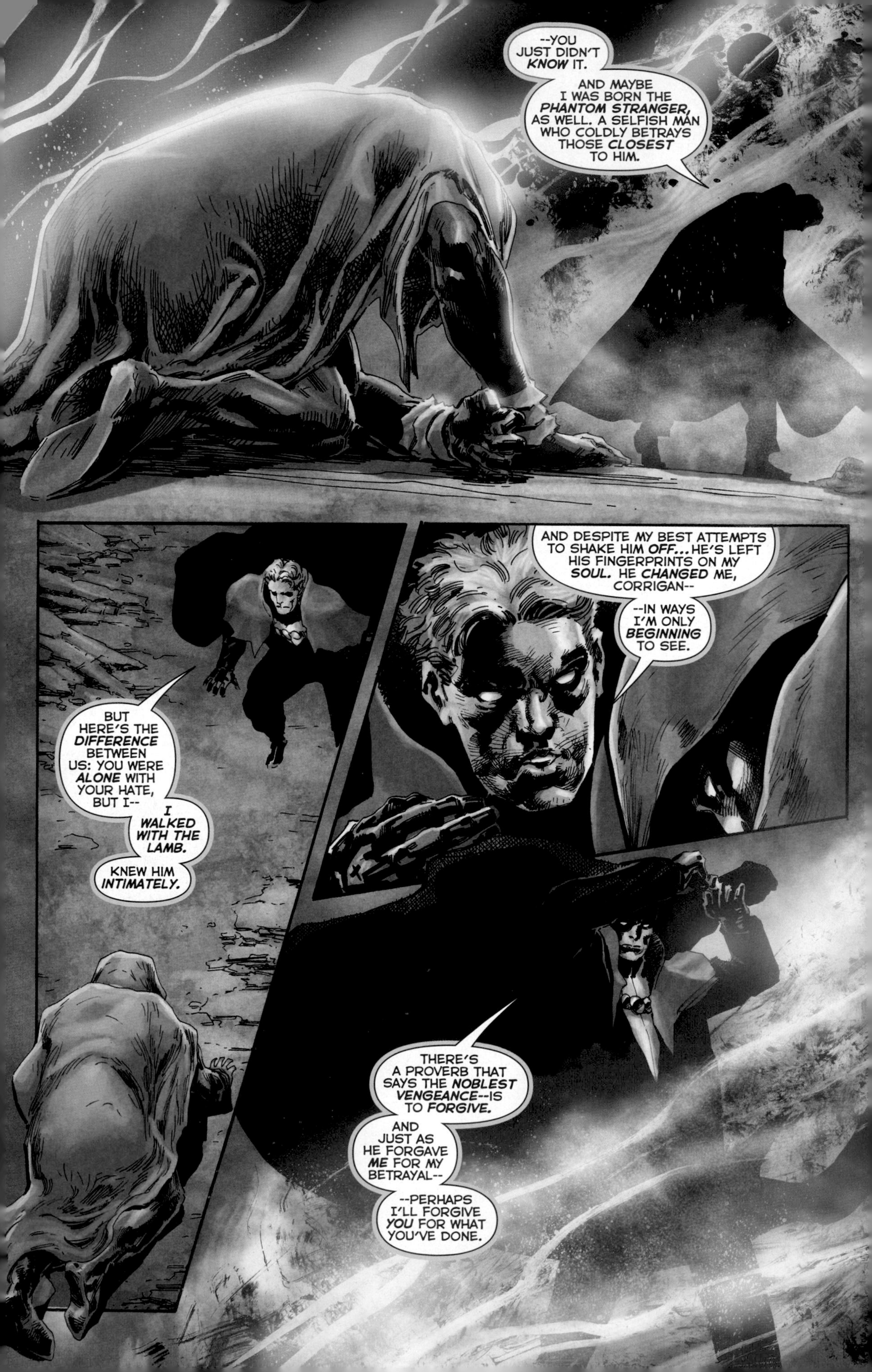
--YOU JUST DIDN'T KNOW IT.
AND MAYBE I WAS BORN THE PHANTOM STRANGER, AS WELL. A SELFISH MAN WHO COLDLY BETRAYS THOSE CLOSEST TO HIM.
BUT HERE'S THE DIFFERENCE BETWEEN US: YOU WERE ALONE WITH YOUR HATE, BUT I--
I WALKED WITH THE LAMB.
KNEW HIM INTIMATELY.
AND DESPITE MY BEST ATTEMPTS TO SHAKE HIM OFF... HE'S LEFT HIS FINGERPRINTS ON MY SOUL. HE CHANGED ME, CORRIGAN--
--IN WAYS I'M ONLY BEGINNING TO SEE.
THERE'S A PROVERB THAT SAYS THE NOBLEST VENGEANCE--IS TO FORGIVE.
AND JUST AS HE FORGAVE ME FOR MY BETRAYAL--
--PERHAPS I'LL FORGIVE YOU FOR WHAT YOU'VE DONE.

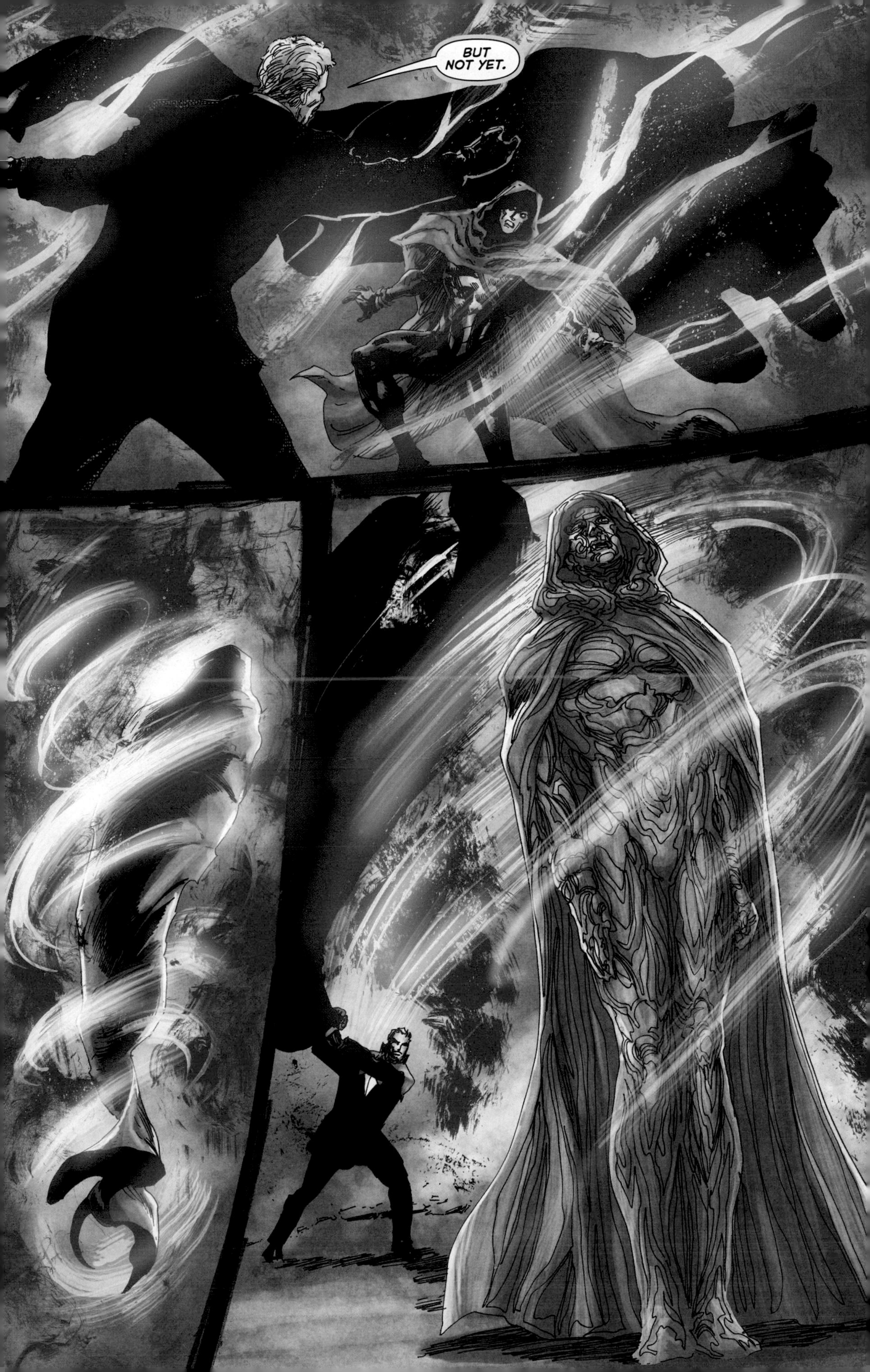
BUT NOT YET.

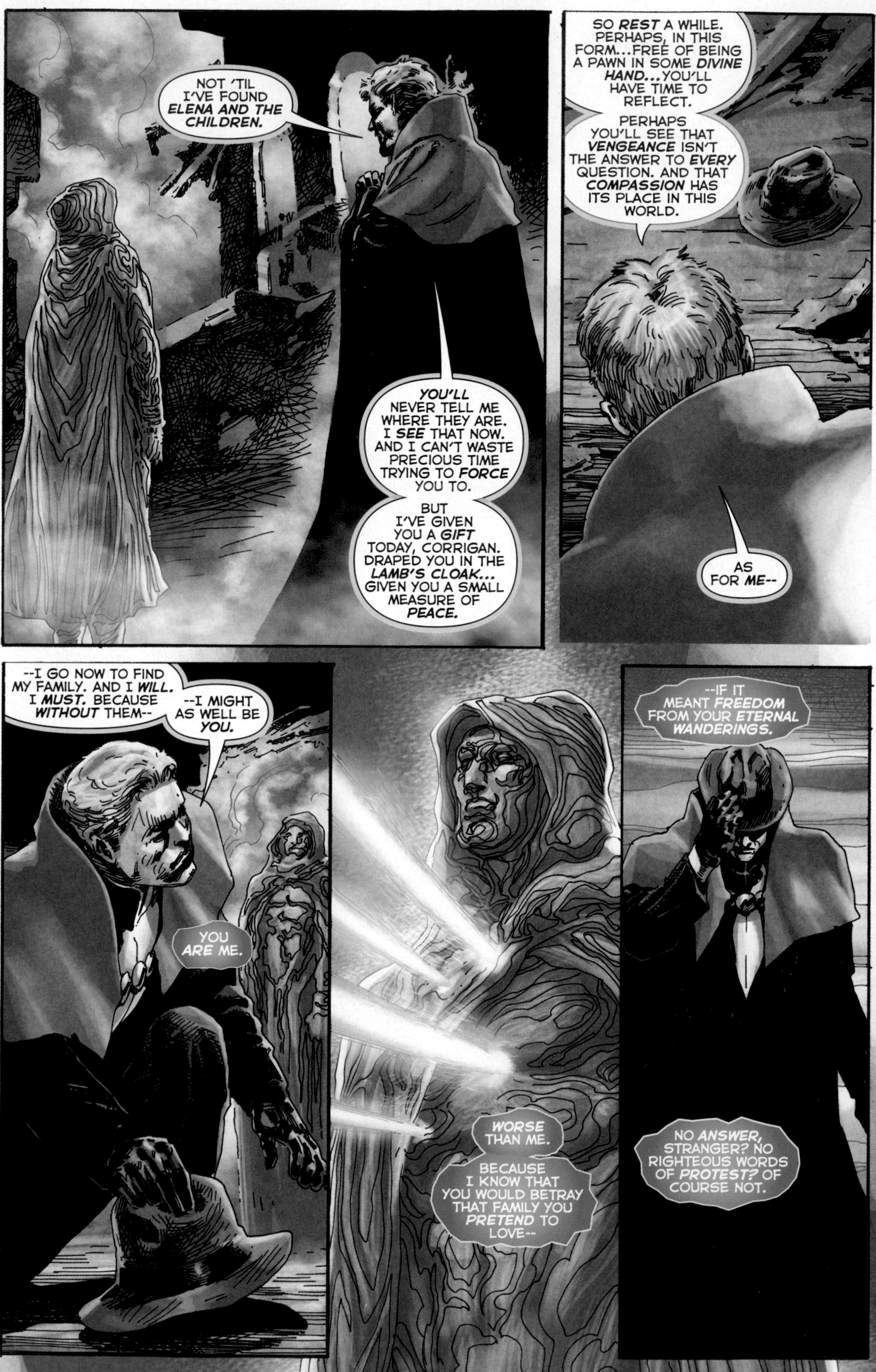
NOT 'TIL I'VE FOUND ELENA AND THE CHILDREN.
YOU'LL NEVER TELL ME WHERE THEY ARE. I SEE THAT NOW. AND I CAN'T WASTE PRECIOUS TIME TRYING TO FORCE YOU TO.
BUT I'VE GIVEN YOU A GIFT TODAY, CORRIGAN. DRAPED YOU IN THE LAMB'S CLOAK... GIVEN YOU A SMALL MEASURE OF PEACE.
SO REST A WHILE. PERHAPS, IN THIS FORM...FREE OF BEING A PAWN IN SOME DIVINE HAND...YOU'LL HAVE TIME TO REFLECT.
PERHAPS YOU'LL SEE THAT VENGEANCE ISN'T THE ANSWER TO EVERY QUESTION. AND THAT COMPASSION HAS ITS PLACE IN THIS WORLD.
AS FOR ME--
--I GO NOW TO FIND MY FAMILY. AND I WILL. I MUST. BECAUSE WITHOUT THEM--
--I MIGHT AS WELL BE YOU.
YOU ARE ME.
WORSE THAN ME.
BECAUSE I KNOW THAT YOU WOULD BETRAY THAT FAMILY YOU PRETEND TO LOVE--
--IF IT MEANT FREEDOM FROM YOUR ETERNAL WANDERINGS.
NO ANSWER, STRANGER? NO RIGHTEOUS WORDS OF PROTEST? OF COURSE NOT.

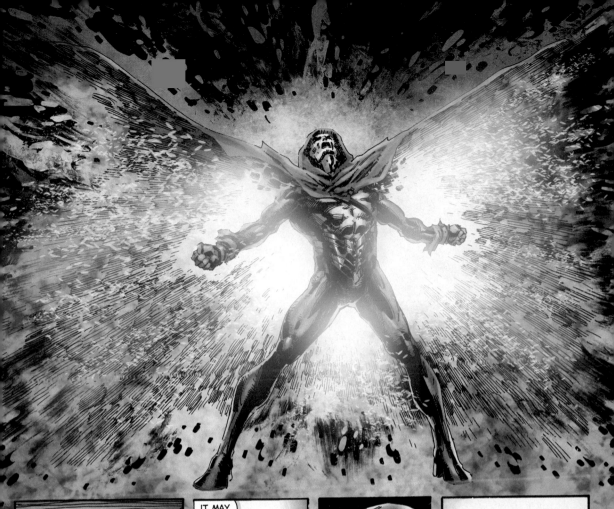

BECAUSE IT'S *TRUE!*

IT MAY *BE.* 'THOUGH I HOPE TO GOD IT *ISN'T.*

BUT *WHATEVER* THE TRUTH, I WANT NO *PART* OF THIS FIGHT. NO PART OF *YOU.*

THE CHOICE ISN'T *YOURS!*

NOR IS IT YOURS, SPECTRE.

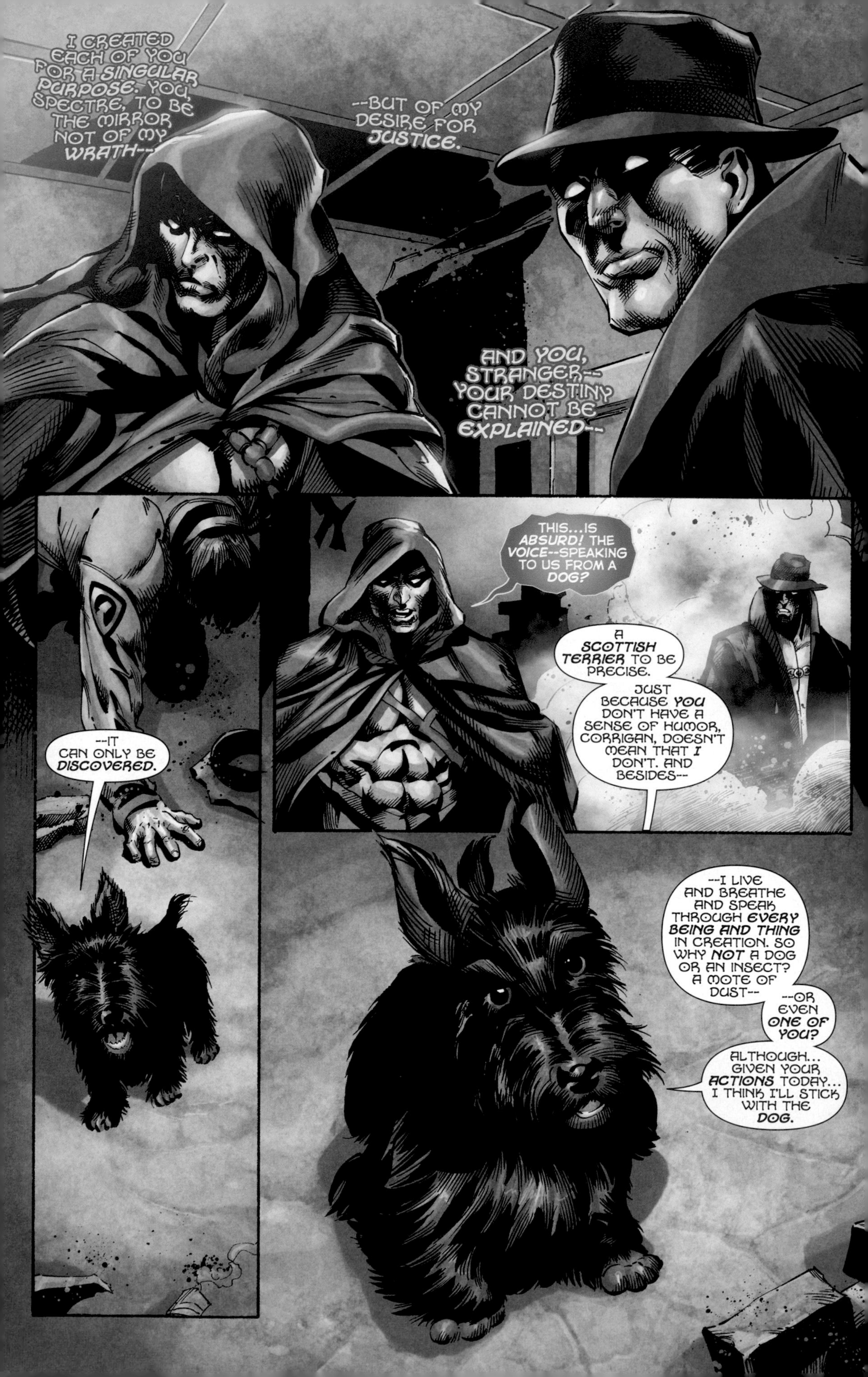
I CREATED EACH OF YOU FOR A SINGULAR PURPOSE. YOU, SPECTRE, TO BE THE MIRROR NOT OF MY WRATH--
--BUT OF MY DESIRE FOR JUSTICE.
AND YOU, STRANGER--YOUR DESTINY CANNOT BE EXPLAINED--
--IT CAN ONLY BE DISCOVERED.
THIS...IS ABSURD! THE VOICE--SPEAKING TO US FROM A DOG?
A SCOTTISH TERRIER TO BE PRECISE.
JUST BECAUSE YOU DON'T HAVE A SENSE OF HUMOR, CORRIGAN, DOESN'T MEAN THAT I DON'T. AND BESIDES--
--I LIVE AND BREATHE AND SPEAK THROUGH EVERY BEING AND THING IN CREATION. SO WHY NOT A DOG OR AN INSECT? A MOTE OF DUST--
--OR EVEN ONE OF YOU?
ALTHOUGH... GIVEN YOUR ACTIONS TODAY... I THINK I'LL STICK WITH THE DOG.

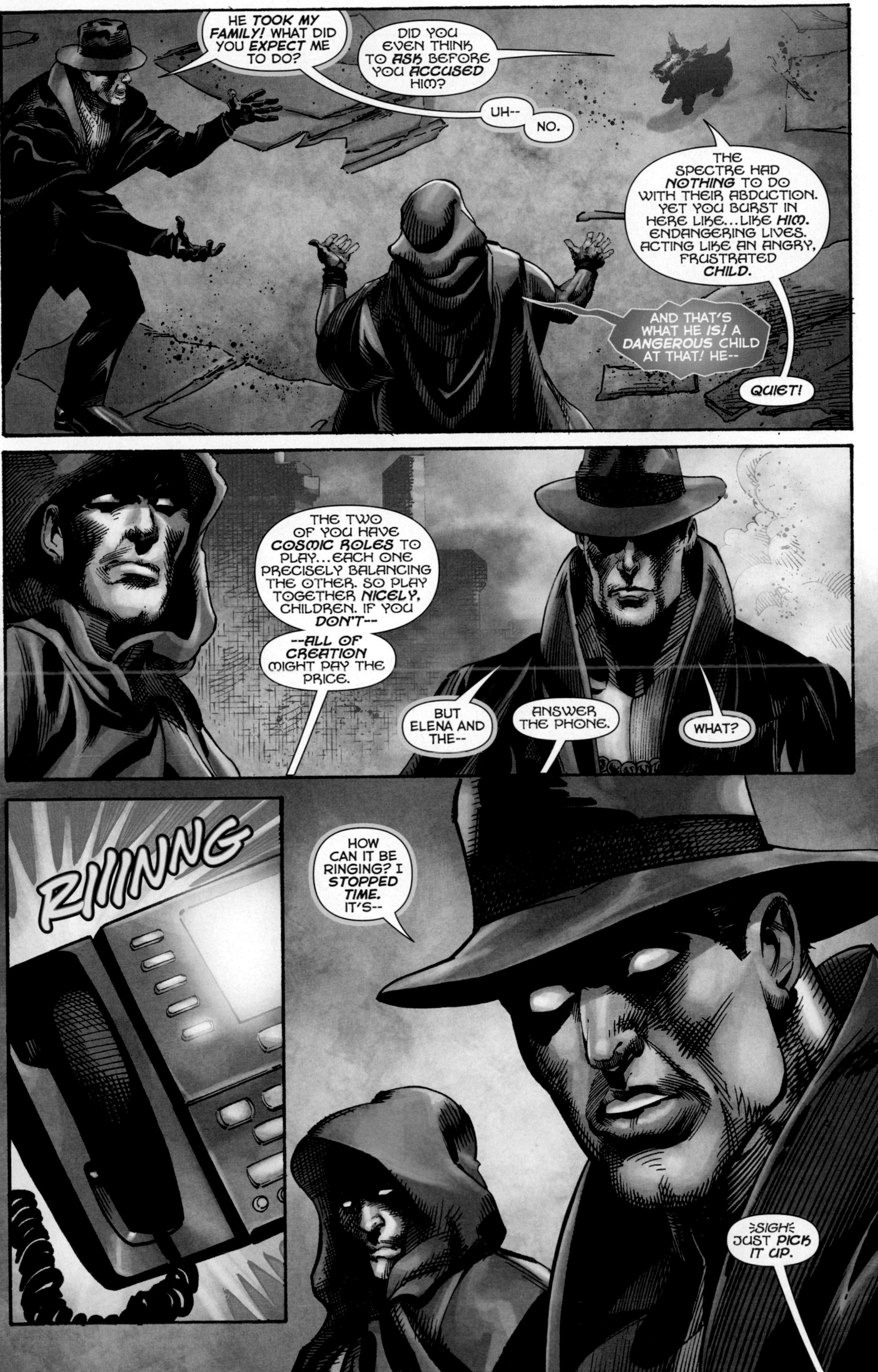
HE TOOK MY FAMILY! WHAT DID YOU EXPECT ME TO DO?
DID YOU EVEN THINK TO ASK BEFORE YOU ACCUSED HIM?
UH--
NO.
THE SPECTRE HAD NOTHING TO DO WITH THEIR ABDUCTION. YET YOU BURST IN HERE LIKE...LIKE HIM. ENDANGERING LIVES. ACTING LIKE AN ANGRY, FRUSTRATED CHILD.
AND THAT'S WHAT HE IS! A DANGEROUS CHILD AT THAT! HE--
QUIET!
THE TWO OF YOU HAVE COSMIC ROLES TO PLAY...EACH ONE PRECISELY BALANCING THE OTHER. SO PLAY TOGETHER NICELY, CHILDREN. IF YOU DON'T--
--ALL OF CREATION MIGHT PAY THE PRICE.
BUT ELENA AND THE--
ANSWER THE PHONE.
WHAT?
RIIINNG
HOW CAN IT BE RINGING? I STOPPED TIME. IT'S--
SIGH JUST PICK IT UP.

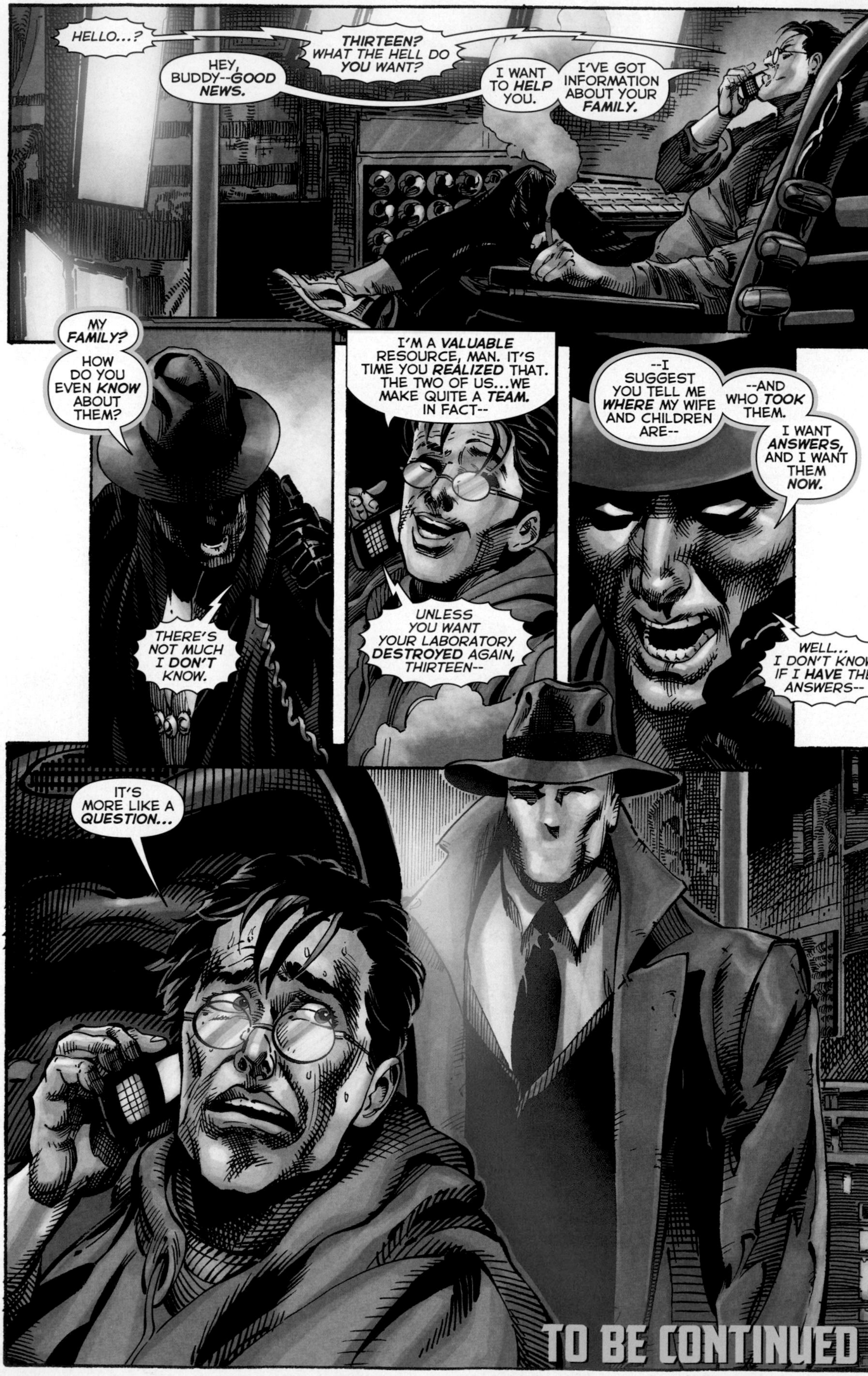
HELLO...?
THIRTEEN? WHAT THE HELL DO YOU WANT?
HEY, BUDDY--GOOD NEWS.
I WANT TO HELP YOU.
I'VE GOT INFORMATION ABOUT YOUR FAMILY.
MY FAMILY?
HOW DO YOU EVEN KNOW ABOUT THEM?
THERE'S NOT MUCH I DON'T KNOW.
I'M A VALUABLE RESOURCE, MAN. IT'S TIME YOU REALIZED THAT. THE TWO OF US...WE MAKE QUITE A TEAM. IN FACT--
UNLESS YOU WANT YOUR LABORATORY DESTROYED AGAIN, THIRTEEN--
--I SUGGEST YOU TELL ME WHERE MY WIFE AND CHILDREN ARE--
--AND WHO TOOK THEM.
I WANT ANSWERS, AND I WANT THEM NOW.
WELL... I DON'T KNOW IF I HAVE THE ANSWERS--
IT'S MORE LIKE A QUESTION...
TO BE CONTINUED

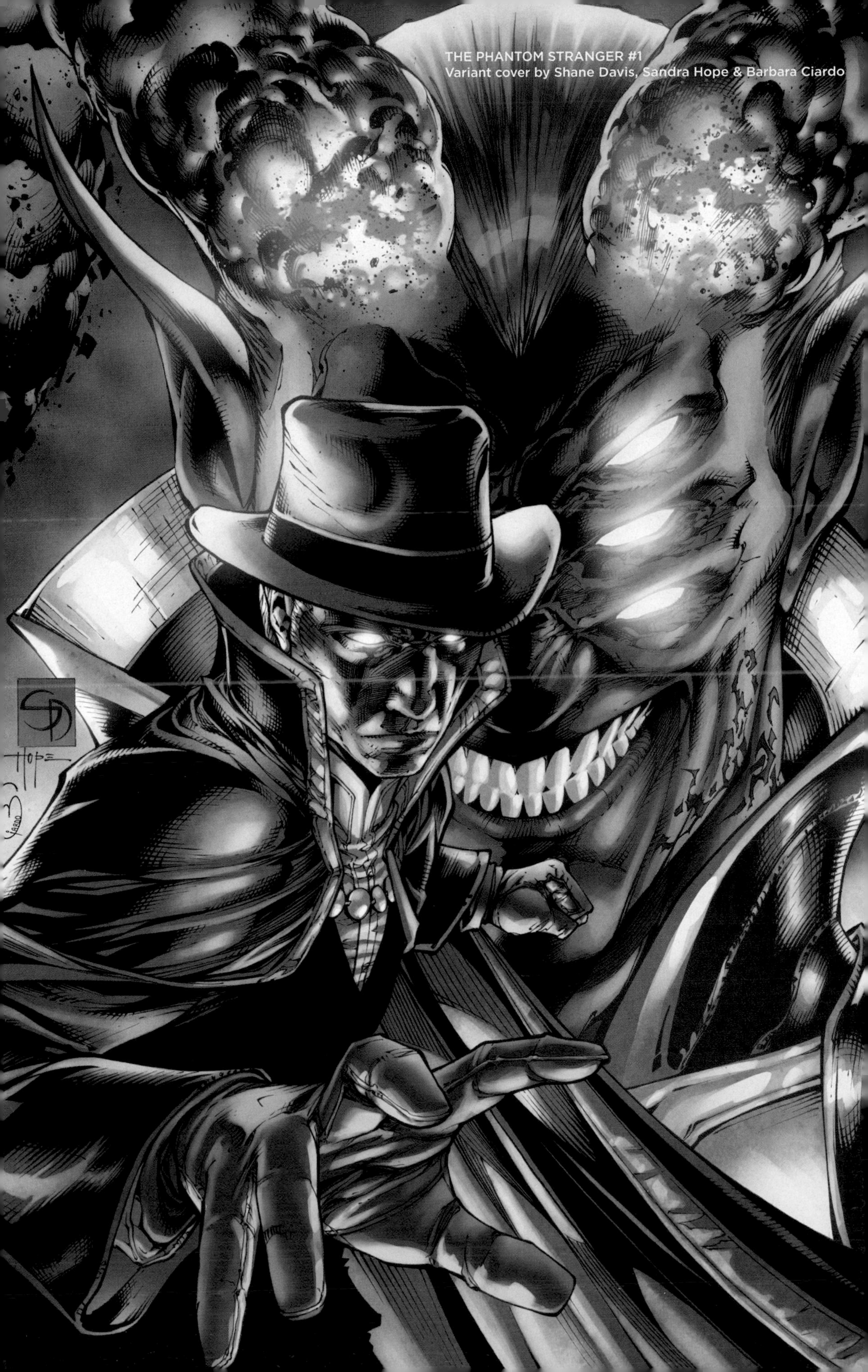

THE PHANTOM STRANGER #1
Variant cover by Shane Davis, Sandra Hope & Barbara Ciardo

THE PHANTOM STRANGER #2
Variant cover by Ethan Van Sciver & Hi-Fi

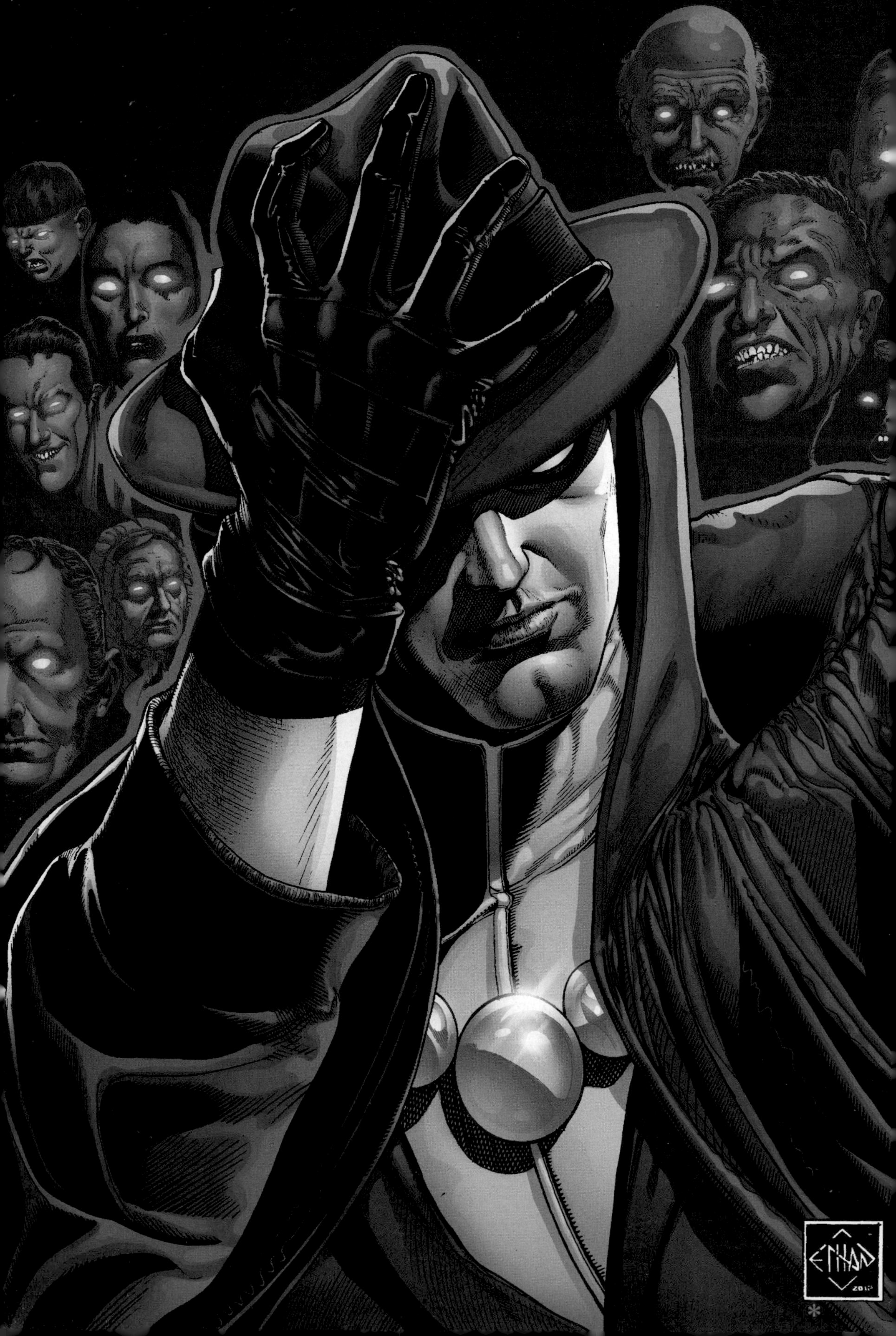

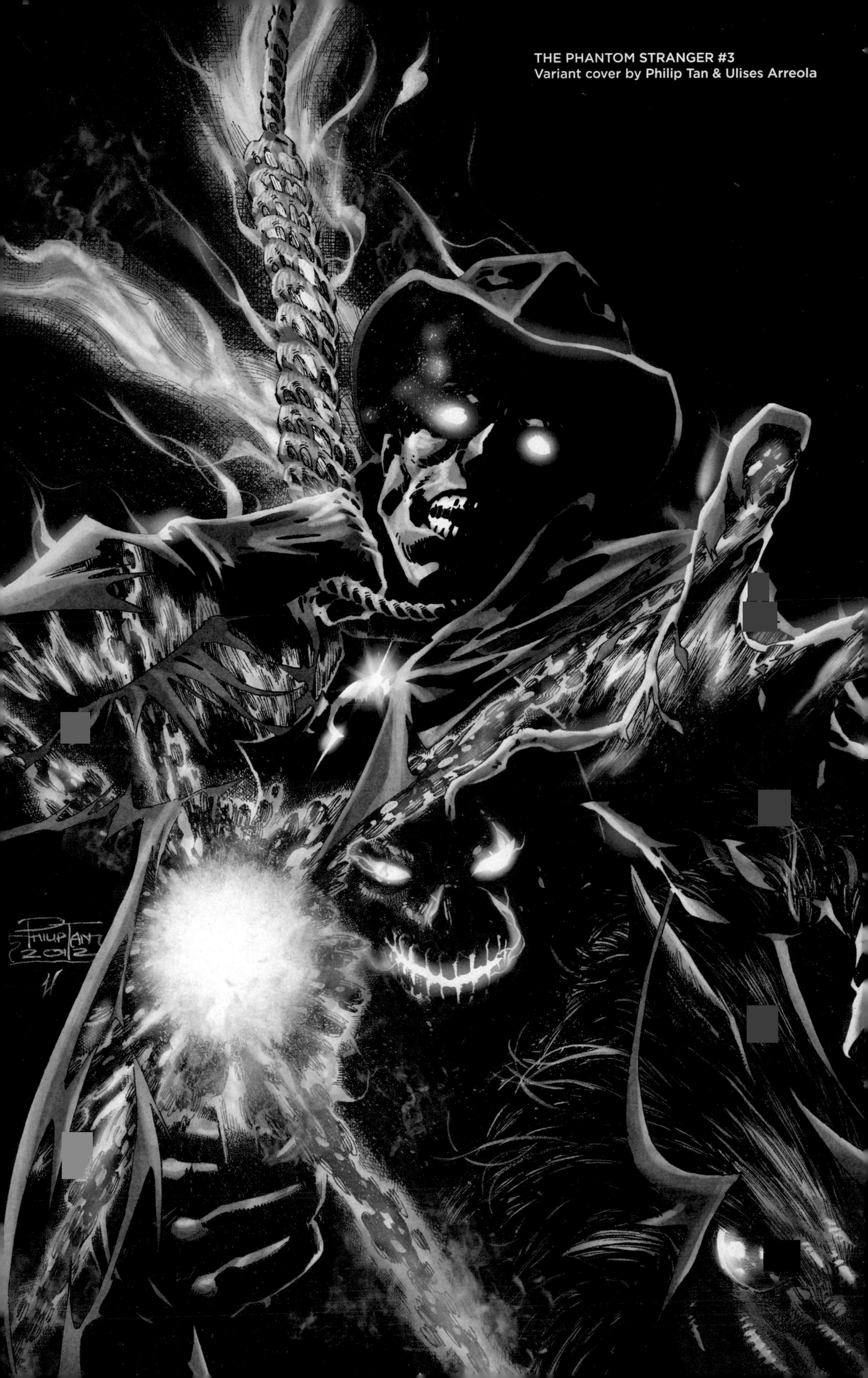
PHILIP TAN
2012

THE PHANTOM STRANGER #3
Variant cover by Philip Tan & Ulises Arreola

TRINITY OF SIN: THE PHANTOM STRANGER
SKETCHBOOK

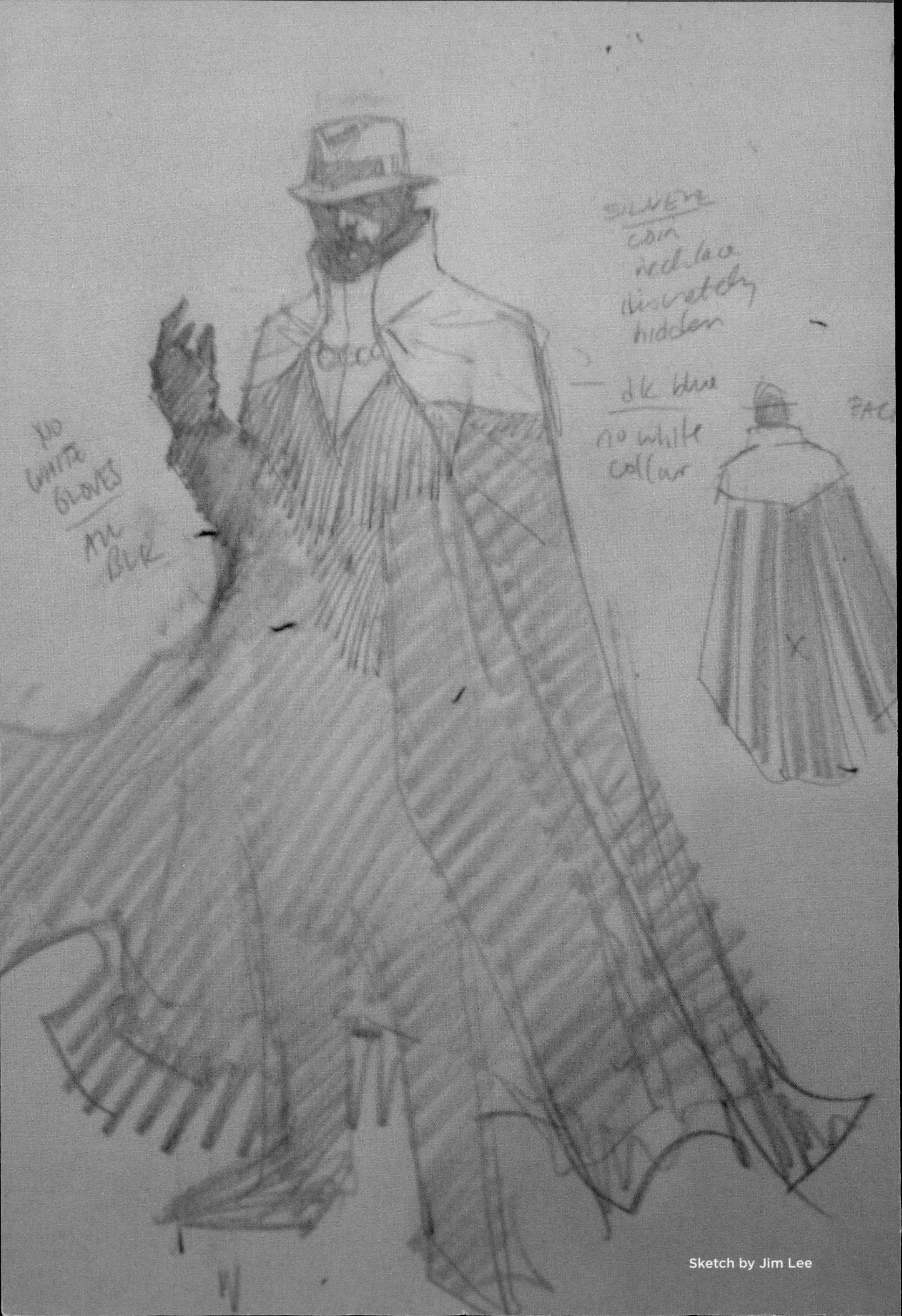
SILVER
coin
necklace
discreetly
hidden
dk blue
no white
collar
NO
WHITE
GLOVES
ALL
BLK

Sketch by Jim Lee

Character study by Philip Tan

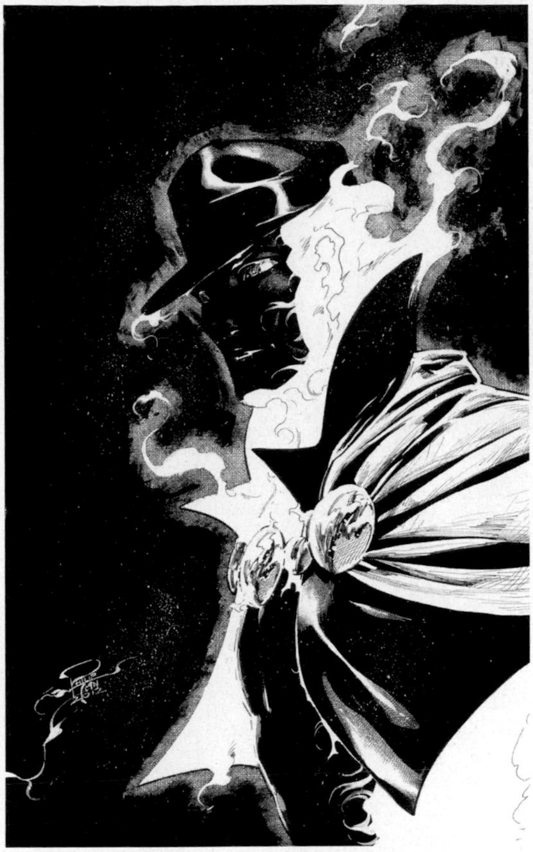

Spectre design by Brett Booth

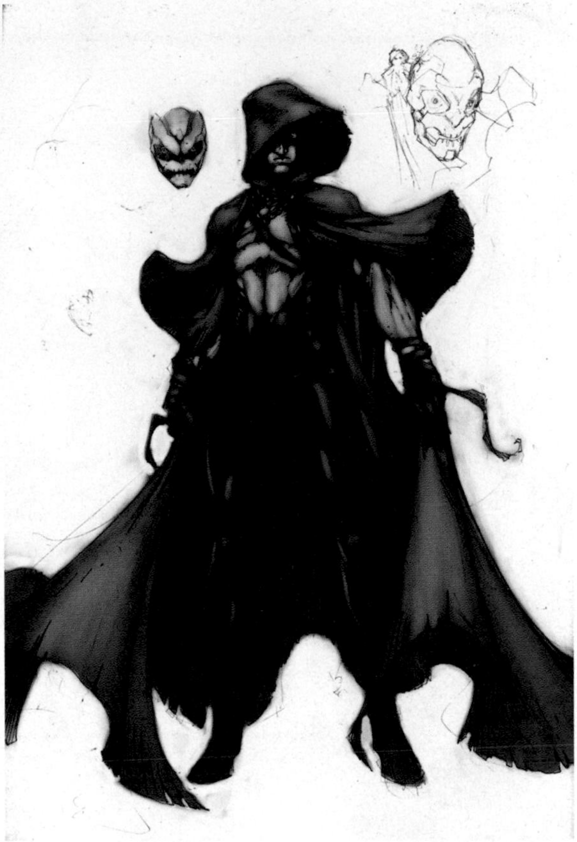

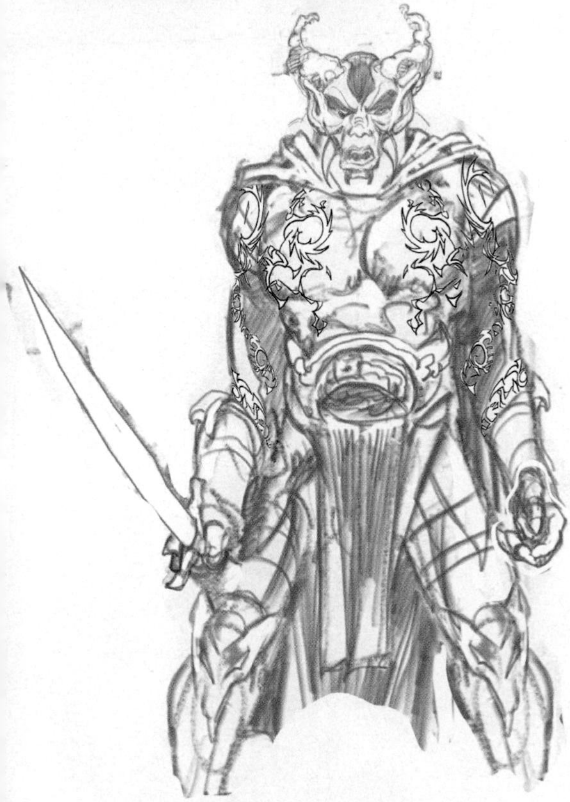

Suge design by Brent Anderson

Ruskoff design by Brent Anderson

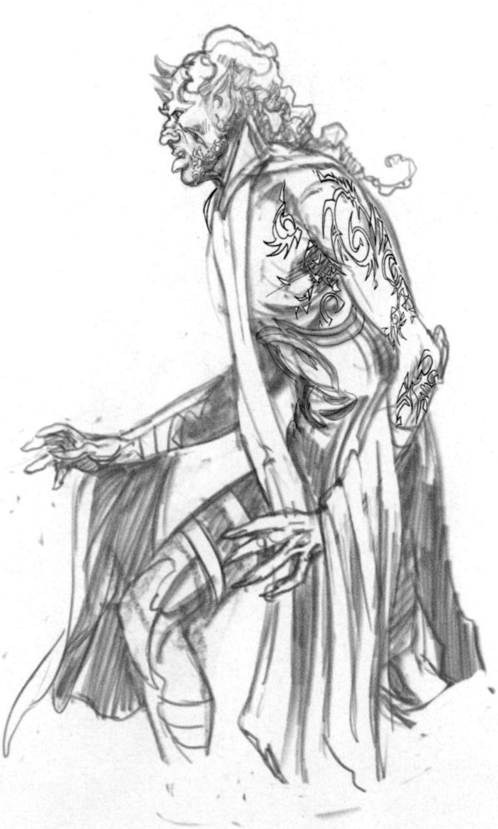

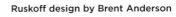

Issue #0 layout by Andy Kubert

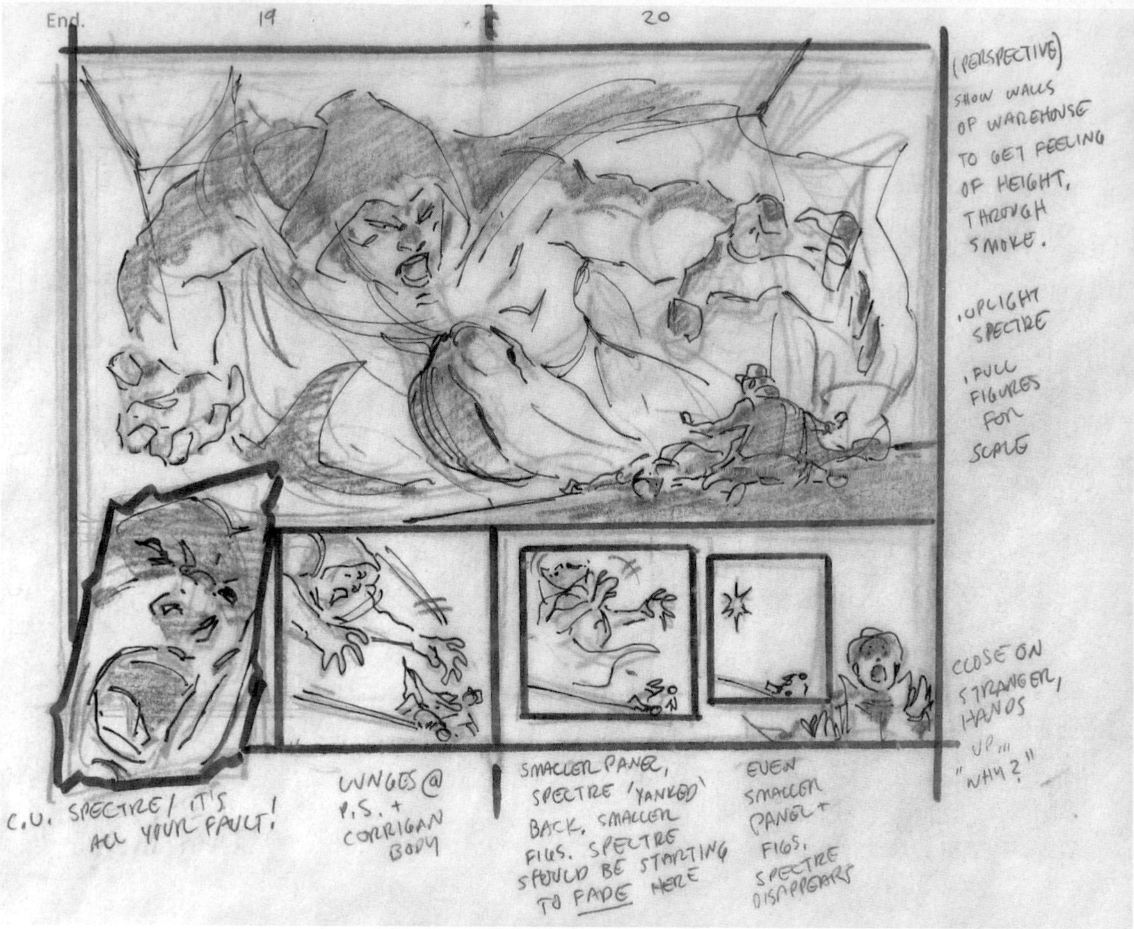
End.
19
20
(PERSPECTIVE)
SHOW WALLS OF WAREHOUSE TO GET FEELING OF HEIGHT, THROUGH SMOKE.
· UPLIGHT SPECTRE
· FULL FIGURES FOR SCALE
CLOSE ON STRANGER, HANDS UP... "WHY?"
C.U. SPECTRE / IT'S ALL YOUR FAULT!
LUNGES @ P.S. + CORRIGAN BODY
SMALLER PANEL, SPECTRE 'YANKED' BACK, SMALLER FIGS. SPECTRE SHOULD BE STARTING TO FADE HERE
EVEN SMALLER PANEL + FIGS, SPECTRE DISAPPEARS

Trigon designs by Brett Booth

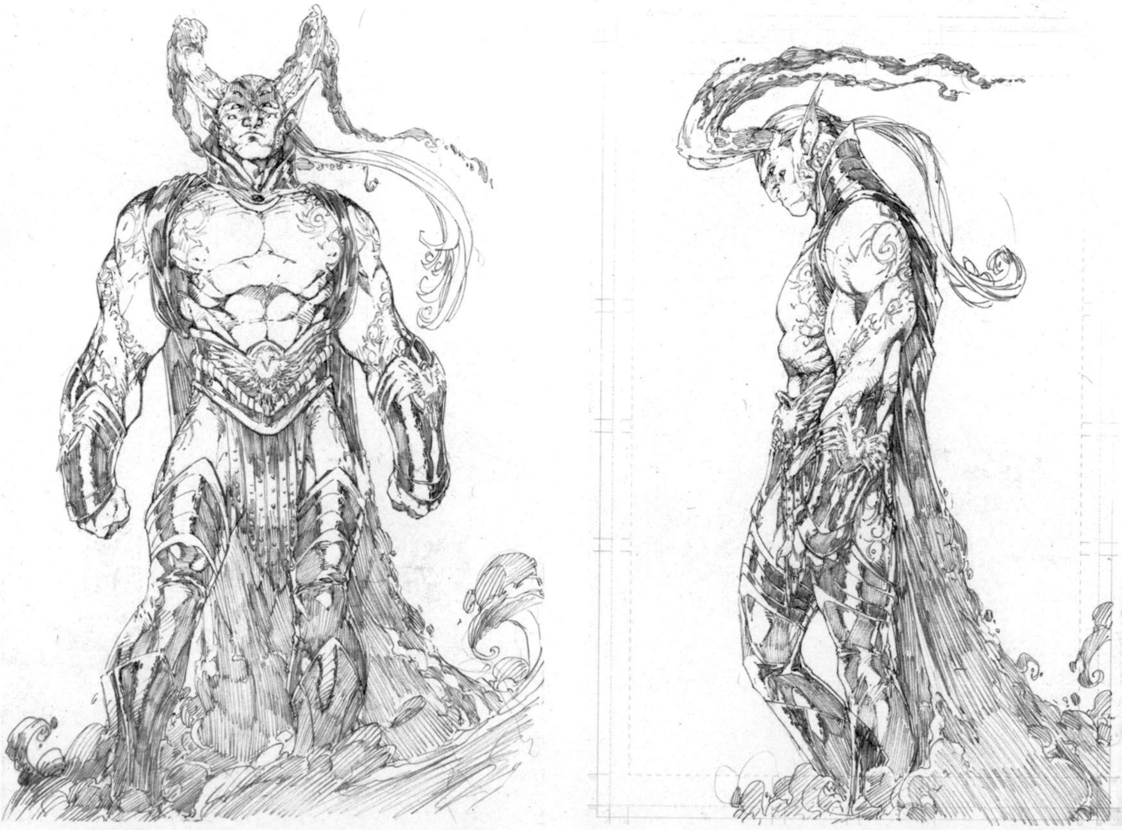

Issue #0 cover sketch by Brent Anderson

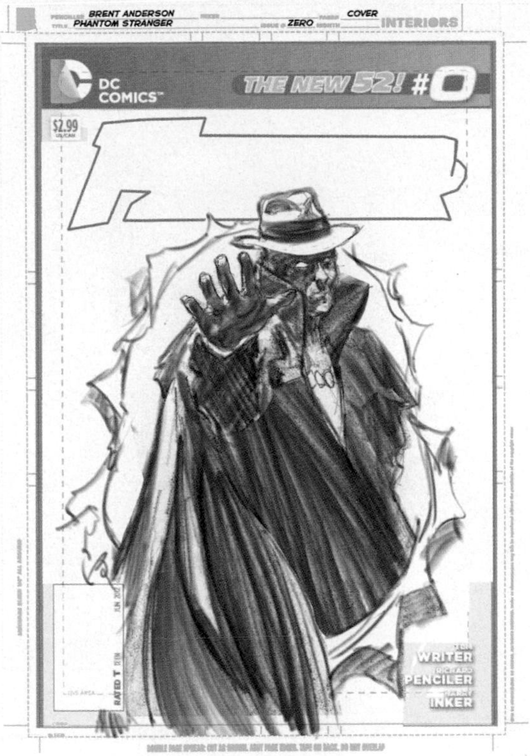
BRENT ANDERSON
PHANTOM STRANGER
ZERO
COVER
INTERIORS
DC COMICS
THE NEW 52! #0
$2.99
WRITER
PENCILER
INKER

Issue #1 initial cover sketch by Brent Anderson

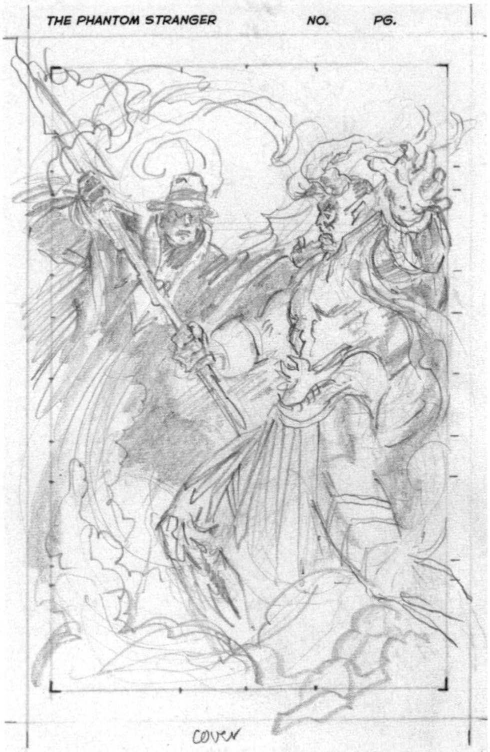
THE PHANTOM STRANGER
NO.
PG.
cover

Issue #2 cover sketch by Brent Anderson

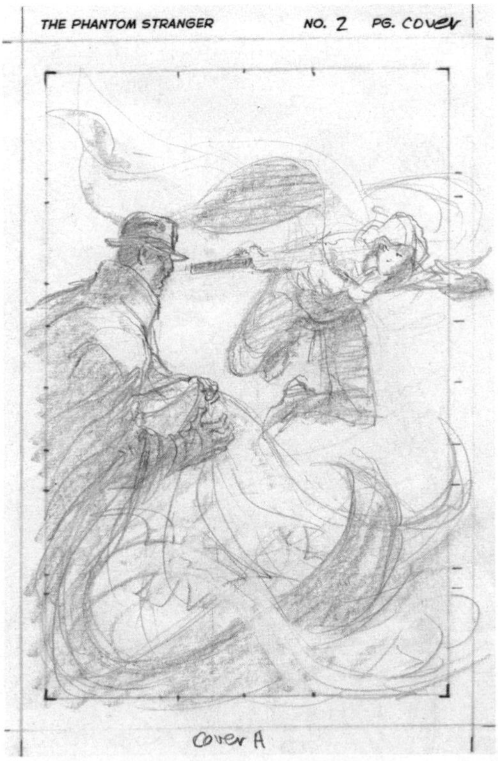
THE PHANTOM STRANGER
NO. 2
PG. cover
cover A

Issue #2 initial cover sketch by Brent Anderson

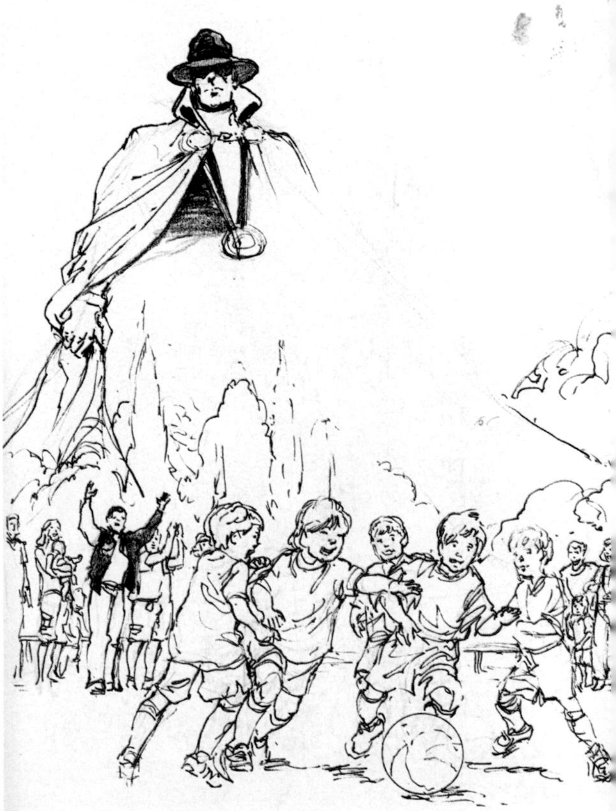

Issue #4 cover sketch by Jae Lee

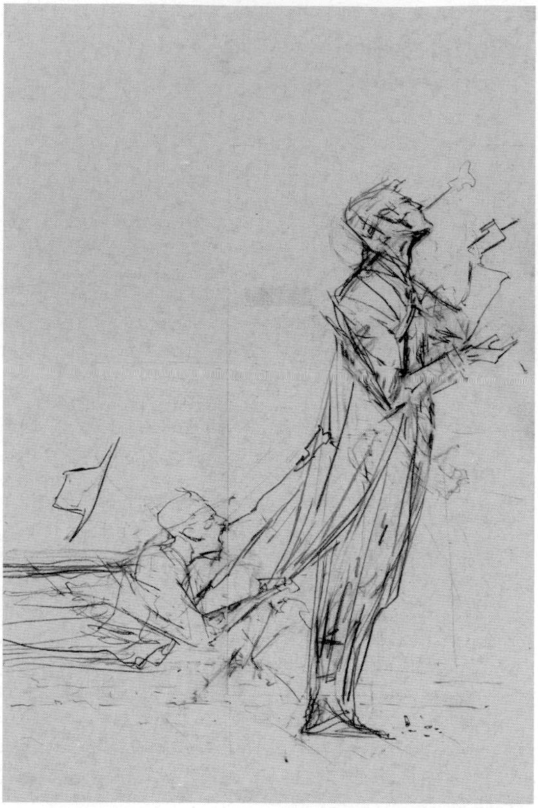

Issue #4 loose pencil cover by Jae Lee

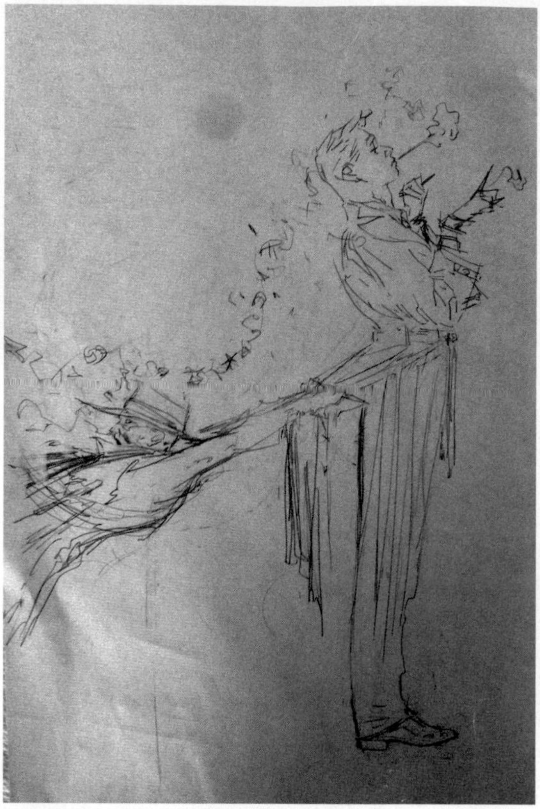

Issue #5 cover sketch by Jae Lee

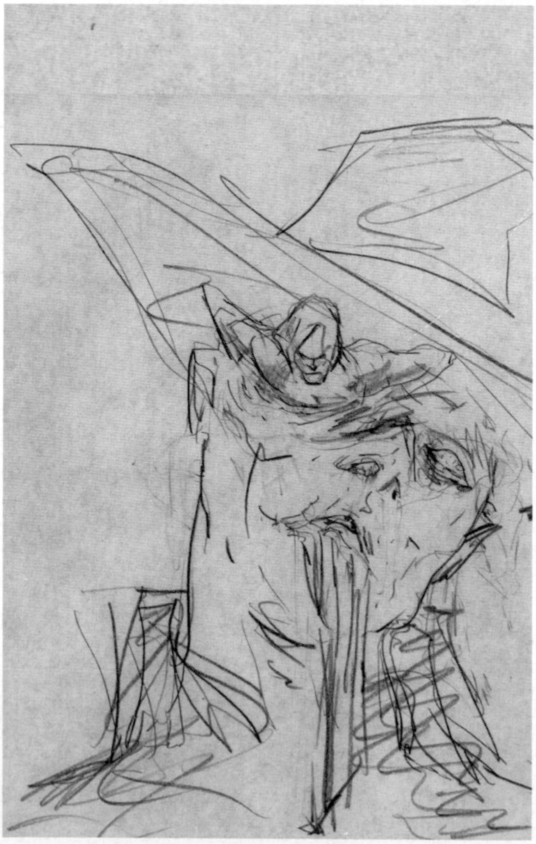

Issue #1 variant cover sketch by Shane Davis

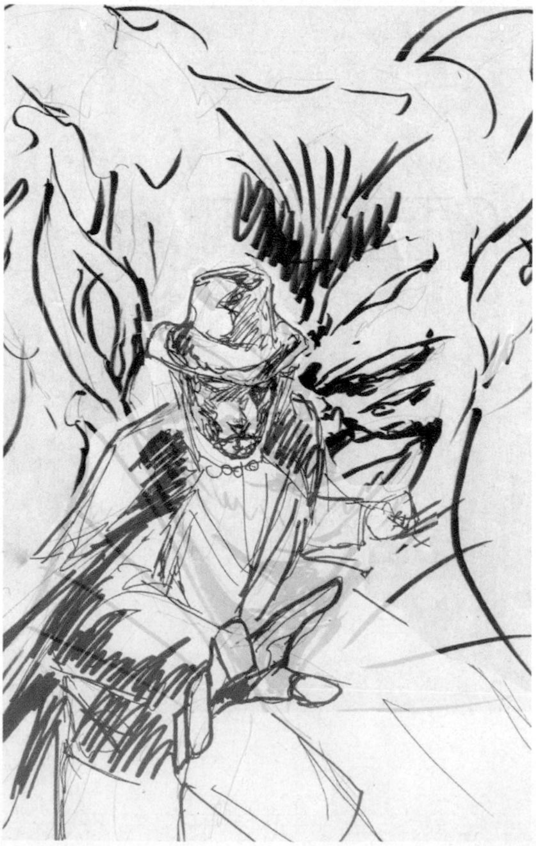